# THE FIGHTIN' PHILLIES

100 Years of Philadelphia Baseball
from the Whiz Kids to the Misfits

**Larry Shenk**

TRIUMPH
B O O K S

Library of Congress Cataloging-in-Publication Data
Names: Shenk, Larry, author.
Title: The fightin' Phillies : 100 years of Philadelphia baseball from the whiz kids to the misfits / Larry Shenk.
Description: Chicago, Illinois : Triumph Books LLC, [2016]
Identifiers: LCCN 2015038342 | ISBN 9781629371993
Subjects: LCSH: Philadelphia Phillies (Baseball team)--History.
Classification: LCC GV875.P45 S52 2016 | DDC 796.357/640974811--dc23 LC record available at http://lccn.loc.gov/2015038342

This book is available in quantity at special discounts for your group or organization. For further information, contact:
**Triumph Books LLC**
814 North Franklin Street
Chicago, Illinois 60610
(312) 337-0747
www.triumphbooks.com

Printed in U.S.A.

ISBN: 978-1-62937-199-3

Design by Sue Knopf

Photos courtesy of The Phillies

*I have been truly blessed with a very loving family—*
*my wife, Julie; our daughter, Debi Mosel, and her husband, Mike;*
*our son, Andy; his wife, Renee; granddaughter, Audrey;*
*and grandson, Tyler.*
*Their endless love, support, and encouragement*
*is monumental and deeply appreciated.*
*Their enthusiasm for this book was of immense inspiration.*
*Julie, Debi, and Andy spent hours as proofreaders, a skill I lack.*
*This book is dedicated to my family, whom I love dearly.*
*I've also been blessed to have a second family,*
*spending over a half century with my Phillies.*
*Support and guidance from the top was enormous.*
*Thank you Ruly Carpenter, Bill Giles, and David Montgomery.*

*The Fight, Fight, Fight-in-Phils!*
*It's a tough, tough team to beat.*
*They're out to win, win ev-'ry day.*
*Every victory is sweet.*
*Watch 'em hit that ball a mile; play a*
*game that's packed with thrills.*
*Get Pa to bring your Mother, Sister,*
*and your Brother.*
*Come out to see the Fight-in' Phils.*
*The fight, fight, fight-in' Phils!*

DEBORAH ARDEN STERN

# Contents

# Foreword

You are not good enough. Those were the words that Seattle Mariners manager Rene Lachemann spoke to me in 1982. To some that may sound like a baseball death sentence, especially because it was the worst team in baseball, but for me it actually led to my baseball heaven. The most fun I ever had in baseball were my six years with the Phils, though it seemed more like 60. It also brought to me a personal relationship with the author of this book, Larry Shenk, also known as "The Baron," who was the VP of public relations for umpteen years. In this book you will read stories of the many faces and places in regards to the last 100 years of Phillies baseball that can only be told by The Baron. Actually, Baron, it is more than 100 years. After all, it's all about accuracy.

We all have faces and places, and they all change over time, but for some the facial changes are not always for the better. I was a cute little baby...well, maybe not little...but cute nonetheless. At least that's what all my ancient friends and relatives said at the time. As we grow, our faces constantly change, and in my case, as I stated earlier, mine was not necessarily for the better. This was truly evidenced by my lack of girlfriends in school. I did eventually lose my baby fat, and because of that—combined with my witty, outgoing personality—I was positive that I would overcome the facial change and be surrounded by girls everywhere. Obviously, along the way I miscalculated and at that time I decided to change course. I was going to be consumed from that point on with nothing more than making sure I had fun in whatever endeavor I followed. The motto for the rest of my life became: "You're only young once, but you can be immature forever."

Former Phillies reliever Larry Andersen insists he was a cute baby. (Courtesy Larry Andersen)

I loved playing sports and certainly had fun doing it. Although I loved football and basketball, my true love was being on a dirt hill 60', 6" from a competitor holding a wooden stick and trying to make me look bad—not that I needed help with that.

After turning 18 and graduating from high school—yes, I actually did—I was chosen by the Cleveland Indians in the seventh round of the 1971 draft. I was stunned that two other pitchers in the state of Washington were picked ahead of me; one was drafted in the fourth round, and the other was in the fifth. That all became a moot point when the Indians threw $10,000 my way to sign with them, convincing me to spurn a football/baseball scholarship to attend the University of Oregon. It was an easy decision at the time, as Oregon didn't offer a major in practical jokes. I'm pretty sure the joke was on me, however, as I opted to buy a souped-up 1968 Mustang instead of investing in property in Aspen, Colorado, consisting of 10 acres at $700 an acre. Did I mention that I'm not very smart?

Most baseball players travel the whole country from small towns to large cities. I went from Yuma, Arizona, to Williamsport, Pennsylvania, from Bellingham, Washington, to Fort Myers, Florida, and numerous cities in between, but I also had the experience of spending six winters of my early career in foreign lands, including four in Puerto Rico and two in Venezuela. The language barrier was somewhat of a challenge. However, I learned early how to use bodily gestures to translate my wants and needs. Apparently I wasn't very good at that either as was proven one winter while playing for the LaGuira Tiburones. When I moved into my condominium, I noticed the toilet was clogged, so I marched down to the *supermercado*, the supermarket as we know it, to pick up some Drano. Using gestures that obviously only I understood, I was sent home with what I later realized was toilet cleanser.

So I lived in six different cities in Major League Baseball over 17 years, 12 cities in the minor leagues spanning 15 seasons, as well as the two foreign lands over six winters. An iPhone with GPS would certainly have come in handy, but in a day when my baseball cards were still printed in black and white, the technology available was restricted to paper maps that can *never* be folded back up the way they were when purchased. I felt like I should have been working for a moving company because my home changed so much.

I was traded, released, loaned out, sent down, optioned out, and purchased, as well as becoming a free agent, six times. Was I that bad? Or was I that good? Either way I felt like I got less respect than Rodney Dangerfield. When you figure the buses; the flights; apartments; hotels and motels; small locker rooms, including trailers; fast food restaurants; and dive bars due to our $5 a day meal money allowance, then maybe, just maybe, you can now see that my face could have been in just about any place.

One of the more trying times in my life was when I got traded to the Boston Red Sox for potential Hall of Famer Jeff Bagwell. To this day I would still feel safer with some tighter security when I travel to Boston. However, I also believe that even throwing just 22 innings for the Red Sox, I was an integral part of us making the playoffs that year. So is it really the worst trade Boston ever made? You may want to check with "The Babe," though that's not possible, but you get the idea.

My baseball heaven, though, was in Philadelphia. At the age of 30, I was one of the younger players on the '83 "Wheeze Kids." But what a thrill. Imagine walking into a clubhouse after leaving a Seattle organization that didn't even want me in Triple A (hence the loan to the Portland Beavers, the Phillies' Triple A affiliate) and seeing no fewer than four future Hall of Famers—Steve Carlton, Mike Schmidt, Joe Morgan, and Tony Perez—as well as Pete Rose, Garry Maddox, Tug McGraw, and the "Sarge," Gary Matthews. Talk about baseball heaven!

Yet by far the greatest thrill of my baseball career began in the spring of '93 when I not only walked in, but also fit in with that band of misfits. We truly were a bunch of rejects, and that was definitely the main thing we had in common. We loved to party, but we loved to play baseball even more. On one spring training bus trip after Dutch (Darren Daulton) had just signed a new and very lucrative contract, Krukker (John Kruk) said to Dutch, "Why don't you build a big mansion, and we can hang out, party, and then play baseball." "Inky" (Pete Incaviglia) replied without hesitation, "If you build it, we will come." Everyone busted up, but that was genuinely how we felt about baseball and each other. We were gruff, scrappy, and played our asses off, both on and off the field. That is why this city loved us so much. Blue-collar, baby, that is exactly what we represented. I doubt there'll ever be another team quite like that one.

An amusing and eccentric personality, Larry Andersen fit right in with the rest of the misfits on the 1993 National League champs. (Courtesy Phillies)

Our postgame celebrations were second to none. With music blaring to the sound of "Two Princes" by the Spin Doctors after every win, we would head to the trainer's room and begin our off-the-field party. This was done much to the chagrin of The Baron, who was constantly on the prowl for a body—any warm body—to accommodate the media. When we clinched the pennant that year in Pittsburgh, we were joined in the trainer's room by Harry the K, Harry Kalas, the father figure to some—and the grandfather fig-ure to others. He was one of us, part of our close-knit family, and we loved him, especially when he led us on his rendition of "High Hopes." When "H of K" passed, I remember trying to choke back tears to no avail, as I did my best to answer questions outside the clubhouse in Washington, D.C.

I can't say I was in my prime during that '93 season, but being around that group of guys certainly made me feel like it. Wearing masks, wigs, coneheads, pinching sunflower seeds on my face, putting in fake teeth, and Mitchypoo (Mitch Williams) spraying instant hair on my head, and on and on. It was immaturity at its best, but we did what we had to do just to get through a grueling 162 games with some sanity. That is still being questioned to this day. "Were those guys really sane?" Bill "Spaceman" Lee, a former pitcher for Boston, asked. "The whole world is insane, so if I'm insane, I'm normal." So I guess then you could say that the '93 team was normal.

In typical Baron fashion, he has filled this book with faces and special places and personalities recounted in/from Phillies history. Although I'm not exactly an astute historian, I do have a memory and cannot figure out why I'm not at least mentioned in the chapter of Unbreakable Records. Consider this: 699 major league games and only one start. Or how about my five career hits, which gives me a lifetime .132 career average? And all that with bruised knees from knocking against each other every time I stepped in the box. Or how about the most seasons with one at-bat or less? Ineptitude at its best. I often used philosophy to help me get over my nervousness, which leads me to one final question: why are they singing "Take Me Out to the Ballgame" when they're already there?

As Ed McMahon used to say to Johnny Carson as Carson was about to do his psychic Carnac skit, "Everything you've always wanted to know is hermetically sealed in this manila envelope." Similarly, everything you've always wanted to know about Phillies teams, players, and the organization can be found in *The Fightin' Phillies: 100 Years of Philadelphia Baseball from the Whiz Kids to the Misfits.*

—Larry Andersen

# Preface

There are Phillies players performing historic moments, the most dramatic home runs in team history, special World Series accomplishments, and Jimmy Rollins breaking one of Mike Schmidt's hallowed records. There are Wall of Fame legends who have a special place at Citizens Bank Park.

There are lesser known faces from the franchise's first 50 years. There's a chapter on those who hold Phillies records that will never be broken. Some of those faces aren't smiley faces. Not to be forgotten are those who have had a cup of coffee wearing a Phillies uniform. Certainly, their faces aren't vividly remembered, but they did reach the majors, a place most of us dreamed about.

There's a chapter of people behind the scenes. What's the life of the bullpen security guard in Clearwater? How are national anthem singers chosen? What does the manager of video coaching services do? What is extended spring training? What is the life of a scout or a minor league manager? There's a day in the life of a radio broadcaster, a person who is heard more than seen, and more personalities that make up Phillies baseball. You will read about spring training places, including two years during World War II, and the Phillies' homes both in Clearwater and Philadelphia.

In summary, you are about to enter a land filled with a potpourri of faces, places, events, and personalities in Phillies history. Enjoy the journey. Seat belts not required—as it is a smooth ride.

# 1

# Historic Performances

Since being established as a National League franchise in 1883, the Phillies have played more than 20,300 games. There have been many great performances and plentiful ones that can be described as duds. History shows the Phillies played their first game on May 1, 1883, losing to the Providence Grays 4–3 at Recreation Park.

No one, including the new management, headed by Alfred J. Reach, made a fuss about that first game. There was no band, no flag raising, no mayor on hand to throw out the first ball. Perhaps it was all old hat to the fans—for many had seen the team do its spring training at home.

According to *The Philadelphia Inquirer* game story of May 2: "The fielding was good on both sides, but the batting was weak." Each team had six hits. The Grays made five errors; the Phillies made three. (So much for good fielding.) Another newspaper reported, "The Phillies started well against Frank Bancroft's crack Providence Club, which had Ole Hoss Radbourne pitching. They got three runs off Radbourne, while, until the eighth, John Coleman, the Phillies hurler, had held the Grays scoreless. But in that eighth, three singles and a double, with a base on balls, brought four runs across, and Providence won the ball game." *The Philadelphia Record* reported "four balls were used up in the game!"

Left fielder William (Blondie) Purcell got the Phillies' first hit and scored the first run. He singled to left center in the first inning and scored on a ground-out. After 17 games (4–13 record), the Phillies replaced manager Bob Ferguson with 29-year-old Purcell. John Coleman, who was 20 years old, went the distance in the season opener and took the loss. The right-hander finished the season with a 12–48 record in 65 games (61 starts) and a 4.87 ERA. Even though his record produced a measly winning percentage of .200, Art Hagan, the No. 2 starter, finished 1–14 for a .067 percentage.

The Phillies began the season 0–8, a start that remains a club record. The first win came on May 14 in Chicago by a 12–1 score. They ended their inaugural season with six losses and a tie and finished last, 17–81, and 46 games out of first place. Their longest winning streak was two games, which occurred three times. Their longest losing streak lasted 14 games.

Some interesting rules and practices were in effect in 1883:

- Gloves were made of thin leather and did not cover the fingers.
- The pitcher's "mound" was a flat surface 50 feet from home plate. (It became 60'6" in 1893.)
- Home plate was a 12-inch square (instead of the present-day five-sided figure, which is 17 inches wide).
- Catchers were positioned 20 or more feet behind the batter and caught the balls on a bounce. They did not wear chest protectors (until 1885) or shin guards (1907).
- Batters were permitted to ask for a high or low pitch. (The rule was abolished in 1886.)

- A pitcher had to throw seven balls in order to issue a walk. Pitchers were required to throw underhanded. (Overhanded began in 1884.)
- Rules prohibited the use of a new ball until the beginning of a new inning, no matter how worn or disfigured the ball might have been.
- Games were not played on Sundays.
- There was one umpire a game. He was paid $5.
- Players had to pay $30 for their uniforms. (Clubs began paying for them in 1912.)
- Player salaries were limited to $2,000 annually. Team rosters only included 11 or 12 players.

## LONG AGO NO-HITTERS

Four Phillies tossed no hitters in the first 23 years of the franchise in 1885, 1898, 1903, and 1906. There was a long dry spell until Jim Bunning's perfect game in 1964. Since then there have been seven, including a gem in 2014, in which four pitchers combined on a no-hitter. Through social media the entire world knew in seconds about that gem. Little was known about the first four Phillies no-hitters until newspaper accounts the next day. With the help of the Baseball Hall of Fame library, the following provides more information about those first four.

### August 29, 1885

*RHP Charlie Ferguson won against the Providence Grays at the Phillies' home field, Recreation Park.*

*Score: 1–0*

*Season record: 26–20, 2.22 ERA.*

*Age: 22*

*Catcher: Jack Clements*

Account from *The New York Times* (August 30, 1885): "Ferguson, the Philadelphia pitcher, accomplished the feat today by retiring the Providence team without a hit in a full nine inning game. Eight of the visitors went out on strikes, one on a foul tip, and seven on short infield flies, only five balls being hit by them to the outfield, all of which were caught. His pitching was very steady, except in the fourth inning when he gave two men their bases on balls. The only run of the game was made by Mulvey in the ninth inning, when he reached first on a hit, stole second, went to third on Fogarty's out and came home on a wild pitch."

## July 8, 1898

*RHP Red Donahue won against the Boston Beaneaters (Braves) at Baker Bowl. Mound was at current distance, 60'6".*

   *Score: 5–0*

   *Season record: 17–17, 3.55*

   *Age: 25*

   *Catcher: Ed McFarland*

Account from *The Cincinnati Enquirer* (July 9, 1898): "Pitcher Donahue today performed the remarkable feat of shutting out the Boston Club without a hit. Donahue did not seem to exert himself in the least in making his great record against the Beaneaters, but he made excellent use of the gray matter beneath his auburn locks. First it was a tantalizing slow one, and then a very speedy curve. His change of pace could not have been excelled, and his opponents were 'shooting ducks' from start to finish. There was not the semblance of a base hit and had it not been for errors by Cross and Lauder only two visitors would have reached first base, these being given bases on balls. Seventeen Boston men were retired on fly catches, 14 of which went to the outfielders."

The first batter he faced reached base on an error. A similar play began the seventh. Overall, he walked two and struck out one, and Boston left four runners on base. The game took one hour, 50 minutes. It was his only shutout of the season and second of his career.

Donahue, a Villanova University product, pitched 13 years in the majors with the New York Giants, St. Louis (NL), Phillies (1898–1901), St. Louis (AL), Cleveland, and Detroit. He was acquired from St. Louis (NL) on November 10, 1897, with Monte Cross and Klondike Douglass for Jack Clements, Lave Cross, Tommy Dowd, Jack Taylor, and $1,000. He compiled a 72–48 record with the Phillies, winning 20 or more games twice.

## September 18, 1903

*RHP Chick Fraser won at the Chicago Cubs in the second game of a Friday doubleheader and the second of six consecutive twin bills. It was the largest margin of victory for a Phillies no-hitter.*

> Score: 10–0
>
> Season record: 12–17, 4.50 ERA
>
> Age: 30
>
> Catcher: Red Dooin

Account from *The Chicago Daily Tribune* (September 19, 1903): "'Chick' Fraser of the Zimmerites shut the Colts out without a run or hit in the second game of the two games played on the west side grounds yesterday, pitching the first full game without a hit in either big leagues this season."

Backed by a 14-hit attack and a four-run first inning, Fraser still had to overcome a shoddy defense as his teammates committed four errors, including three by shortstop Rudy Hulswitt. That's the most errors for any player in a no-hitter. Fraser walked five and struck out four. The game took one hour, 40 minutes. The losing pitcher was Peaches Graham, and it was the only game he pitched in the majors.

Fraser pitched 14 seasons in the majors with Louisville (NL), Cleveland (NL), Phillies (1899–1901 and 1902–04), Philadelphia (AL), Cincinnati (NL), and Chicago (NL). He was purchased from Cleveland on December 16, 1898, for $900 or $1,000. He compiled a 175–212 record, including 74–75 with the Phillies.

### May 1, 1906

*LHP John Lush won at Brooklyn's Washington Park. He was the youngest Phillies pitcher to toss a no-hitter (20 years, 8 months) and shortest (5'9") to do so.*

*Score: 6–0*

*Season record: 18–15, 2.37 ERA*

*Age: 20*

*Catcher: Jerry Donovan*

From the *Detroit Free Press* account (May 2, 1906): "The most notable pitching performance of the year in the major leagues—the first no hit and no run game recorded—was played this afternoon at Washington Park, Brooklyn. Hugh Duffy's Philadelphia Nationals, meeting the Superbas, performed the shutting out process, and Johnnie Lush, of Duffy's staff, did the record pitching. Lush is a left-hander who has been doing some remarkable work this spring. Already he had pitched a two-hit game, but today he pulled off the hitless stunt without anything occurring in the way of doubtful decisions on hits or errors that could cast the slightest reflection on his right to his record. Lush's feat was the more remarkable from the fact that he further contributed to his record performance by striking out eleven of the locals. He passed three men to first on balls, two of these being in succession, in the second inning. This was as far as any of the Brooklynites got."

With a 2–3 record, Lush faced Mal Eason, who would throw a no-hitter two months later. The Phillies scored twice to start the game and finished with 11 hits and three errors. Lush walked three and struck out 11. The game lasted one hour, 45 minutes. Born in Williamsport, Pennsylvania, Lush attended Girard Prep in Philadelphia. He pitched seven seasons in the National League for the Phillies (1904–07) before being traded to the Cardinals on June 10, 1907, for Buster Brown. During his Cardinals career (1907–14), he tossed a six-inning no-hitter on August 6, 1908, vs. Brooklyn to win 2–0. He compiled a 66–85 career record, including 23–26 with the Phillies.

## ALEXANDER'S 16 SHUTOUTS IN '16

*"A shutout is a statistic credited to a pitcher who allows no runs in a game. No pitcher shall be credited with pitching a shutout unless he pitches the complete game, or unless he enters the game with none out before the opposing team has scored in the first inning, puts out the side without a run scoring, and pitches the rest of the game without allowing a run. When two more pitchers combine to pitch a shutout, the league statistician shall make a notation to that effect in the league's official pitching records."*—Major League Baseball rule 10.18.

That's the rule, and the pitcher who rules the world for most shutouts in a season is right-hander Grover Cleveland Alexander of the Phillies in 1916. At age 29 he did it 16 times, breaking his own club record of 12 set the previous season. Almost half of the 33-game winner's victories were shutouts, a very rare feat.

Along the way, he broke the major league record of 13 by Jack Coombs (a 31-game winner with the Philadelphia A's in 1910). Alexander's 30th win came in the first game of a Saturday, September 23rd doubleheader against Cincinnati, which the Phillies won 7–3. Manager Pat Moran approached his ace after that game and said, "I'll have to ask you to pitch the second game. We have only a little more than an hour to catch the train. Get it over fast." He did winning 4–0 in two hours and seven minutes.

- The 16 shutouts were split evenly between the road and Baker Bowl.
- In addition he had six games (all wins) in which he allowed one run. On June 12 Pittsburgh scored its run in the top of the ninth inning.
- He was shut out four times, and three of them were 2–0.
- He pitched back-to-back gems three times, including three consecutive once.
- By opponent his shutouts were: Cincinnati (five), Boston (three), Pittsburgh, Brooklyn, and St. Louis (two each), Chicago and New York (one each). The five against Cincinnati tied a major league record for the most against one team.
- His best months were May and August with four each.
- Four were 1–0 decisions, including a 12-inning game vs. Chicago.
- His fastest shutout took one hour, 22 minutes.
- He pitched 144 total innings in the shutouts while only issuing nine walks.

Alexander also owns the club record for consecutive shutouts (four), which took place on September 7, 13, 17, and 21. This feat didn't occur in 1916—but in his rookie season in 1911 when he posted seven shutouts. During that streak he had 41 consecutive scoreless innings—yet another Phillies record that hasn't been matched. Cliff Lee came the closest with 34 innings in 2011.

When the Phillies won the pennant in 1915, Alexander was the ace, throwing a club-record 12 shutouts with four being one-hitters. Right-handed pitcher Joe Oeschger was a teammate. Rich Westcott wrote a story about the 91-year-old Oeschger in *Phillies*

*Report* in December 1983, in which Oeschger discussed Alexander. "The key feature of the 1915 club was hitting," Oeschger said. "We had power hitters in Cravath and Luderus. We won a lot of close games. Of course, Alexander was our top pitcher. If you got him one or two runs, you would win the game. He was a stopper and could prevent a long losing streak. If I were to classify all the pitchers that I had contact with or witnessed, I would say Alexander was the greatest...He was fantastic. In a way, he was just a natural pitcher, had wonderful control, his stuff was sharp and he was very difficult to hit safely. Alexander never threw the ball over the heart of the plate. It was either a little inside or outside. When you batted against him, you better start swinging or he would have a couple of strikes on you before you knew it. He worked every fourth day. He never had to be relieved. In those days if you couldn't pitch nine innings, you better start looking for another job."

In Alexander's career that also included stints with the Chicago Cubs and St. Louis Cardinals, he amassed 90 shutouts— second only to Walter Johnson's 110. Sixty-one came in a Phillies uniform, a club record that will never be broken. Steve Carlton's 39 are a distant second. So how do three Phillies Hall of Fame pitchers stack up for most shutouts in a season? Carlton's high mark was eight in 1971, Jim Bunning's was seven in 1965, and Robin Roberts' was six in 1951.

## YOUNGEST TO WIN A GAME

Roger McKee, a left-handed pitcher, did something special, something that no one else has done in the modern era of Major League Baseball on October 3, the last day of the 1943 National League season. McKee beat the Pittsburgh Pirates in the second game of a doubleheader. His pitching line was: nine innings, five hits, three runs, five walks, one strikeout, and two wild pitches. It was his only decision in a five-game big league career, but that's been done many times.

What separates him from thousands of other pitchers is that he was the youngest pitcher to win a game. He was 17 years, 17 days old when he took the mound at Forbes Field. His uniform number? 17.

The feat wasn't recognized in record books or Phillies archives. McKee wasn't even aware of it for a long time. "Many years later, a fan from New York state sent me a letter asking for an autograph," the late McKee once said. "The letter said, 'By the way, you are the youngest pitcher to win a game in the 20th century.' I hadn't thought about it."

The Phillies were notified of the feat by a friend of McKee's. Unable to locate any information, the club turned to the research department at the National Baseball Hall of Fame and Museum library in Cooperstown, New York. Freddy Berowski, a research associate, confirmed the fact after some digging. "He is the youngest to win a game in the modern era and second youngest in Major League history," Berowski said. "Willie McGill, age 16, won 11 games in 1890. The only possible person who could have been younger is Ed Knouff, who pitched in 1885. His exact birth date is unknown."

So there you have it. Roger McKee stands alone, and very few people knew. Imagine if that happened in today's world of multimedia outlets and social media.

McKee was an outstanding high school and American Legion (Post 82) pitcher in Shelby, North Carolina. "We won the legion state championship in 1942. We were eliminated in the semifinal round the following summer," he said. "That night Cy Morgan, a Phillies scout, wanted to see my dad and me. We met at a hotel in town. He offered $3,000 to sign with the Phillies. When he said I would report right away to Philadelphia, pitch some BP, perhaps an exhibition game, and make the final road trip. That was the selling point."

His debut came on August 18 when he was 16 years of age at Shibe Park. He threw three relief innings and allowed one run. He turned 17 on September 16 and won his historic game 17 days later, a game that took one hour, 48 minutes.

Because of World War II, big league clubs didn't hold spring training in the South. "We had spring training in Wilmington, Delaware, the next year [1944]," McKee said. "It was cold, and there was snow on the ground. We worked out every day in a big fieldhouse for a couple of weeks. Finally, we got to go outside one day. I don't know what it was, but the speed of my pitches wasn't there anymore. I had thrown a lot of American Legion innings with little rest the year before. That could have been it. Maybe I threw too hard the first time we worked outdoors."

McKee pitched in one game for the Phillies in 1944 (September 26) after spending the season with the Wilmington minor league team, pitching and playing first base. He wound up bouncing around the minor leagues until 1957 or 1958. He returned to Shelby, helped coach his high school and American Legion teams, worked in the fiber industry briefly, and retired after 30 years with the postal service. During the 2009 alumni weekend, he and his family were guests of the Phillies. McKee passed away on September 1, 2014, at age 87.

## MOST DRAMATIC HOME RUN

A number of Phillies sluggers have led the league in home runs, including Gavvy Cravath, Cy Williams, Chuck Klein, Mike Schmidt, Jim Thome, and Ryan Howard. Although they hit a ton of home runs, the single most dramatic home run in club history was by a 29-year-old left-handed hitting left fielder who finished with 39 home runs in 508 career games with the Phillies. His 13th homer in the 1950 season ranks No. 1 for drama.

"One ball, two strikes. Now Newcombe's set, in the stretch, delivering, swinging...A fly ball, very, very deep to left field, moving back Adams, way, way back...He can't get it...It's a home run—WOW!... A home run for Dick Sisler, the Phillies lead 4–1."

Those were the words of radio broadcaster Gene Kelly as he described Sisler's pennant-winning home run against the Dodgers in Brooklyn on October 1, 1950. "He threw me a fastball on the outside and then came in a little," Sisler recalled years later. "I was fortunate enough that it carried. I didn't know it was going all the way until after I had rounded first base." And in a neat sidenote, his Hall of Fame dad, George Sisler, was the director of minor leagues for the Dodgers and looked on from the third-base side of the park.

The big blast put the Phillies in the World Series for only the second time in the club's history. The "Whiz Kids," drained from a tough pennant race, were no match for the New York Yankees, losing the World Series in four straight.

Sisler's home run was a welcome sight for the ballclub. They took first place on July 25 and led by five games with only seven games remaining. But Curt Simmons (17–8) was drafted in the Army in early September, and two other starters, Bob Miller (11–6) and Bubba Church (8–6), were injured. Knowing a loss on October 1 would force a one-game playoff with Brooklyn for the National League pennant the following day, manager Eddie Sawyer decided to go with his ace, Robin Roberts, in the big Sunday afternoon game at Ebbetts Field. For Roberts it was his fourth start in the last nine games and a bid for his 20th win.

Two-out singles by Sisler, right fielder Del Ennis, and third baseman Willie Jones staked Roberts to a 1–0 lead in the sixth inning. In the bottom of the same inning, shortstop Pee Wee Reese sent a two-out drive deep to right field. Ennis retreated, and the ball hit a screen above the fence and dropped down to a one-foot coping. To the Phillies' disgust, the ball stayed there, and Reese circled the bases to tie the game.

Roberts and the Phillies appeared to be on the brink of disaster in the last of the ninth inning. Cal Abrams walked to start the inning, and Reese singled him to second. Duke Snider followed with another hit to center. Richie Ashburn made the throw of his life, as described by Kelly:

"A line drive single to center...Ashburn races in with the ball and here comes the throw...he is...OUT!"

In a twist of fate, Brooklyn's third-base coach, Milt Stock, who sent Abrams, was an infielder on the Phillies' 1915 pennant-winning squad.

Despite the great throw by Ashburn, Roberts remained in a huge jam. The talented Dodgers had a runner on first base and the winning run on third base with one out. Roberts walked Jackie Robinson intentionally to load the bases. He then retired Carl Furillo on a foul to first base and Gil Hodges on a routine fly ball to Ennis, sending the game to extra innings.

Roberts remained in the game and singled off Don Newcombe to start the 10th inning. Eddie Waitkus' single moved Roberts to second. Ashburn laid down a sacrifice bunt, but Roberts was thrown out at third. Sisler followed with his pennant-winning home run on a 1–2 pitch. Roberts retired three straight in the 10th setting off celebrations in Brooklyn and Philadelphia. The Whiz Kids were so popular that one of their longtime fans, Deborah Arden Stern, wrote a song about the team, "Fightin' Phils."

## RELIEVER EARNS FIRST MVP

Pennant winners traditionally have a closer that dominates. The Phillies are no exception with Jim Konstanty (1950), Tug McGraw 1980), Al Holland (1983), Mitch Williams (1993), and Brad Lidge

(2008–2009) leading the way. What about the 1915 pennant-winning Phillies? It was a different era then as teams didn't have closers. Konstanty's season was more historic than for any of the just mentioned closers. He relieved 74 times—then a major league mark—but a record that has been toppled multiple times. He was 16–7, setting a Phillies record for most wins by a reliever. That record remains.

His most historic moment came after the season was over—November 2 to be specific. The Baseball Writers Association of America voted him the National League's Most Valuable Player (286 votes to 158 for Stan Musial). The 33-year-old right-hander was the first relief pitcher to win the award. As of today, he's the *only* NL reliever to do so.

He finished 62 games—then a club record—and his 152 innings rank second for a Phillies reliever. His walks and strikeout totals (50 and 56) were unusual. Saves were not an official record in that era. Play-by-play research reveals he would have 22 under today's save rule. "By today's standards, Jim really wasn't a closer," says ex-teammate Curt Simmons. "By that I mean he just didn't pitch one or two innings. He could come in the seventh inning and finish a game. His fastball was just so-so, and he didn't use it. He had two outstanding pitches, a palm ball and slider, and his control was outstanding…Jim used the palm ball as his change-up and he threw it off the plate. Left-handed hitters couldn't touch him. He'd throw his slider on the corners. What was really strange was he'd throw his slider from one side of the pitching rubber and palm ball from the other side, and he got away with it. Hitters just didn't make good contact. We didn't win in '50 without him."

His ability to throw multiple innings stood out in two games that pennant-winning season. On August 25 the Phillies defeated the Pirates 9–7 in 15 innings at Forbes Field. Konstanty entered in the seventh inning, which was a 6–6 tie. The Phillies went ahead with a run in the 10th, but Konstanty gave up a game-tying home run to Ralph Kiner, who led off the bottom of the 10th, ending a 22-inning scoreless streak. He allowed two singles the rest of the way. He allowed one run in nine innings of relief.

On September 15 the Phillies defeated the Reds 8–7 in 19 innings, the second game of a Shibe Park doubleheader. This time he came in for the top of the ninth inning with the Reds leading 5–3. The Phillies tied the game in their at-bat, sending the game into extra innings. Konstanty pitched a total of 10 innings and allowed two runs in the top of the 18th inning. The Phillies tied it with two runs in the 18th and won on a walk-off RBI single by Del Ennis in the next inning. It is doubtful a Phillies reliever will ever pitch nine innings in a game again, let alone 10.

With 20-game winner Robin Roberts starting three times in five days and 17-game winner Curt Simmons in the military, manager Eddie Sawyer shocked the world by naming Konstanty as the starting pitcher in Game 1 of the World Series against the New York Yankees on October 4 at Shibe Park. He lost 1–0, allowing four hits in eight innings.

## ROBERTS' 17-INNING DANDY

When you win 20 games or more and throw 300 innings six consecutive seasons, that's a career that will lead you to being enshrined in Cooperstown, New York. Toss in five straight seasons, in which you lead the league in complete games, and that's hefty stuff. Well, say hello to Robin Roberts, the workhorse of Major League Baseball in the 1950s.

Obviously "Robbie" had a lot of amazing individual accomplishments. One game that stands out as a testimony of his durability happened on September 6, 1952—the first game of a scheduled twi-night doubleheader. He pitched all 17 innings in beating the Boston Braves 7–6 at Shibe Park before a scant 12,474 fans. The second game was suspended by a 1:00 AM Sunday curfew in the bottom of the eighth inning with Boston leading. Nearly as impressive was Phillies catcher Smoky Burgess, who caught all 25 innings and went 5-for-11.

Robbie's pitching line was: 17 innings, 18 hits, six runs, three walks, and five strikeouts. He faced 71 batters. Assuming he averaged five pitches per batter, he threw 355 pitches. Say he averaged four per batter, his pitch count would have been 284. (Tom Cheney of the Washington Senators went 16 innings in a win in 1962, throwing 228 pitches, the most officially recorded.)

Five days after Roberts' longest game, he went nine innings in a 3–2 win against the St. Louis Cardinals, one of five more wins the rest of the season, which were all complete games. Complete games were nothing new for the Phillies right-hander. The 17-inning gem was No. 3 in a run of 28 consecutive complete games from August 28, 1952, through July 5, 1953. His record during that streak was 21–6. (One game of the 28 was a tie.) In today's game complete games are nearly extinct. Specialization and pitch counts have taken over. Starters are expected to go six innings and then turn it over to a bullpen of relievers and closers to finish a game.

In Robbie's 14-year career with the Phillies, he averaged 18 complete games per season. He led the National League for five straight seasons starting in 1952 when he had 30. His high was 33 in 1953. Putting it in perspective, the complete game high for the Phillies this decade is 18...by the whole 2011 staff.

His 17-inning marathon was a true feat. "We won the game when Del Ennis hit a home run into the upper deck off Bob Chipman leading off our 17th inning," Roberts said. "There's nothing more exciting than a walk-off home run—unless you are the guy who gave it up," he laughed. "We didn't count pitches back then so I don't know how many I threw. I do know I pitched better in the second game than I did in the first game," he again laughed. Robbie blanked the Braves from the ninth through the 17th innings.

Today pitchers ice their shoulders and elbows after they pitch. It was different back then. "I always took a hot shower and ran hot water on my arm," Roberts said. "I was told one time that it would increase circulation. I did the same thing my whole career. It's hard to say that was right, and ice is wrong."

Since this 17-inning game in 1952, the Phillies have played six other games of the same length and used a total of 37 pitchers. By the way Robbie's the last major leaguer to pitch 17 innings in a game. Although that may have been his single-most impressive outing, that season was also his most impressive single season.

Robin Roberts, who delivered many historic performances for the Phillies, stands to the left of Major League Baseball commissioner Bowie Kuhn during his Hall of Fame enshrinement in 1976. (National Baseball Hall of Fame and Museum)

He finished 28–7, the most wins for a National Leaguer since Dizzy Dean won that many in 1935. He was 7–5 on June 17 but won 21 of his next 23 decisions. No Phillies pitcher since has matched 28 wins. Robbie led the league in wins, games started (37), complete games (30), innings pitched (330), and hits allowed (292). There was no Cy Young Award back then—just the Most Valuable Player. Hank Sauer, a Chicago Cubs outfielder, won the award—the biggest farce in the history of the award.

### ASHBURN EDGES MAYS

Willie Mays .346, Richie Ashburn .344. That's the way the National League batting championship race stood with just three games left on the 1958 schedule.

Mays was heading home to San Francisco for three games with the St. Lois Cardinals. Ashburn just finished an unbelievable year at Connie Mack Stadium in which he batted .378. His final three games were in Pittsburgh. Going into the final week of the season, Ashburn was batting only .262 versus Pirates pitching.

Six hits during the doubleheader in Philadelphia against the Pirates on September 22 put him in the race as the end neared. "There were four of us in the race that week," Ashburn recalled. "Hank Aaron, Stan Musial, Willie, and myself. I remember *Sports Illustrated* did a big story on the batting title, and they listed odds for each. I was the last of the bunch. It really got me peeved."

Friday, September 26 saw Ashburn pass Mays. Richie went 2-for-4 to go to .3448 while Mays was hitless in three at-bats to drop to .3440. Ashburn increased his average to .3469 with a 3-for-5 Saturday, while Mays climbed to .3445 on the strength of two hits in five at-bats.

It all came down to the final game Sunday afternoon. Right-hander Bennie Daniels was pitching for the Pirates. Ashburn singled to left in the third, beat out a single to third in the sixth, and was walked by left-hander Bob Smith in the eighth. That walk led to a run, which put the Phillies on top 4–3. Pittsburgh tied the game in the eighth, and the game went into extra innings.

Ashburn singled to center against another lefty, Bob Gross, to open the 10th. He wound up scoring the decisive run in a 6–4, 10-inning victory, coming across the plate on Harry Anderson's looping single. Ashburn, who hit .478 after September 11, was finished for the season, a .350 figure. But Mays was just getting started on the West Coast. "I figured the pressure was on him," Ashburn said.

The great center fielder of the Giants needed a perfect 5-for-5 to tie Ashburn. Mays gave Ashburn a scare by going 3-for-5, which put him at .347. "I really didn't know I won until sometime that night," Ashburn said. "I don't remember exactly when. I know the team was flying back to Philadelphia, but I had driven to Pittsburgh and was continuing on home to Tilden [Nebraska]." Not only did he lead the league in hits (215), Richie also led in walks (97). He was the first player to do that since Rogers Hornsby (1924). No Phillies hitter has won a batting title since.

Ashburn became only the second Phillies player to win two batting titles. His first Silver Bat came in 1955. He had 180 hits and walked 105 times but didn't lead the National League in either, but his .338 average was 19 points better than Mays and Musial. Richie went hitless in seven at-bats in a season-ending doubleheader in the Polo Grounds, but it didn't matter.

### Phillies Batting Champions

| YEAR | NAME | BATTING AVERAGE |
|------|------|-----------------|
| 1891 | Billy Hamilton | .340 |
| 1893 | Billy Hamilton | .380 |
| 1899 | Ed Delahanty | .410 |
| 1910 | Sherry Magee | .331 |
| 1928 | Lefty O'Doul | .398 |
| 1933 | Chuck Klein | .368 |
| 1947 | Harry Walker | .363 |
| 1955 | Richie Ashburn | .338 |
| 1958 | Richie Ashburn | .350 |

## MAHAFFEY'S 17-STRIKEOUT GEM

There have been some great strikeout pitchers in Phillies history, including Grover Cleveland Alexander, Robin Roberts, Jim Bunning, Steve Carlton, and Curt Schilling. The honor of having the biggest strikeout game in franchise history, however, belongs to Art Mahaffey, who spent six seasons with the Phillies (1960–65). The right-hander from Cincinnati, Ohio, struck out 17 Chicago Cubs in the second game of a Sunday afternoon doubleheader at Connie Mack Stadium on April 23, 1961. Nine went down swinging.

Mahaffey, 23, threw 146 pitches that afternoon, of which only 48 were called balls. He fanned Don Zimmer, Ron Santo, Ernie Banks, and Frank Thomas three times each in matching the major league record for most strikeouts in a day game set by Dizzy Dean of the St. Louis Cardinals against the Cubs on July 30, 1933.

"I remember everything about it," Mahaffey said. "Matter of fact, I was at a golf tournament with Frank Thomas one time, and he was telling me I didn't strike him out that day. He was wrong. He was 3-for-3, three Ks. Early in the game, Pancho [Herrera] dropped a foul pop-up hit by Thomas. I struck Frank out on the next pitch."

During those days the Phillies and Blue Cross had a Pitchometer built by Dr. I. M. Levitt of the Franklin Institute. The Pitchometer was used throughout the city to test the throwing speed of young athletes. Mahaffey remembered hitting 100 mph on the machine one time. "Against the Cubs that day, I had an unbelievable fastball and curveball," he recalled. "I threw mostly fastballs, particularly in the late innings. Earlier, I got maybe five or six strikeouts with my curve." Mahaffey had 15 strikeouts through seven innings. He struck out only one in each of the last two innings. "I had two strikes on the last four hitters but only got one strikeout," he said. "I came so close to having more than 17."

One batter who didn't fan that day was ex-Phil Richie Ashburn. He pinch hit in the eighth inning. "Whitey was tough to strike out. I remember he hit a line drive out to [Johnny] Callison in right field," said Mahaffey, an All-Star in both 1961 and 1962. "It is amazing how many fans remember this game. There's a photo of Connie Mack Stadium from that day, and I've signed many an autograph, always including 4/23/61."

Prior to Mahaffey's big day, the Phillies record for strikeouts in a game was 13 shared by three pitchers: Ray Benge on June 16, 1929, Robin Roberts on May 2, 1957, and Jack Sanford on June 7, 1957. Oddly, the opponent in each case was the Cubs.

One other note about the day: Frank Sullivan, a 6'6" right-hander, blanked the Cubs 1–0 in the first game. It marked the last time the Phillies had two shutouts in a doubleheader. Three Phillies pitchers came close to Mahaffey's record, falling one short: Steve Carlton on June 9, 1982 vs. the Cubs, Curt Schilling on September 9, 1997 vs. the New York Yankees, and Cliff Lee on May 6, 2011 vs. the Atlanta Braves. Chris Short did fan 18 on October 2, 1965 at the New York Mets, but that game went 18 innings.

## CARLTON'S 3,000TH STRIKEOUT

Through his first 14 big league seasons, Steve Carlton averaged 212 strikeouts per year. Barring injury, he would become the first left-hander ever to reach 3,000 strikeouts as he entered the 1981 season. Lefty picked up 28 strikeouts in his first four starts (3–0 record, 2.45 ERA), setting the stage for some baseball history at Veterans Stadium. On Wednesday, April 29, he faced the first-place Montreal Expos.

Carlton needed three strikeouts to reach 3,000 and become the sixth pitcher ever to reach that lofty height. He handed the Expos a 6–2 loss. His first pitch came at 7:40 PM. Always a fast worker, Carlton left little doubt as he struck out the side in *four minutes*. Tim Raines went down swinging, Jerry Manuel was called out, and Tim Wallach took a 3–2 pitch for strike three. The crowd rose to its feet, the scoreboard flashed a message about 3,000 strikeouts, and Lefty tipped his cap to the 30,141 appreciative fans.

Longtime umpire Frank Pulli was behind the plate. "For some reason, I knew he needed three going into the game," he said. "I believe I was more pumped than Lefty. After I called Wallach out on the 3–2 pitch, he complained a little. He thought it was high. I didn't. I told him, 'Tim, you'll be the answer to a trivia question someday.'"

The game was televised on PRISM that night. Chris Wheeler and Tim McCarver were the broadcasters. Lefty didn't speak with reporters during this period of his career. He did a brief postgame interview with McCarver on PRISM:

"Since your first year here in 1972, I don't think I've ever seen since then a crowd respond to you like they did tonight when you got your 3,000th strikeout," McCarver said. Carlton responded: "They like to see people achieve different goals. They are right there plugging with you, and you're always happy to have a nice crowd like this."

Later that same season (September 21), Lefty fanned Montreal's Andre Dawson in Montreal for No. 3,118, the most for any National League pitcher. When Carlton's career ended after the 1988 season, he ranked second to Nolan Ryan on the all-time strikeout list.

Acquired in an unpopular trade for Rick Wise in spring training of 1972, Carlton became a quick hero as he won 27 games (10 losses) for a Phillies team that had only 59 wins. "Super Steve" won 15 consecutive games at one point, setting a new club record. When Lefty pitched shortstop Larry Bowa called it "Win-day."

When it was all said and done, Steve Carlton was acclaimed as the greatest pitcher in Phillies history.

## ROSE BREAKS MUSIAL'S RECORD

The year was 1981, and baseball was returning to the playing field after a players' strike had wiped out 55 games. Baseball interest in Philadelphia was at an all-time high as the Phillies were the defending world champions. The first game back was on August 10, a Monday night ABC telecast. Pete Rose was one hit shy of breaking Stan Musial's 17-year-old record for most hits in National League history.

There was no better way for baseball to resume than in front of a jam-packed Veterans Stadium and a national television audience. The St. Louis Cardinals, for whom Musial starred, were the opponents. Ironically, Musial's 3,630th and last hit came in 1963, a ground-ball single to right past a Cincinnati rookie second baseman named Pete Rose.

Rose had tied Musial on June 10. His record-tying hit was a single off Nolan Ryan of the Houston Astros. It came in the first inning, and then Ryan closed the door with three straight strikeouts. The next day the players went on strike. Baseball stood still for two months.

Facing Bob Forsch on August 10, Rose reached base on an error by the shortstop in the first inning, grounded to the pitcher in the third, and grounded to the second baseman in the fifth. Leading off the Phillies' eighth, Rose hit another grounder, but this one went between short and third for the record-breaking 3,631st hit. Mark Littell was the pitcher. Fireworks exploded from the Vet roof, 60,561 fans stood as one and roared, Rose tipped his helmet, and Musial entered the field to congratulate him followed by hugs from Pete Jr. and the rest of the Phillies. It was one of the great historic moments in Phillies history. "The whole thing about breaking records is the reaction of the fans. It was very special because it happened at home in front of so many Phillies fans. Musial being there was icing on the cake," Rose said. "There was no pressure attached to this record. It's not like a hitting streak. I needed one more hit, and it was going to happen. It was just a matter of where, when, the kind of hit, and the pitcher."

Following the game, a large media mass squeezed into a room behind home plate for a press conference. A red phone that had a direct line to the White House was positioned on the podium. President Ronald Reagan was going to call and congratulate Pete. It turned out to be a hilarious phone conversation:

**White House operator:** "Mr. Rose, hold on please..."

**Pete:** "Tell the President, I'll be with him in a minute."

**White House:** "Mr. Rose, hold on please..."

**Pete:** "Good thing there isn't a missile on the way."

**White House:** "Mr. Rose, hold on please..."

**Pete:** "I've waited 19 years for this, I can wait another minute."

**White House:** "Mr. Rose, hold on please..."

**Pete:** "Larry [Shenk], I'll give him my home phone."

**White House:** "Hello Pete, this is President Reagan calling."

**Pete:** "Hey, how ya' doing?" (That response brought down the house.)

Rose played two more years with the Phillies before moving on to the Montreal Expos in 1984 for part of one season and closing out his playing career back in Cincinnati from 1984 to 1986. He finished with 4,256 hits, 826 coming in a Phillies uniform.

Honus Wagner held the National League record before Musial, and his 3,430th and final hit came in 1917 at age 43. Wagner's

3,000th hit—a double—was against the Phillies, June 9, 1914, at Baker Bowl off Erskine Mayer.

## BUNNING'S PERFECT GAME

It was only fitting that Jim Bunning, then a father of seven, would do something special when he took the mound in 90-degree heat at Shea Stadium on Father's Day on June 21, 1964. The slender right-hander entered the record book by throwing a perfect game against the New York Mets on that Sunday afternoon 6–0. It was the first perfect game in the National League since John Ward, pitching for Providence, blanked Buffalo 5–0 on June 7, 1890.

Bunning struck out 10, including pinch-hitter John Stephenson to end the masterpiece in the first game of a doubleheader. Of the 90 pitches he threw, only 21 were out of the strike zone. He had a three-ball count twice. By the inning he threw eight, 11, eight, 12, nine, seven, 10, 12, and 13 pitches. "My slider was my best pitch, and I had a pretty good curve. I had just as good stuff in my other no-hitter, but I think I'm a better pitcher now," he said at the time.

(While pitching for the Detroit Tigers, he authored a no-hitter against the Boston Red Sox on July 20, 1958, at Fenway Park. The last hitter he retired was future Hall of Famer Ted Williams. Bunning walked two and struck out 12 that Sunday afternoon.)

The only potential hit in New York was wiped out by a sensational diving stop by second baseman Tony Taylor of a drive by Jesse Gonder in the fifth inning. Taylor knocked down the line drive, crawled after the ball, and got Gonder at first base.

Generally, when a pitcher is working on a no-hitter it is a no-no for players to talk about it on the bench. But in his book, *Jim Bunning, Baseball and Beyond*, Bunning described how he and his teammates talked at length about his approach during the game. "The other guys thought I was crazy, but I didn't want anyone tightening up. Most of all, I didn't want to tighten up myself,"

Bunning said. "I started thinking about it around the fifth inning. By then you know you have a chance."

Manager Gene Mauch said after the game, "He acted like he knew something early. He was moving the infielders around early. Then late in the game when he was coming back to the dugout, he was yelling, 'Nine more, six more, three more. Do something out there, dive for the balls.'" Said right fielder Johnny Callison: "It was the strangest thing. You don't talk when you have a no-hitter, right? But he was going up and down the bench and telling everybody what was going on. Everybody tried to get away from him, but he was so wired that he followed us around." Catcher Gus Triandos added: "He was really silly. He was jabbering like a magpie."

As the Shea Stadium fans were on their feet and cheering, Bunning took the mound for the ninth inning. With two outs away from immortality, Bunning motioned Triandos to the mound. "He calls me out and says I should tell him a joke or something, just to give him a breather," Triandos said. "I couldn't think of any. I just laughed at him."

Up stepped George Altman as a pinch-hitter, someone Bunning figured would get to bat. With a 1–2 count, Bunning recorded his ninth strikeout. That brought up a second straight left-handed pinch-hitter, Stephenson, who had a .047 average. "I knew if I got Stephenson up there with two out, I had it," Bunning said. "I knew I could get him out on curveballs, no matter what." Curveballs were all Stephenson saw. A swing and a miss on the first pitch, then strike two looking, a curveball outside, another one outside, then a swing and a miss ended the game. Twenty-seven down and none to go.

Bunning pounded his fist into his glove, and his teammates flooded the field while Mets fans continued to cheer. Mary Bunning and their oldest daughter, Barbara, had driven to New York for the game. The rest of the family was back in Bunning's

South Jersey residence watching the classic on television. Mary was ushered to the field where she hugged and kissed her husband. A postgame dinner was planned, but that didn't happen. They drove back to Philly late that night.

Bunning got a phone call from Ed Sullivan, host of the popular TV show that aired live on Sunday nights out of New York. Bunning appeared on the show and received $1,000. "We added a pool and bathhouse to our home in Kentucky," he said.

Only one other pitcher—the legendary Cy Young— had tossed a no-hitter in each league. In 1887 he threw one while in the National League and in 1904 and 1908 he accomplished those feats in the American League. Bunning's gem was the first no-hitter by a Phillies pitcher since 1906 when John Lush stopped the Dodgers by the same score in Brooklyn.

**Hall of Fame Artifacts from Bunning's Perfect Game**

- Raincheck ticket signed by Gene Mauch and broadcasters Richie Ashburn and Bill Campbell
- Bunning's cap
- Ticket stubs
- Official scoresheet

## WISE NO-HITS CINCINNATI

As a rookie in 1964, Rick Wise won his first game on June 21 at Shea Stadium, the second game of a Sunday afternoon doubleheader. No one noticed because it followed Jim Bunning's perfect game. Seven years later, though, the 25-year-old Wise got big time attention for his right arm and big bat.

On a Wednesday night in Cincinnati's Riverfront Stadium, Wise did something no one had ever done up to that date. And it hasn't been duplicated since. He belted two homers while pitching a no-hitter. Only a sixth-inning walk to Davey Concepcion kept him from a perfect game. "I went 3–0, got a strike but then overthrew a fastball up in the zone," he recalled. "It was one of the few pitches I threw out of the strike zone." He threw 95 pitches that historic night. Fifty-six of them were fastballs, and 39 were breaking pitches.

Wise remembered it was scorching hot in Cincinnati that day. "By late morning it was already in the 80s," he said. "On top of that, I was not feeling well at all. I was fighting the effects of the flu, which I'd had for five or six days. The thought of skipping my start never crossed my mind. My warm-up pitches seemed to stop halfway to home plate. I felt very weak and thought to myself, *You'd better locate your pitches very well or you won't be around long.* The first nine batters went down in order, and I felt myself getting stronger, possibly because I had sweated out the remnants of the flu. While [I was] batting in the fifth inning, Ross Grimsley left a slider up in the zone, and I hit it for a home run to left field. Meanwhile, the Reds were offering at my pitches early in the count, and it made for quick innings. My tempo increased, my focus increased, and my command and location were excellent, except to Concepcion in the sixth inning.

"I led off the eighth inning against Clay Carroll, who fell behind in the count 2–0. I checked the third-base coach for a sign, and he just turned his back on me. In other words the green light was on—swing at it! Clay threw the next pitch right down Broadway, and I was ready. Home run No. 2 to left center. The Cincinnati fans rose to their feet as I started the ninth inning. That was special. I retired the first two batters, and low and behold, Pete Rose came to the plate and stood between me and a no-hitter. He was the last hitter you wanted to see with one out remaining in a no-no. The count went to 3–2, and I went with a fastball, low and away. A semi-line drive to John Vukovich, and the game was complete. My greatest game ever!" His record stood at 8–4, and time of game for this gem was an hour, 53 minutes.

Wise's 16th win that same season came on Saturday, September 18, against the Chicago Cubs at Veterans Stadium. In this game he retired 32 consecutive batters, which was four short of the major league record. Tim McCarver again was the catcher. No Phillies pitcher has come close to Wise's single-game gem. Oh, Curt Simmons, Robin Roberts, Jim Bunning, and Roy Halladay each have had games in which they retired 27 consecutive batters. But thanks to extra innings, Wise went beyond 27.

**Hall of Fame Artifacts from Wise No-Hitter**
- Wise's cap, glove, and bat
- Game-used baseball

A home run leading off the second inning by catcher Frank Fernandez gave the Cubs a 3–1 lead. Wise didn't allow another base runner until Ron Santo singled with two out in the 12th inning. Once again, Wise's bat came into play. He was 3-for-6 and drove in the winning run. With a runner on third with one out, Don Money and Ron Stone were walked intentionally to get to Wise, who followed with a walk-off single to right for a 4–3 decision. "The best part about that game was that I fell behind 3–1 on a two-run homer in the first and a solo home run in the second," Wise said. "I got a visit from the pitching coach and then retired 32 in a row."

His pitching line was: 12 innings, five hits, three runs, two earned runs, no walks, and 10 strikeouts. He faced 41 batters. In addition to 10 strikeouts, there were 11 ground-ball outs, six infield pop-ups or line drives, and only five fly balls to the outfield.

## SCHMIDT'S HISTORIC HOME RUNS

As a 23-year-old rookie in 1973, Mike Schmidt hit .196 with 18 home runs in 132 games. That might not have been the greatest start, but when his 18-year career with the Phillies ended in 1989, he had amassed 548 home runs. Without a doubt he's the greatest player in Phillies history. His career featured many great moments, but two home runs stood out. Both occurred in April, and they were exactly 11 years and one day apart.

## April 18, 1987

Schmidt couldn't have written a more dramatic script for his 500th home run. The 37-year-old unloaded his historic home run on a 3–0 pitch with two runners on base and two out in the top of the ninth inning and the Phillies losing 6–5 to the Pittsburgh Pirates. Schmidt drilled Don Robinson's pitch into the sand-colored wall behind the Phillies left-field bullpen, giving the Phillies an 8–6 win in Pittsburgh's Three Rivers Stadium.

Only 13 other players had reached that level in baseball history. "I started 1987 needing five home runs for No. 500," Schmidt said. "It was scary as the possibility of choking on those five was real, as everyone was focused on how long it would take me. The team was having a rough start, I believe 1–8, as we went to Pittsburgh for a three-game series. I had hit three in the first seven games and was rolling, feeling pretty good myself."

Schmidt moved to within one of 500 by homering off Bob Patterson in the first game of a series on Friday night. It came in the second inning. He was hitless in three more at-bats, adding a 10th-inning walk.

The next afternoon Schmidt popped out in the first with two runners on base, walked in the third, and flied to left in both the fifth and seventh innings. "We were behind by two in the top of the ninth as a rally started," Schmidt recalled. "[We] got two men on base, Juan Samuel beat out a double play, and Von Hayes walked on four pitches. I came up with two on and ran the count to 3–0 and got the green light. A little known fact is that I finished the game at shortstop."

The greatest personal thrill for Schmidt and his good friend, Harry Kalas, came precisely at 4:53 PM. Kalas' emotional call was brief but elicited goose bumps: "Swing and a long drive, there it is! No. 500. The career 500th home run for Michael Jack Schmidt!"

"Schmidt pumped his arms and legs for a giddy moment before he reached first base, then continued his tour of the bases in his normal, stately majesty," wrote Paul Hagen, *Philadelphia Daily News* baseball writer. "It's a relief," Schmidt said in Hagen's article. "I had a lot of pitches to hit lately, but all those at-bats I was fighting that adrenaline, fighting the image of the ball flying out to left field."

Going into the season, it was a guessing game for many as to when Schmidt would reach the milestone. He did it in only 11 games. Schmidt had his own prediction: "Without looking at the schedule or even knowing who we're playing, I'd say around April 20, give or take a couple of days."

Hagen indicated Schmidt had considered kissing home plate after the historic trip around the bases. "There were two reasons I didn't: one was that all my teammates were standing there," said the beaming Schmidt. "The other was that the plate looked kind of dirty."

### April 17, 1976

Schmidt and the Phillies were in Wrigley Field for a two-game series Saturday and Sunday afternoon. In the Saturday game, he set a club record hitting four consecutive home runs, including a 10th-inning game-winner off right-hander Paul Reuschel as the Phillies hung on 18–16. Their record stood at 2–3.

"I arrived in Chicago in a slump. I was demoted to sixth in the batting order that day. I was definitely pressing and not relaxed," Schmidt said. "Before the game my friend, Dick Allen, pulled me aside and said, 'Lets you and I just concentrate on having fun today.' The game started, and we fell behind immediately, so it was comeback baseball all game. We came back from 11 runs twice [12–1 after three innings and 13–2 after four]."

For the record he hit a two-run homer in the fifth inning (a curveball, according to Schmidt) off Rick Reuschel, a solo home run in the seventh (fastball up and in) again off Rick, a three-run blast in the eighth (another fastball) off Mike Garman, and a two-run homer in the 10th (fastball up and in) off Paul Reuschel. "I wasn't thinking anything special when I went up there in the 10th," Schmidt recalled. "I was feeling good and was nice and relaxed. I don't think moving from third to sixth in the order meant anything. I did use a Tony Taylor bat and wore a Terry Harmon T-shirt that he said had a lot of hits in it. Five-for-six with four homers and eight RBIs—pretty good day! The important thing… we won 50 games out of the next 63 to reach the postseason for the first time."

How significant was that afternoon in Chicago? Schmidt became the second player in National League history to hit four *consecutive* home runs in a game, joining Boston's Bob Lowe, who did it in 1894. Overall, 10 players hit four home runs in a game up until 1976. Seven of the elite were in the National League, including two Hall of Fame Phillies—first baseman Ed Delahanty (1896) and outfielder Chuck Klein (1936).

## MULHOLLAND NO-HITS FORMER TEAM
### By Paul Hagen

There was no foreshadowing that something extraordinary was going to happen at Veterans Stadium on the muggy, buggy night of August 15, 1990. No hint that a dog days matchup between a Phillies team on its way to a fourth straight losing season and the visiting San Francisco Giants would become the framework for one of the most memorable nights in franchise history.

When Terry Mulholland threw his first pitch to Giants lead-off man Rick Parker, he was a 27-year-old left-hander with a 6–6 record and a 4.34 ERA. Coming into the season his career numbers were 7–15 and 4.67. He had been shuttled back and forth between the bullpen and the rotation all season. Two hours and nine minutes later, he was the author of the first no-hitter pitched in Philadelphia in that century. "I still keep feeling like it was somebody else who did it," he said later. "These things don't happen to Terry Mulholland. They happen to Nolan Ryans, Tom Seavers, guys like that. Not guys from Uniontown, Pennsylvania...I think in the back of my mind it will always seem like a dream because that's what it is: a dream come true."

It was a game that was laced with coincidences, starting with the fact that Mulholland was pitching against the team that drafted and signed him and then had traded him to the Phillies just over a year earlier. In that deal the Phillies also got left-hander Dennis Cook and third baseman Charlie Hayes. Hayes was charged with the throwing error in the seventh inning that cost Mulholland his perfect game...then redeemed himself by snagging pinch-hitter Gary Carter's line drive for the final out to preserve the no-hitter.

The batter who reached base on the error was Parker, who was drafted by the Phillies in 1985 and was the player to be named later who was sent to San Francisco, along with Steve Bedrosian for Mulholland, Cook, and Hayes.

By the time Carter came to the plate, all the normal baseball superstitions had been observed. Nobody talked to the pitcher between innings. Everybody sat in the same seat in the dugout. Catcher Darren Daulton, who normally used more than one glove during hot summer nights, stuck with the same sweat-soaked mitt.

Carter took the first pitch for a ball. The fans groaned. Mulholland's second pitch was fouled straight back. A rhythmic clapping began. Carter swung and missed. The count was 1–2 now, and the crowd rose. Someone started a chant: "TER-RY! TER-RY!" Mulholland stepped off the mound. "My right leg was beginning to feel kind of wobbly," he said later. "I didn't feel 100 percent behind the next pitch, so I huddled with myself." The next pitch was fouled in a soft arc into the seats down the left-field line. Home-plate umpire Eric Gregg asked for more baseballs. The chant became more urgent: "TER-RY! TER-RY!"

Then Carter smoked one, a tracer toward left that ran parallel to the foul line. Before the crowd even had a chance to gasp, Hayes took a quick step to his right, reached across his body, and made the catch. Daulton rushed to the mound. Mulholland threw his glove in the air and embraced him as the rest of the team converged. The normally reserved pitcher waved to the wildly cheering crowds and even tossed his maroon hat into the seats.

Later in the clubhouse, he would be doused with champagne. Giants manager Roger Craig sent over his lineup card as a souvenir. Club president Bill Giles gave both Mulholland and Daulton bonuses. The Hall of Fame came calling, asking for artifacts. "That game certainly brought my name far above my career numbers," Mulholland reflected. "If it helps get things moving for me, that's great."

**Hall of Fame Artifacts from Mulholland's No-Hitter**

• Mulholland's uniform jersey
• Game-used baseball

And maybe it did. From that point to the end of the season, his ERA was 1.99. For the next three seasons, he was the Phillies Opening Day starter and totaled 41 wins. He led the league with 12 complete games in 1992 and played an integral role in helping the Phillies make it to the World Series for the first time in a decade in 1993. He had many memorable moments in his career. But he never did anything like what he did on August 15, 1990, a game that started out just like any other and ended up being anything but.

*(Paul Hagen is a columnist for MLB.com and 2013 recipient of the J. G. Taylor Spink Award for lifetime of excellence in baseball writing.)*

## GREENE NO-HITS MONTREAL

*By Tommy Greene*

May 23, 1991 was a day like any other day for me except it was a 12:35 PM getaway game in Montreal. I had been pitching out of the bullpen up to that point except for a spot start for Jose DeJesus because of back spasms. Mentally, I told myself I was going to treat this start like I treated my relief appearances: be aggressive and go as long and as hard as I can. My thought was if I run out of gas they will put someone else in for me.

I knew my body and how long it took for me to get ready to pitch. Dennis "Oil Can" Boyd had already finished warming up in the bullpen for the Expos and was walking back to the dugout before I threw my first pitch in the bullpen. By the time both anthems were played and he threw his first pitch of the game, I was sitting in the dugout ready to go.

As the game progressed, we took an early lead (1–0). Except for some walks there was nothing but routine plays made behind me. The walks that I had that day (seven) were high, but considering that the game was 1–0 until the ninth, I did not give in to the power guys that could hurt me with the long ball. I had four

**Hall of Fame Artifacts from Greene's No-Hitter**

- Greene's cap
- Game-used baseball

3–2 pitches to them but just missed on the last pitch. Most of them were with two outs.

It wasn't until after the seventh inning that I realized I hadn't given up a hit. When I did that, I immediately thought of the three no-hit bids I had coming up through the minor leagues that I lost with two outs and two strikes in the last inning. I said to myself, *Take one batter at a time.* In the bottom of the ninth, I was facing the meat of their order.

The first batter I struck out. *One down.* The second batter grounded out. *Two outs.* Before Tim Wallach stepped in the box, I thought of what my pitching coach with the Atlanta Braves (Leo Mazzone) said to me numerous times through the minor leagues: "When are you going to finish one of these bleeping games off?" I thought, Leo, *This one is for you.*

I then told myself I was going straight after Tim. I wasn't getting two strikes again unless he fouled pitches off. Darren Daulton put down the sign for a fastball. By then I had thrown probably over 100 fastballs out of my 135 pitches. I agreed with his sign and said to myself, *stay aggressive*, and threw the fastball on the outer half of the plate. He swung and hit probably the hardest ball all day, but it was a one-hopper right back to me. I gloved it. I couldn't believe it. I was so excited that I ran all but 20 feet over to first base and didn't toss it to Ricky Jordan until I realized he was screaming at me to toss it to him, which I did. It was over! I finally finished one off! Where it counted the most in the big leagues!

*(Tommy Greene pitched 36 games for the Phillies in 1991 and went 13–7.)*

## SCHILLING'S WORLD SERIES SHUTOUT
### By Hal Bodley

Curt Schilling oozed with confidence as he walked to the mound in the opening game of the 1993 World Series against Toronto. The big right-hander was giddy after winning the MVP Award as his Phillies shocked the favored Atlanta Braves to win the pennant in the just-completed National League Championship Series.

The energized Phillies jumped to a 2–0 lead in the first inning against Toronto at the SkyDome, and now it was up to Schilling to put down the Blue Jays. And maybe trick them. Instead to the delight of 52,011 fans, Toronto did the tricking. Powered by Devon White and John Olerud homers, the Blue Jays sent the Phillies and Schilling reeling 8–5. "I lost the game because for the only time in my postseason career, I went 100 percent against my instincts," Schilling remembers. "I thought I could trick 'em. I threw my first change-up of the second half of the season, and Devon White sent it to the second deck!" Schilling was nursing his wounds—and ego—after the game "when Vuk [bench coach John Vukovich] chewed my butt out, told me to pitch like me!"

That's exactly what Schilling did when he returned to the mound in Game 5 with the Blue Jays leading the best-of-seven series 3–1, and the Phillies hanging by a thread—or Schilling's right arm.

What Curt did was give the Phillies, facing elimination, arguably the most impressive one-game pitching performance in their World Series history. He shut out the Blue Jays 2–0, allowing just five hits for an offense that had scored 37 runs in the first four games, including an awesome 15–14 come-from-behind triumph on a rainy night at Philadelphia's water-logged Veterans Stadium in Game 4 the day before.

Of course, Joe Carter's dramatic walk-off three-run homer in the ninth inning against the Phillies' Mitch Williams in Game 6 will forever be the face of the 1993 World Series. That resulted in an 8–6 victory, which gave the Blue Jays back-to-back World Series titles. They were deprived of the chance of making it three in a row because major league players were on strike in 1994, and the series was cancelled.

But had the admittedly strong-minded Schilling not gone back to what made him one of the National League's premier starters, there wouldn't have been a historic Game 6. "For me it was the most exciting game I'd ever been in," said Schilling, who later had his share of great World Series moments pitching for the Arizona

Diamondbacks and Boston Red Sox. "It was my first win-or-go-home start."

Schilling still wonders how good he was that night. "At the time, I didn't know how to measure how good the game was," he says. "Recently, though, I looked at the lineup. Wow, I had no idea it was that good—and that deep. That was a juggernaut!" The Blue Jays' batting order included John Olerud (.363 batting average), Paul Molitor (.332), and Roberto Alomar (.326), the American League's 1-2-3 hitters during the regular season. And, of course, Carter, who'd driven in 121 runs that summer.

"Schilling was just untouchable that night," recalled Cito Gaston, who skippered the Blue Jays to their back-to-back World Series titles. "We came back with six runs in the eighth inning the night before but got nothing going against Schilling. He had an excellent breaking pitch and, of course, his fastball. Just to shut down our three guys who were the top hitters in the league says a lot. I wish he had been on the other side that night."

Gaston concurred that this was undoubtedly the best single World Series game ever pitched for the Phillies. The former manager also is quick to point out how Schilling changed his style from Game 1. "That's why he was a great pitcher. I call people like that 'coachable,'" Cito explained. "He knew he had to change the way he went at our team the next time out. He made those adjustments. You have to do that in the big leagues. A lot of people, especially kids, aren't willing to do that. By him looking at himself and listening to his pitching coach, he recognized it and made some big changes. Hey, he beat us 2–0—one heckuva game."

All five Blue Jays hits were singles, and only in the sixth and eighth innings did they get runners past first base. In the sixth with one down, Rickey Henderson and White walked, but Alomar grounded into a double play to end the threat. Pat Borders opened the eighth with a single to left; Willie Canate was sent in to pinch run and raced to third on Rob Butler's single to center. Henderson followed with a bouncer back to Schilling. Curt rifled the ball to catcher Darren Daulton, who chased Canate back toward third where Dave Hollins tagged him out. Alomar grounded out to second base, and the threat was over. "Getting Henderson was the big play," said Daulton, who doubled and scored the Phillies' second run in the second inning. "That was such a huge win for us. Schilling had never pitched better. He had unbelievable location, was painting the corners of the plate."

Said Schilling: "I cannot say enough for the game Dutch [Daulton] called." Daulton added, "Schill just put on a show that night. He had everything working—and it was in the World Series! Toronto had an awesome lineup, but there wasn't much they could do against him. When you have a guy who has so many weapons working, it was just one of those games. We needed that win." When Molitor lined out to center to end the shutout, Daulton remembers running to the mound. "I still have the picture of me hugging him," Dutch said. "When I got to the mound, I yelled in his ear, 'You put on quite a show tonight, big guy!'"

Before Carter's homer in Game 6, Schilling recalls sitting in the dugout for several innings pleading with manager Jim Fregosi and "begging him to let me pitch. Vuk was sitting next to me and said, 'Mitchy Boy has got this,' and about 15 seconds later Joe hits *the* home run. I said to myself then, *Oh, my God, I just witnessed one of the greatest moments in baseball history.* That was quickly followed by, *Holy shit, our season's over!*"

There would have been no 1993 World Series for the Phillies had Schilling not pitched so well in the NLCS against Atlanta. He didn't record a win but started two games, worked 16 innings, and allowed just three earned runs against one of the most potent offenses and best pitching staffs in the NL. The Braves had played in the previous two World Series and were heavily favored to return for a third. "We wanted to show them they weren't better than we were in every way," said Schilling, whose 1.69 ERA and 19 strikeouts were enough to earn him the NLCS MVP. "We knew we were tougher, but that didn't mean crap if we couldn't beat them when it counted." The Braves, of course, had Greg Maddux, Tommy Glavine—both 20-game winners—and John Smoltz, now all in the Hall of Fame.

Schilling, 16–7 during the regular season, set the tone for the underdogs in Game 1 when he established a NLCS record by striking out the first five Atlanta batters he faced—Otis Nixon, Jeff Blauser, Ron Gant, Fred McGriff, and David Justice. With Justice and his 40 dingers setting the pace, followed by McGriff (37) and Gant (36), the Braves led the NL that season in homers. Schilling, who fanned 10, had a 3–2 lead after eight innings when he was replaced to start the ninth by Mitch "Wild Thing" Williams. The Braves tied with an unearned run, but the Phillies scored in the 10th to win 4–3.

The Phillies also won Schilling's next start in Game 5 4–3 in 10 innings. Curt was unable to get past the ninth inning, giving way to Williams and Larry Andersen. Ah, yes, the Wild Thing. Aside from celebrating the Game 5 shutout, the lasting memory of Curt Schilling is him sitting on the bench with a white towel draped over his head when Wild Thing, obviously known for his lack of control, pitched. "I have few regrets in my career, but the towel thing was one," Schilling says solemnly. "I did it because I had issues watching him pitch. He joked about it all year, but I never saw the humor. That being said, it was gut-wrenching. I had no idea I was being so disrespectful. Then one day Dave Hollins came to me and said, 'Dude, you can't do that; it's just so wrong.' After Dave said that, I realized how right he was. I was mortified. I went directly to Mitch and apologized profusely. 'Dude, I can't watch myself either,' was his reply. Then, he had buttons made—'I

SURVIVED WATCHING MITCH PITCH IN THE 1993 WORLD SERIES' and handed them out."

*(Hal Bodley, dean of American baseball writers, is a senior correspondent for MLB.com. He has been covering Major League Baseball since 1958.)*

## MILLWOOD NO-HITS SAN FRANCISCO
### By Greg Casterioto

In a historic season that the Phillies organization has dubbed "Field of Memories," Kevin Millwood gave the fans a memory that the 40,016 in attendance on April 27, 2003, will never forget. With the Phanatic's birthday taking center stage on a gorgeous Sunday afternoon, the big right-hander from North Carolina walked the first San Francisco batter he faced but then took care of the Giants in the first inning with a strikeout, fly-out, and a batter caught stealing on a great throw from his battery mate, Mike Lieberthal.

In the second inning, Millwood got two more strikeouts (both called) on beautifully placed fastballs that looked like they came out of the arsenal of Hall of Fame-bound Greg Maddux, a former mentor and teammate of Millwood. After striking out two more batters looking in the third inning, a few fans started to come to their feet, perhaps realizing that on this day that Millwood was on.

When Giants catcher Yorvit Torrealba grounded out to end the fifth inning, if you didn't know Millwood was pitching a no-hitter, all you had to do was listen to the crowd. "It was like the playoffs or the World Series," said Millwood, who should know having made one start in the 1999 Fall Classic. "After the fifth they got a little louder every inning. You can say all you want about blocking out the fans, but from the sixth inning on, I heard 'em. It helped me. It got my adrenaline going."

The fans hung on to every pitch, every pop of the mitt and—loudest of all—every strike. They were the 10th man on the field, roaring and cheering for their newest chosen son. The edge-of-your-seat anxiety is exactly what makes Major League Baseball America's Pastime. The announced crowd of 40,016 fans sounded more like 140,016.

**Hall of Fame Artifacts from Millwood's No-Hitter**

- Kevin's cap
- Game-used baseball
- Tickets from the game

In the ninth inning, the crowd got so pumped up and excited that Millwood claimed he couldn't hear himself think. That final out was recorded on his 108th pitch—a fly ball to center field that was appropriately caught by Ricky Ledee, who had homered to account for the only run of the game and made a spectacular catch late in the game to preserve the no-hitter.

Millwood and his fans raised their arms in the air in unison and celebrated a kind of victory that most only dream about. "It's a little hard to put into words," said Millwood moments after pitching just the second no-hitter ever in the 33-year history of Veterans Stadium. Both were against the Giants.

Phillies fans of all ages were united that day and had their eyes focused on one man. It was one of those afternoons at the ballpark that years from now people who weren't there will claim they were. It was special. It was magical. And it proved that, yes, baseball is alive and well in the City of Brotherly Love.

*(Greg Casterioto is the director, baseball communications for the Phillies.)*

## THOME'S 400TH HOME RUN

*By Greg Casterioto*

With Citizens Bank Park on the immediate horizon, the Phillies signed free-agent first baseman Jim Thome to a six-year, $85 million contract on December 6, 2002, signaling the start of a new era in franchise history. Not only were the Phillies opening a new ballpark a year later, but they had a prolific power hitter in their lineup. The arrival of the 32-year-old slugger helped revive the fan base. In 13 seasons with the Cleveland Indians, Thome had amassed 337 home runs. In his first Phillies season, he hit a league-leading 47, including the last homer ever hit in Veterans Stadium. That was the second of a two-homer game on September 27, 2003.

Entering 2004 Thome needed just 19 home runs for 400. Barring injury, there was little doubt he'd reach the milestone prior to the All-Star break. When the Phillies embarked on a 10-game road trip in early June to Atlanta, Chicago, and Minnesota, Thome was sitting on 393 home runs. His numbers at U.S. Cellular Field were good (14 home runs in 57 games), and in Minneapolis they were even better (22 in 62 games). Chances were—much to Phillies fans' dismay—he would make history on the trip rather than at home.

Through the first four games at Turner Field, Thome hit two home runs, needing just five. With most major league players, five home runs could easily take a month to hit but not with Thome. When he gets hot, there's not much opposing pitchers can do to stop him. In his final season with Cleveland, he set a franchise record by homering in seven consecutive games. In contrast, the Phillies' record is five straight games shared by Dick Allen, Mike Schmidt, Bobby Abreu, and Chase Utley, who did it twice. Thome came close the year before, hitting two-run homers in four consecutive games.

So hitting five home runs in six games didn't seem like a long-shot. "The main thing was, going to Chicago and then Minnesota, they are comfortable surroundings," Thome said. "I had my parents on the road trip, I was seeing some friends in Chicago, and, honestly, I wasn't thinking about it too much. There were other things going on in my life then just as far as seeing friends and family, so I wasn't sitting in my room thinking about it all day."

The first night in Chicago, Thome hit two against the White Sox. The next night, he hit another. Now with four games to go, he needed just two and he was on a roll. It looked as if he might do it in Chicago, which seemed appropriate, considering it's in his home state. Mother Nature had other plans, though. The third game of the series was postponed due to rain.

Arriving in Minnesota, there was definitely a buzz in the air with the players. Everyone was aware of Thome's upcoming milestone, and even more were familiar with his power numbers at the Metrodome. During batting practice on the first day, Thome put on a power display, launching home runs into the upper deck with ease. One time the ball went so far that Thome turned and looked at manager Larry Bowa's expression and just laughed. For once, Bowa was speechless.

Later on that night, the Phillies won 11–6, but Thome did not homer. The night belonged to Ricky Ledee, who hit two (one into the upper deck) and collected five RBIs. The next night, however, Thome *did* hit one out. That was No. 399. With one game to go at the Metrodome, Thome was about to make history. "You don't really ever try to think that you have a chance because then you don't want to start swinging for it," Thome said.

That Sunday came and went without a Thome homer. He did, however, leave the Metrodome with 23 career home runs, which stand as the most by any visiting player in the 23-year history of the building. His 400th, though, would have to wait another day, and Phillies fans couldn't have been happier.

The buzz in Minnesota was nothing compared to Philadelphia the next day. In a makeup game from a rainout in April, the Phillies had to give up a day off to play the Reds. As fate would have it, Thome was on 399 home runs, and Ken Griffey Jr. was on 499. Never before in baseball history had two players hit their 400th and 500th home runs in the same game. Now, it was a possibility. "I remember coming in that Sunday night, and the talk was Junior's got a chance to hit his 500th and I have a chance to hit 400," Thome recalled. "Let's face it: we're all living a dream. To be put in that situation, to slow that moment down was really a neat experience." History would have to be put on hold as Junior sat out that game. Now the night belonged to Philadelphia's favorite son, Jim Thome.

In typical Thome fashion, he didn't waste any time. In the first inning, he fell behind 0–2 to Cincinnati right-hander Jose Acevedo. After working the count full and with myriad flashbulbs going off around him, he launched the next pitch into the left-center field seats. A few days later, a bronze plaque was placed at—Section 147, Row 4, Seat 6—the exact location of the historic blast. "On the first pitch, I saw all the flashbulbs" he said. "I thought, *Wow, this is pretty cool.* And then when it got to 3–2, I was glad I had seen a lot of his pitches. When he threw the fastball in, I fouled it back. Then I thought there's probably not a good possibility that he's going to double up here. I think he'll go with the next one, which was a breaking ball. And I guessed right."

In a postgame press conference, Thome admitted how glad he was to be able to hit a milestone home run like No. 400 in front of his hometown fans rather than on the road. "I was very excited for the city of Philadelphia," he said. "After what happened and watching the way people reacted, no question. My wife got to be here.

The only thing I regret is my parents weren't here, but they were on the road trip, and they had seen a lot of the home runs up to that point. My wife called my mom right when it happened."

TV cameras caught his wife, Andrea, and their one-year-old daughter Lila, celebrating in one of the private suites. Jim saw the video after the game. "It was neat because Lila didn't know what was going on, and someday when she sees the film, it'll be cool to say this happened, this is what your dad did and this is what Mommy did. Mommy was excited. Lila has no concept right now."

Thome has many memorable home run balls. "They're in a box. Someday I'll make a special room up with all the people." That box became quite full as Jim continued to pile up home run numbers that someday will put him in Cooperstown. Thome was traded to the Chicago White Sox after the 2005 season before moving on to the Los Angeles Dodgers (2009). His career continued with the Minnesota Twins (2010–11), back to Cleveland (2011), and then the Phillies (2012) before ending in Baltimore that same year.

No. 500 came in a White Sox uniform and No. 600 in a Twins jersey. His last Phillies homer was No. 609, and the very final one (No. 612) was for the Orioles on September 26. No. 1 occurred on October 4, 1991 with the Indians.

## HOWARD'S 58-HOME RUN SEASON

When it comes to Phillies single-season home run record holders, six players are on a short list. Of the half-dozen, only Schmidt is a right-handed hitter. He, Sam Thompson, and Chuck Klein are enshrined in the Baseball Hall of Fame in Cooperstown, New York.

As a 25-year-old rookie in 2005, Ryan Howard hit 22 home runs in 88 games—good enough to earn National League Rookie of the Year honors. Power was his forte as he hit 112 in 515 minor league games. Yet no one could forecast what he would do in his second major league season. Bottom line: Howard obliterated Schmidt's record by blasting 58 home runs.

Howard, nicknamed "The Big Piece" by manager Charlie Manuel, tied Schmidt's record on August 29. It was the fourth consecutive game in which he went deep. It was a simple matter of when, not if, he would surpass Schmidt's 26-year-old record. Two days later in Washington, D.C., Howard did it in typical fashion with a mammoth home run into section 461 of the upper deck. He destroyed a 2–2 fastball from Pedro Astacio at 8:04 PM. Ken Mandel of MLB.com wrote: "A few feet

**The Not-So-Dirty Half-Dozen**

OF Sam Thompson, 20 home runs (1899)

RF Gavvy Cravath, 24 home runs (1915)

CF Cy Williams, 26 home runs (1922)

CF Cy Williams, 41 home runs (1923)

RF Chuck Klein, 43 home runs (1929)

3B Mike Schmidt, 48 home runs (1980)

1B Ryan Howard, 58 home runs (2006)

higher and it would've been considered a hostile flying object in restricted D.C. airspace."

Manuel said, "That had lift. It kept going. He's a special player and legit." Battling for a wild-card spot, the Phillies lost the game in 10 innings 6–5 to the Nationals. His historic homer had tied the game at 2–2 in the fourth inning, the 25th time that one of his bombs either tied a game or gave the Phillies a lead. "It was great, but the big thing is that we lost the game," Howard said. Losses were critical as the Phillies were trying to earn the wild-card berth and their first postseason appearance since 1993.

Sitting on 49 home runs, where would he finish? Returning to Citizens Bank Park, Howard quickly did some major damage. The date was September 3, a Sunday afternoon against Atlanta. Facing right-hander Tim Hudson, Howard hit three consecutive home runs on a total of nine pitches. His bid to hit four straight ended with a one-out single in the eighth inning off Macay McBride. The Big Piece had just become the 23rd player ever to reach 50. "Howard's performance electrified the building, as standing ovations, curtain calls, and chants of 'MVP' dominated the afternoon," wrote Dennis Deitch in *The Delaware County Daily Times*.

Howard's total now stood at 52, the most ever hit by a player in his sophomore big league season. Hall of Famer Ralph Kiner of the Pirates held the distinction with 51 in 1947. Visons of 60 began dancing in the heads of fans and the media. Would he become the sixth to reach that lofty plateau? Twenty-six games remained, and he needed eight more. On September 22, game No. 153, he became the eighth player to reach 58 with a three-run blast off Ricky Nolasco of the Florida Marlins. It matched Jimmie Foxx, who hit 58 for the Athletics in 1932, setting a Philadelphia record.

### Ryan Howard's 58-Home Run Season: By the Numbers

- Became the 23rd player to reach 50 home runs
- Had seven multi-home run games, matching Dick Allen's 1968 club record and equaled by Chase Utley also in 2006
- Set a club record by homering in 16 of the 19 parks he played in, missing Fenway Park, Miller Park, and PNC Park
- 28 home runs either tied the game or gave the Phillies a lead
- 26 came when the count was even
- 13 came in the sixth inning, the favorite inning for No. 6
- 32–18 (.640) Phillies record when he homered
- One pinch-hit home run on May 4
- To no one's surprise, he lacked an inside-the-park home run

With nine games remaining, two more for 60 seemed within his grasp. As we all know, he didn't get there. Ryan got 10 hits and walked 10 times with six being intentional in those nine games. "Someday in the offseason, when I look back at this season, it will be special," he said at the time. "I try to stay locked in and try to win games. One day I'll wake up and realize what happened."

Critics pointed to the fact Howard played in hitter-friendly Citizens Bank Park. Well, he hit 29 there to match Schmidt's 1979 record for most home runs at home in Phillies history and 29 on the road, equaling Chuck Klein's club record set way back in 1932. "You hear talk about the ballpark we play in and things like that," Manuel said. "Honestly, it doesn't matter where Ryan plays. His home runs are legitimate."

Howard also set club records for most home runs in August (14) and RBIs for that month (41). His 37 intentional walks was yet another record. His 149 RBIs were second only to Klein's 170 in 1930, and his .659 slugging percentage trailed only Klein's .687 in 1930. He also led the team with a .313 average. The last Phillie to lead in average, home runs, and RBIs was another left-handed hitting first baseman, John Kruk, in 1991.

Those fan chants of "MVP, MVP, MVP" became a reality when he was named the National League's Most Valuable Player after the season. He joined legend Cal Ripken Jr. (1982–83) as the only players to win Rookie of the Year and MVP awards in back-to-back seasons.

## UTLEY'S HISTORIC WORLD SERIES

When Chase Utley scored from second base on a routine ground-out against the Atlanta Braves on August 9, 2006, Phillies Hall of Fame broadcaster Harry Kalas exclaimed: "Chase is going to keep going and he's safe at home plate! Chase Utley, you...ARE...the man!" During the 2009 World Series, Chase was indeed "the man."

It is the greatest offensive show of any Phillies player in the Fall Classic. After hitting .429 in the National League's Division Series against the Colorado Rockies and just .211 in the National League Championship Series win over the Los Angeles Dodgers, Utley stepped into the batter's box for his first at-bat in Game 1 of the World Series. The date was October 28, and a loud New York crowd at Yankee Stadium awaited him. Facing the big left-hander of the New York Yankees, CC Sabathia, is no picnic in the park. Up until that moment, Utley was hitless—with three strikeouts—in five career at-bats against Sabathia.

A year earlier in the World Series against the Tampa Bay Rays, Utley hit a two-run homer in his first-ever World Series at-bat, setting a tone and silencing the cow bell ringing throng in St. Petersburg's Tropicana Field. Sabathia and Utley were in a tug-of-war at-bat in the third inning of a scoreless game. Finally, on the ninth pitch—a 3–2 offering—Utley drilled a home run into the right field to silence a revved-up crowd. It was the first home run Sabathia had allowed to a left-handed hitter in Yankee Stadium all season long.

Three innings later on a 96-miles per hour two-strike fastball, Utley did it again—a solo shot deeper into the right-field seats. "My approach was trying to make him work a little bit," the reserved Utley said. "I was trying to hit the fastball. It was nice for us to get off to a good start. The goal isn't to hit home runs. The goal is just to put good at-bats together." No Phillies player had ever hit two homers in one series game, and Chase became the first major leaguer to hit multiple home runs in a World Series game since Reggie Jackson drilled three in the old Yankee Stadium in 1977.

As was the case in St. Petersburg, the Phillies won the first game. The Yankees took the next two and sent Sabathia to the mound for Game 4 in Citizens Bank Park. This time the big lefty was leading 4–2 in the seventh when Utley came to bat with two outs. He saw five straight sliders and fell behind in the count 1–2. He hit the sixth slider into the right-field seats to make it a 4–3 game. The Phillies tied it in the eighth, but the Yankees scored three times in the ninth to take a commanding lead in the series 3–1. Chase had rebounded from his slow start against Sabathia, slugging a double and three homers in his six at-bats against the towering lefty.

With their backs to the wall in Game 5, the Phillies took the field in front of a raucous Citizens Bank Park crowd that was quieted when the Yankees scored a first-inning run. Facing A.J. Burnett, Jimmy Rollins singled, and Shane Victorino was hit by a pitch to start the Phillies' first inning to set the stage for the Phillies' No. 3 hitter. Utley brought the crowd back in the game by hitting Burnett's first pitch for a three-run homer. With the Yankees trailing 6–2, lefty reliever Phil Coke was brought in to face the Phillies in the seventh inning. Utley battled through the first six pitches before sending Coke's seventh pitch into the right-center field seats. "First home run was a fastball. The second one was a fastball as well," Utley explained after the game. Three-at bats, three runs, two homers, four RBIs, a walk, and a stolen base was Utley's night.

Hitting five home runs in five series games tied Jackson's 1977 feat. Utley became the second player with a pair of two home-run games in one World Series. Phillies fans witnessed the other one, Willie Aikens of the Kansas City Royals, in 1980. The Phillies survived Aikens' heroics by winning their first world championship. The Yankees did the same by holding Utley in check (0-for-3) in Game 6, depriving the Phillies of winning back-to-back titles for the first time in franchise history.

In 49 career World Series at-bats, Utley went deep a club-record seven times, which ties him for 10th place on baseball's all-time list. Including all 164 postseason at-bats, he hit 10, which is second in club history to his close friend, Jayson Werth, who hit one more. When Utley homered in the postseason, the Phillies' record was 7–1.

Chase's World Series slugging percentage (.795) ranks sixth all-time, putting him ahead of Jackson, Babe Ruth, and Lou Gehrig. That's pretty hefty company.

Following Utley's second two-home-run Series game, Charlie Manuel had this to say about his second baseman: "He's quiet and he goes about his business in a real good way. He's a pleasure to be around and a pleasure to manage. I don't want to embarrass him or nothing like that, but sometimes I tell our players, 'Just play with Chase.' Because if you play with Chase you've got a chance to be a pretty good player."

## HALLADAY'S HISTORIC YEAR

Three Hall of Fame pitchers—Grover Cleveland Alexander, Robin Roberts, and Steve Carlton—won a combined 665 games wearing a Phillies uniform. They threw zero no-hitters. Halladay came to the Phillies in a big trade after the 2009 season. In his first season in pinstripes, he won 21 games in the regular season and was 1–0 in the National League Division Series. Two of his first 22 wins with the Phillies were no-hitters. *Yep, two.*

His seventh win of the 2010 season was a perfect game in Miami on the last Saturday night in May by the score of 1–0. His 22nd win came in his first ever postseason start, a 4–0 no-hitter against the Cincinnati Reds on a Wednesday night at Citizens Bank Park five months later.

The 33-year-old right-hander attained a plateau never reached in baseball history with a no-hitter in the regular season and post-season. He became one of seven pitchers in baseball history with two no-hitters in the same year, one of six with a no-hitter and perfect game in a career, and one of two with a postseason no-hitter.

In throwing the second perfect game in Phillies history, Halladay did it on 115 pitches, 72 of which were strikes. He had six 3–2 counts and one 3–1 count. He struck out 11, including six looking. His team scored an unearned run in the third inning, and that's the way it stood going into the bottom of the ninth inning.

Roy Halladay and Carlos Ruiz celebrate after the Phillies right-hander tosses a no-hitter in his first postseason game. (Miles Kennedy)

The crowd of 25,086 was on its feet cheering every pitch. Three Miami Marlins pinch-hitters stood between Halladay and immortality. It didn't take long—just three pitches per batter. Mike Lamb flied to Shane Victorino, who caught the ball at the edge of the centerfield warning track; Wes Helms was called out on strikes; and Ronny Paulino grounded out to third baseman Juan Castro.

The celebration was on. "The fans were awesome," Halladay said after his masterpiece. "To be on the road and see them that into it was really special. It made it all the more memorable. It's not something you think about. It's hard to explain. There are days when things just click. It's not something you try to do."

Carlos Ruiz caught his first no-hitter. "I can't say enough about the game he called," Halladay said. "After four to five innings, I just let him take over. It was a no-brainer for me. See the glove, hit the glove."

**Hall of Fame Artifacts from Halladay's Perfect Game**

- Halladay's cap
- Game-used baseball
- Tickets from the game

Jayson Stark of ESPN.com summed up the night this way: "In a way, Roy Halladay was the—ahem—perfect pitcher to have this kind of a night because all he does, every minute of every day, is pursue perfection."

As a 22-year-old, Halladay came ever so close to a no-hitter in 1998 with the Toronto Blue Jays. Making his second big league start on September 27, Detroit outfielder Bobby Higginson, a Philadelphia product, hit a solo home run as a pinch-hitter with two out in the top of the ninth to break up the no-no. Halladay won 2–1. According to Jim Salisbury, CSNPhilly.com, Halladay smiled following his Miami perfecto and said, "It's a great feeling. A lot better than eight and two-thirds."

The National League Division Series got started in historic fashion as Halladay no-hit the Cincinnati Reds—the league's best offensive team—in the opening game. Only a two-out walk to Jay Bruce—on one of three 3–2 counts—in the fifth inning kept him from a second perfect game. He was more economical than in his perfect game, throwing 104 pitches and 79 of them for strikes. He struck out eight, including Scott Rolen three times. Five of the eight strikeouts were swinging. Only four balls were hit to the out-field. Perhaps the most amazing stat of the night: of the 28 batters Halladay faced, he threw a first-pitch strike to 25.

With 46,411 fans on their feet Halladay walked to the mound in the top of the ninth inning, facing the eighth, ninth, and lead-off hitters. Ten pitches are all it would take. Catcher Ramon Hernandez popped up to Chase Utley, and pinch-hitter Miguel Cairo fouled out to third baseman Wilson Valdez to bring up a tough hitter, second baseman Brandon Phillips. On an 0–2 pitch, Phillips' bat struck a tapper in front of the plate. Ruiz pounced on the ball and fired to Howard from his knees to set off another cel-ebration. "I was panicking," admitted Ruiz after the game.

Halladay joined Dan Larsen as the only pitchers with a no-hitter in the 107-year history of post-season baseball. Pitching for the New York Yankees, Larsen threw a perfect game against the Brooklyn Dodgers in Game 5 of the 1956 World Series.

> **Hall of Fame Artifacts from Halladay's No-Hitter**
> - Roy's jersey
> - Game-used baseball
> - Tickets from the game

For his feat Halladay acknowl-edged the crowd. "When it gets that loud, it's hard to ignore," he said. "Especially the last three innings, it seemed like it got louder every inning. It's obviously one of the most electric atmospheres I've ever been in. It's something you obviously can't ignore, so it was a lot of fun."

By the middle innings, Halladay admitted he sensed a no-hit-ter was within reach. "You're definitely closer," he said. "As soon as you try and do it, it kind of takes you out of your plan a little bit. I was definitely aware of it, knew what was going on in the fifth or sixth inning." Ruiz felt it earlier. "Warming up in the bullpen, it was like wow. Everything was working in the bullpen," the catcher said. "His stuff was so good he could have pitched another perfect game."

For each of his gems, "everything" included cutters, sinkers, change-ups, and curveballs. Command of each was exceptional. In most no-hitters, there is a defensive gem or two that plays a role. Halladay was backed by his defense in each game. Shortstop Wilson Valdez and Castro made key plays in Miami. Shortstop Jimmy Rollins made two excellent plays, and right fielder Jayson Werth made a nice catch on the only hard hit ball by the Reds.

Pitching coach Rich Dubee felt his ace was better against the Reds than the Marlins. "I thought he had four pitches, never really lost any of those four," Dubee said. "He had four pitches throughout nine innings that he pretty much could throw at any time and to both sides of the plate. He was like that in Miami, but he wasn't as consistent."

Halladay actually had more hits than he allowed. He had a run-scoring single in a three-run second inning against Reds pitcher Edinson Volquez. Halladay's no-hitter was the first in Citizens Bank Park history. And the last time the Reds were no-hit was in 1971 by the Phillies' Rick Wise.

### COMBINED NO-HITTER

Something took place on Labor Day of 2014 that had never happened before in 20,105 games the Phillies had played in their history. Facing the Braves on a sweltering Monday afternoon in Atlanta's Turner Field, four Phillies pitchers combined on a no-hitter to win 7–0.

The starter, Cole Hamels, struggled with his control, allowing five walks and hitting a batter on 108 pitches in six innings. He threw 21 pitches in the first inning, including three-ball counts on the first three batters. Four of the five walks and the hit batsman came in the first three innings. The three relievers were much more efficient with three up and three down each for Jake Diekman, Ken

Giles, and Jonathan Papelbon, including 39 total pitches and five strikeouts.

When asked if he had ever thrown a no-hitter, Hamels ran his fingers through his black hair. "No. Not in high school or any other place. I always left after six innings," he said, laughing, "just like I did in Atlanta.

"It was fun because it was a complete team effort. During no-hitters, you sit there, fingers crossed. No one talks. This was different. Everybody was into it on the bench, wondering who was coming in next. Cooch [Carlos Ruiz] did an outstanding job, handling four different guys with different personalities and stuff."

Added Ruiz: "Cole struggled with his consistency and command, but he really made the big, tough pitches when he needed to."

Leading 2–0, Hamels was lifted in the top of the seventh. "He was pretty well spent there," manager Ryne Sandberg explained. "He had some stressful early innings and wasn't going to go nine." The Phillies, though, extended their lead, scoring three runs in the top of the inning.

Diekman relieved in the bottom

**Hall of Fame Artifacts from the Combined No-Hitter**

- Sandberg's lineup card from the dugout
- Hamels' cap
- Game-used baseball removed from play in the top of the ninth

half. "I was running in and looking at the scoreboard because they normally have who was due up," the lefty reliever said. "And that's the first time I realized it was a no-hitter. And I was like, 'All right.'" Giles entered in the eighth and struck out the side. "A once-in-a-lifetime experience," he called it. Papelbon used only nine pitches in retiring the Braves in the ninth in a no-save situation. "It was different. I didn't have the adrenaline that I would usually have," Papelbon said. "I tried to focus on location over velocity and do what I could to preserve the no-hitter."

The no-hitter also came to be because of some great fielding. Right fielder Marlon Byrd made a belly-flopping catch of a liner off the bat of Chris Johnson to end the third inning. Two runners were on base. In the ninth inning, Johnson hit a little squibber past Papelbon, but shortstop Jimmy Rollins made the play for the 26th out. The 27th out was routine—a soft liner caught by Darin Ruf who was inserted at first base for defense in the bottom of the inning.

Ruiz became the first Phillies catcher behind the plate for three no-hitters. (The first two were by Roy Halladay.) Twelve other catchers have done that in baseball history. Jason Varitek of the Boston Red Sox is the leader with four. Only two other teammates—Chase Utley and Ryan Howard—were in the three no-hitters.

It was the 12th no-hitter in Phillies history. The first was by Charles Ferguson in 1885 in the franchise's third season. It was the 11th combined no-hitter in baseball history and the first since six Mariners pitchers did it to the Dodgers in 2012. Sandberg, though, had never been in a no-hitter as a player or manager. Also of note: leadoff hitter Ben Revere drove in a career-high five runs.

Hamels decided the game ball would go to club president David Montgomery, who was on a leave of absence as he battled cancer. "We're going to dedicate it to David. He has been a paramount person in the Phillies organization," Hamels said. "It's really nice to be able to give it to him because of what David and his family has gone through."

## ROLLINS PASSES SCHMIDT

Jimmy Rollins thrilled Phillies fans with leadoff home runs. He hit 46 of them to be exact—by far the most in team history. He excited fans by hitting more doubles than anyone who ever wore a Phillies uniform and got people out of their seats with his electrifying triples in the alleys or corners.

Mike Schmidt congratulates Jimmy Rollins in 2014 after he breaks the Hall of Famer's club record for the most career hits. (Miles Kennedy)

Yet it was a simple line-drive single to right field that set him apart from everyone else who played for the Phillies. Ripping a fifth-inning fastball from Cubs right-hander Edwin Jackson for a single vaulted him into first place for the most hits in franchise history with 2,235. The history-making moment happened on June 14, 2014, at Citizens Bank Park before 32,524 fans, who immediately stood to salute the new hit king.

Upon reaching first base, Rollins clapped his hands, took off his helmet, waived to the cheering crowd, and broke into that infectious smile of his. The incumbent hits leader, Mike Schmidt, charged out of the Phillies dugout, picked up Jimmy's bat near home plate, and headed to first base. Then, passing the torch, Schmidt raised Rollins' left arm. Fireworks exploded overhead as play was halted for a few minutes. Jimmy's teammates rushed from the dugout for a hug-a-thon.

"Schmidt coming down the line shocked me," Rollins said after the game. "I knew he was going to be here, but I didn't know he was going to have a part in it. I hit first base, and he was halfway down the line, charging with my bat. That was pretty nice. That was a surprise."

Mike's message was simple. "Congratulations, it couldn't happen to a better guy," he said. "I appreciate your friendship." Schmidt wanted to be there when Jimmy broke his record. He arrived in town on Wednesday when Jimmy was four hits shy and stood behind manager Ryne Sandberg once the game started on Saturday. Chase Utley was the last player to greet Rollins at first base. The two shook hands and hugged and Chase left with a message: "Now, score a run." Jimmy did. His two-out stolen base was followed by a three-run homer by Dominic Brown that decided the 7–4 win.

Schmidt and Rollins, both second-round draft picks, wound up as the greatest third baseman and shortstop in Phillies history. Mike's a Hall of Famer and so should Jimmy be some day. When it comes to awards, he was the National League MVP (2007), NL All-Star (2001–02, 2005), Silver Slugger (2007), and Rawlings Gold Glove (2007–09, 2012).

Scout Bob Poole followed Rollins and filed this exact report prior to the 1996 draft: "This youngster can pick and throw. He has range, quickness, supple hands, strong/accurate arm. Excellent instincts and field smarts. Switch hitter; swing is compact with short stride, makes sharp contact from both sides. Tool wise, it's all there, except power, but it comes in a small package. Will be an early pick by a club that will go for tools over size. He CAN play and he can play shortstop in the major leagues."

## 2,000 Hit Club

*Shortstop Jimmy Rollins (2,306 hits)*
Drafted in the second round in 1996 out of Encinal High School (California) where he held 10 school records, including highest batting average (.484) and most stolen bases (99), Rollins spent 15 seasons with the Phillies from 2000–2014. His first hit was a third-inning single on September 17, 2000, off Marlins starter Chuck Smith at Veterans Stadium in his first major league game and second plate appearance. (He drew a walk in his first plate appearance.) His last Phillies hit was a fourth-inning triple on September 8, 2014, off Pirates starter Jeff Locke at PNC Park.

*Third baseman Mike Schmidt (2,234)*
Drafted in the second round in 1971 out of Ohio University, Schmidt played his entire 18-year career with the Phillies from 1972 to 1989 (2,404 games). He was inducted into the National Baseball Hall of Fame in 1995. His first hit was a fifth-inning single on September 12, 1972, off Mets starter Jim McAndrew at Veterans Stadium. His last hit was an eighth-inning single on May 25, 1989, off Dodgers starter Tim Belcher at Dodger Stadium.

*Outfielder Richie Ashburn (2,217)*
Signed by the Phillies as a catcher in 1945, Ashburn played 1,794 games with the Phillies from 1948 to 1959. He was inducted into the Hall of Fame in 1995. His first hit was a third-inning single on April 20, 1948, off Boston Braves starter Johnny Sain at Shibe Park. His last Phillies hit was a fifth-inning single on September 27, 1959, off Milwaukee Braves starter Bob Buhl at Milwaukee County Stadium.

*Outfielder Ed Delahanty (2,214)*
Eldest and most talented of five brothers who played in the majors, Delahanty played for the Phillies from 1888 to 1889 and 1891–1901 (1,557 games). He died at age 35 when he was swept over Niagara Falls during the 1903 season. Reports varied as to whether he fell or jumped. He was elected to the Hall of Fame by the Veterans Committee in 1945. The date of his first hit is unknown, but his last Phillies hit was a single on October 2, 1901, in the first game of a doubleheader at Cincinnati.

Mike Arbuckle was the director of scouting in 1996. "I saw him play one road game in high school that spring, an all-dirt infield, which played really quick. He handled everything defensively,"

Arbuckle said. "He had all the raw ingredients, soft hands, strong arm, above average running speed, bat speed, and really enjoyed playing. From that one game, I saw intangibles, a personal confidence. He stood out. I saw a little Lenny Dykstra in Jimmy. Small in stature but body strength and wanting to be the guy in tough situations. Because of his size, we pegged him as a second rounder. I foresaw him as a steady defensive shortstop, making the exceptional play but also very consistent, the guy who always made the play with two out and the tying run on their base. I under-projected him as a hitter, never figured he would set the Phillies record. I tell you what, if you compare him with other shortstops in Cooperstown, he belongs there."

**Jimmy Rollins: By the Numbers**

- Games: 2,090, ranks second in franchise history
- At-bats: 8,628, first
- Runs: 1,325, third
- Hits: 2,306, first
- Singles: 1,500, third
- Doubles: 479, first
- Triples: 111, third
- Home runs: 216, ninth
- RBIs: 887, sixth
- Extra-base hits: 806, second
- Total bases: 3,655, second
- Walks: 753, sixth
- Strikeouts: 1,145, fourth
- Stolen bases: 453, second

Lee Elia rejoined the Phillies as director of minor league instruction in the fall of 1999. "First time I saw him was in the instructional league program. He was impressive from the get-go. He could steal a base, played a good shortstop, a switch hitter who could drive the ball from either side. I remember talking to him about playing the little man's game, you know, draw walks, bunt, steal, hit-and-run, put the ball in play. He told me, 'I'm not a little man.' He thought he could do better and he did. He turned out to be a very special player. I don't think any of us thought he would become the Phillies' all-time hit leader."

Shortly after being named manager after the 2000 season, Larry Bowa got his first glimpse of Rollins in the Florida Instructional League. "Jimmy put on a show—single, triple, stolen base, and two great defensive plays," Bowa said. "He had great hand-eye coordination as a hitter. Despite his speed, he didn't get many leg hits. I thought he could be a good hitter but didn't believe he would have the power he showed. He was a lot stronger than people thought. He thrived in late-inning situations. [It] didn't bother him what he had done earlier in the game."

Broadcaster Chris Wheeler saw every one of Jimmy's hits. "[In] spring training, 2000, Lee Elia, Darold Knowles, and I were returning from playing golf," Wheeler said. "I was in the back seat and started asking them about our young prospects because they were in our minor league system then. I'll never forget when I got to Jimmy, Lee and Knowlsey lit up. I recall Lee saying, 'I see him as a big-time player, an All-Star, Gold Glover winner, you name it. The Phillies won't need another shortstop for 15 years.' Jimmy turned out to be one of the best, most consistent players in our history. He was a great run producer and saved tons of runs with his over-the-top defense. We knew if we ever got to the postseason, the rest of the baseball world would soon see what we were seeing. He was a red-light player and the bigger the moment the more he liked it. The day after he passed Mike [Schmidt], I went to the clubhouse to congratulate him. I said I think I may be one of the few people who can say he saw every one of the hits. J-Roll gave me that amused, wide-eyed look of his that appeared when you said something that really interested him. Then with that great gap-toothed smile, said, 'Wheels, that's probably true, and it's sure been a lot of fun.' It sure was a lot of fun watching him. He should get serious Hall of Fame consideration when his time comes around."

## HAMELS NO-HITS CUBS

On July 25, 2015, the Twitter rumor mill was churning with the Rangers, Cubs, Dodgers, and Red Sox all interested in Cole Hamels. *Rangers are out...Favorites are now Dodgers and Cubs...Rangers are back in…Giants have entered the picture…Astros are making a strong push.* Speculation was swirling like hurricane winds.

With six days left until the July 31 trading deadline, Hamels took the mound on a sunny Saturday afternoon in Chicago's Wrigley Field. A dozen scouts were seated behind home plate zeroing in on every pitch. Cole's two previous outings were the worst of his career. He allowed 14 runs in six and one-third innings. He hadn't won since May 23. Questions of his health, trade value, and rumors that the Phillies might wait until the offseason filled the Twittersphere.

But after giving up 16 hits to his 29 previous batters, Hamels faced 29 Cubs and no-hit them. The Cubs hadn't been no-hit in 50 years when another lefty—Sandy Koufax of the Dodgers—threw a perfect game against them. The No. 1 song on the hit parade back then was "Help" by the Beatles. Gas was 31 cents a gallon. That's how long ago Koufax did his thing.

Hamels had some help on a hard one-hopper back to him by pinch-hitter Kyle Schwarber to end the eighth inning and two breath-taking catches by rookie Odubel Herrera, a Rule 5 pick from the Rangers. Herrera, originally an infielder, was converted to center field where he had played only two games in six minor league seasons, both at Myrtle Beach in the Carolina League in 2014. The no-hitter was just his 67th game in center in the majors. "Odubel made two phenomenal catches," Hamels said after the game. "I hung a breaking ball on the last pitch, but the wind was in my favor. He picked me up, picked up the team."

The wind was blowing in at Wrigley, which had an effect on two fly balls. David Ross sent a drive to deep left-center field in the eighth, but Herrera got there and went into a dive on the dusty warning track after making a great catch, saving the no-hitter for the moment. The start of the inning was delayed slightly as Herrera forgot his sunglasses. Kris Bryant worked a full count as the last batter of the game. He sent a drive to deep center. Herrera overran the ball, came back, and caught it while falling down. After that pitch Cole walked off the mound toward the first-base foul line, a journey pitchers will make after a bad pitch. Following the catch, he smiled, raised his left arm, and gave Carlos Ruiz a high five as Ryan Howard emerged setting off a hug-a-thon. The wind didn't stop Howard from hitting a three-run homer to left center, padding Cole's lead. The Phillies added two runs in the eighth taking any kind of pressure off Hamels. "Asked what his thoughts were when he took the mound in the ninth, he laughed: "I hadn't pitched in the ninth for a couple of years, just tried to stay focused. It was pretty exciting and a full team effort. Nothing will top winning a World Series, but this is right under it."

Hamels and Ruiz had been battery mates more than any other current pitcher-catcher combination. Game No. 207 for them was historic in more ways than one as

> **Hall of Fame Artifacts from Hamels' No-Hitter**
> - Hamels' cap
> - game ball

Ruiz became only the second catcher behind the plate for four no-hitters. Jason Varitek in the American League is the other one. Ruiz caught both of Roy Halladay's gems in 2010 and the combined no-hitter last September in Atlanta. Cole was the starter that day when four Phillies tossed the first combined no-hitter in Phillies history.

Following his two bad outings, Hamels worked on some mechanical flaws. He had been up with many of his pitches and did the same when he walked Dexter Fowler, the first batter of the game. He also walked Fowler in the sixth inning. "I just wanted to pound the zone today," he said. And he did. He threw 129 pitches, 83 for strikes. Cole had 27 swings and misses, the most since 29 in a game during his rookie season in 2006. There was one broken bat. Right fielder Jorge Soler broke the bat over his left knee after his third strikeout in the seventh inning.

Following a dousing of cold water during a postgame interview with Phillies broadcaster Greg Murphy, Cole did an interview from the dugout with Phillies radio voices Scott Franzke and Larry Andersen, went to a media interview room, and then returned to a joyous clubhouse behind the first-base dugout. It had been 7,921 games since a pitcher walked in that clubhouse after no-hitting the Cubs. Finally, after checking his cell phone, Cole saw he had over 50 messages from family, friends, and former teammates. As he exited Wrigley Field, Hamels stopped to sign autographs and thank the Cubs fans. There were 41,683 there, and all stood in the top of the ninth witnessing history.

Hamels not only held the Cubs hitless, but he actually out-hit them thanks to an eighth-inning double. In doing so, Hamels extended the recent trend of no-hit pitchers outhitting their opponents. Each of the last five pitchers to throw a no-hitter in a National League ballpark did just that. And each of the last 12 no-hitters have come in the National League.

Hamels' nickname is Hollywood. Well, Hollywood couldn't have written a better script for his last start with the Phillies. Cole was traded to the Texas Rangers in an eight-player deal on July 31.

# 2

# 1915 Phillies

## SPRING TRAINING IN FLORIDA

*By Bob Warrington*

"This is your bread and butter as well as mine," declared Phillies manager Pat Moran in a pep talk to his players at spring training in 1915. A lot was new about the club that year. A reserve catcher with the team since 1910, Moran had become manager after a disappointing sixth-place showing in 1914. Restructuring the roster was needed, and some Phillies had been jettisoned, including former manager Red Dooin, while others were brought into the fold.

Even the location of spring training had changed. The Phillies practiced at Coffee Pot Park in St. Petersburg, Florida, for the first time. Located at First North Street and 22nd Avenue, the ballpark—located in what is now a residential community—was the home of the St. Louis Browns the previous preseason, but a dispute over who should pay certain bills ended that relationship. St. Petersburg's mayor Al Lang enticed Phillies president William F. Baker to train at Coffee Pot Park by—among other inducements—

supplying the baseballs used at spring training and providing a discounted room rate for players at the Fifth Avenue Hotel.

The Phillies' stay at Coffee Pot Park ran from March 1 to March 25, 1915, but even getting to spring training proved something of an adventure. The Phillies, along with players from the Philadelphia Athletics and Brooklyn Dodgers, boarded the steamer *Apache* in New York harbor for a trip down the Atlantic seaboard to Jacksonville, Florida. After a few hours at sea, the British cruiser *Essex* approached and hovered around the *Apache* as it proceeded on its journey. World War I was raging in Europe in 1915, and the *Essex* was patrolling along America's East Coast intercepting merchant ships attempting to smuggle war goods from the United States—still a neutral country—to Germany. Initially suspicious of the *Apache*, the *Essex* eventually became satisfied the steamer carried ballplayers—not military supplies—and pulled away to resume its patrol duties.

A stern disciplinarian with a canny baseball mind, Moran was relentless in drilling his players on the fundamentals of the game, or what he called "inside baseball." Bunting, fielding, cutoffs, hit-and-run plays, signaling, double steals, and double plays were part of the daily practice routine. Pitchers spent entire sessions learning how to hold a runner close to the bag through deceptive moves and quick deliveries. Moran also had his men walk the two miles from their hotel to the ballpark and back again every day as part of their conditioning. He jokingly called them "Tipperary hikes" after a popular World War I British Army marching song, "It's a Long Way to Tipperary."

Training and exhibition games were held Monday through Saturday but never on Sunday. Laws and cultural mores prohibited professional sports on a day that was then regarded as reserved for religious worship, family togetherness, and meditation. With no practice on Sunday, March 21, the Phillies decided to go on a fishing excursion, which led to "one of the most eventful days of the training campaign."

The boat *Frank E* departed at 6:00 AM with manager Moran and all but two Phillies players on board for a day of fishing in the Gulf of Mexico. Once the boat was far beyond the sight of land, however, a stiff wind arose that made fishing all but impossible. Soon, the sea became so rough that the captain ordered all passengers to don lifejackets and get below deck. The situation grew worse when the engine conked out. At first amused by their predicament, those on board soon became very serious. Some players removed pieces of clothing in case the boat foundered and they had to swim, though conditions never became that dire. The crew restarted the engine, and the boat returned to port that afternoon. Passengers disembarked with some bumps, bruises, and many cases of seasickness. Only a few Phillies ate in the dining room that evening, but one who did appear was the wife of Phillies player Beals Becker. She chose to join her husband and was the only woman on board *Frank E.* According to one report, she "stood the trip bravely."

There also was time for veteran players to play pranks on newer members of the team during spring training. The second-string squad (rookies and reservists) was scheduled to leave early one morning and travel to play a two-game series against the Birmingham Barons of the Southern League. Several of these players left their suitcases in the hotel's front office the night before. Learning of this some veterans put paving blocks taken from the street in the suitcases. When the players picked them up the next morning, they were bewildered as to why they were so heavy.

Spring training today bears little resemblance to 100 years ago. Conditions then were primitive. There was one shower at the ballpark, and it spouted only cold water. The grandstand was made of wood and seated a mere 500 fans. Players were responsible for washing their uniforms. Lunch often consisted of a fried fish—typically with the head still on—between two pieces of bread. Players would raid nearby orange groves to supplement their meager meals. There was one trainer whose main job was to rub down players after practice.

Less than half of the Phillies' 30-game exhibition schedule was against other big league clubs. Opponents in most games were minor league teams, including seven games against a roster of stars from the Cuban League called the Havana Reds. There also were a number of intrasquad games in which the regulars faced the "Yanigans"—a term used during the period to refer to a team comprised of rookie and reserve players. The regulars had to play hard to avoid the risk of losing their roster spots to ambitious Yanigans, who were eager to move up and become regulars themselves.

Once the Phillies broke camp on March 25, the team migrated north, playing additional exhibition games until the regular season started on April 14. This included two games against the Philadelphia Athletics in Jacksonville and then a series of games against the Atlanta Crackers of the Southern League, the Norfolk Tars of the Virginia League, the Washington Senators, and then a four-game "City Series" in Philadelphia with the A's, which the clubs split 2–2. Preseason wound up with three games against the Providence Grays of the International League. By the time the Phillies finished their last preseason game on April 13, they had compiled a record of 18 wins, seven defeats, two ties, and three rainouts.

Near the end of spring training, a perceptive reporter who had followed the Phillies predicted, "Boss Moran's team will be one of the surprises of the National League season." With a strong pitching staff led by the brilliant Grover Cleveland Alexander; a potent offense spearheaded by home run king Gavvy Cravath; and talented new players, including future Hall of Famer Dave Bancroft,

The 1915 Phillies pose for a team photo. On the bottom, left to right, are: Al Demaree, Bert Adams, Bill Kellefer, Ed Burns. Second row: George McQuillan, George Chalmers, Ben Tincup, Grover Cleveland Alexander, manager Ed Moran, Stan Baumgartner, Erskine Mayer, Eppa Rixey, Joe Oeschger. Third row: Fred Luderus, Bert Niehoff, Bobby Byrne, Dave Bancroft, Oscar Dugey, Milt Stock. Fourth row: Gavvy Cravath, Bud Weiser, Dode Pasket, Possum Whitted. Not pictured: Beals Becker. (Phillies)

the club was skilled in and ready to play inside baseball. The 1915 Phillies would indeed be one of the surprises of the season, winning the NL pennant for the first time in franchise history.

*(Bob Warrington is a native Philadelphian who writes about the city's baseball history.)*

## FIRST PENNANT WINNER

A roster of only 23 players and a rookie manager etched their place in Phillies history by winning the franchise's first National League pennant in 1915. The league's most dominant pitcher and leading power hitter anchored the champions who started the season with an eight-game undefeated streak, a club record that still exists.

The roster was a balance of rookies and veterans, including new faces that were brought in following a sixth-place finish the year before. The pitching staff included two future Hall of Famers, a lad born in Scotland, a native American Indian, an offseason cartoonist, and a future sportswriter.

In the first 32 seasons of the franchise, three second-place finishes were the best any team could do. The Phillies didn't win another pennant for 35 years. While we have lived through later championship clubs, we know little about the team from 101 years ago. Their faces and names are obscure, but they have a special place in the team's history.

After 14 years as a catcher with three different National League clubs, including 1910–1914 with the Phillies, Pat Moran replaced Red Dooin. Moran caught only one game in 1914 and basically served as the pitching coach. He was credited with changing the delivery of a rookie pitcher in 1911 and convincing Dooin not to send the hurler to the minors. That pitcher was Grover Cleveland Alexander. The 39-year-old Moran became baseball's first manager since the turn of the century to win a championship without prior experience.

Moran brought in eight new players, including starters at second base, shortstop, and left field. Bobby Byrne, the incumbent second baseman, moved to third base, giving the team different players at three infield positions. He made one roster move during the season, acquiring pitcher George McQuillan on waivers on August 20.

The average Opening Day age was 26. The oldest were outfielders George Paskert and Gavvy Cravath (34); the youngest was pitcher Stan Baumgartner (20).

College grads included Eppa Rixey (University of Virginia), Baumgartner (University of Chicago), and Joe Oeschger (St. Mary's College of California and a master's degree from Stanford

University). Pitchers included a Cherokee Indian (Ben Tincup), one of the era's rare Jewish players (Erskine Mayer), a cartoonist (Al Demaree), a Scottish player (George Chalmers), and two future Hall of Famers (Alexander and Eppa Rixey). Rookie shortstop Dave Bancroft was also enshrined in Cooperstown, New York. The latter two earned their credentials primarily with other teams.

Great nicknames were plentiful, including: Clifford (Gavvy) Cravath, George (Possum) Whitney, (Dode) Paskert, (Dut) Chalmers, (Bareback) Oeschger, (Old Pete) Alexander, (Beauty) Bancroft, (Eppa Jephtha) Rixey, Milt (Handle Hit) Stock, Bill (Paw Paw or Reindeer) Killefer, and (Whiskey Face) Moran.

Alexander threw a six-hit shutout as the Phillies opened the season with a 3–0 win against the defending champion Braves before 12,000 fans at Fenway Park in Boston on April 14. The shutout was the first of 12 for Alexander. He would blank Rudolph and the Braves again 168 days later in Boston's Braves Field to clinch the Phillies their first National League pennant. It was his fourth one-hitter of the season. The game took one hour, 35 minutes.

The 8–0 start expanded into winning 11 of their first 12 games. They took over first place for good on July 13, clinched the pennant on September 29, and ended seven games ahead of Boston. The Phillies finished 90–62, reaching 90 wins for the second time in franchise history. Their longest winning streak was the eight games at the start of the season while the longest losing streak was four games. The season included 20 postponements and 22 doubleheaders, in which the Phillies had an 8–5–9 record. All games were played in the day.

The pitching staff led in earned run average (2.17), complete games (98), and shutouts (20). Offensively, their 58 home runs were the most. The Phillies led the league in attendance (449,898) and average (5,290). By comparison, the 1914 Phillies drew a meager 138,474.

## THE ROSTER

### C Bert Adams

*Opening Day Age: 23*
*B–S: T–R*
*6'1", 185*

In his 24 games, he hit zero homers, two RBIs, and had a .111 average. Acquired by the Phillies in a trade with the New York Giants prior to the season, he did not play in the World Series. His big league career ended in Philadelphia four years later.

### RHP Grover Cleveland Alexander

*Opening Day Age: 28*
*B–R: T–R*
*6'1", 185*

In 42 starts, he went 31–10 with a 1.22 ERA. He led NL in wins, ERA, complete games (36), shutouts (12), innings (376⅓), and strikeouts (241). He won the pennant-clinching game and Game 1 of the World Series, the Phillies' lone win. He won 33 and 30 games the next two seasons, including 16 shutouts in 1916, a record that still stands and was elected to the Baseball Hall of Fame in 1938.

### SS Dave Bancroft

*Opening Day Age: 23*
*B–S: T–R*
*5'9", 160*

He led club with 153 games. Bancroft also had 85 runs, seven homers, 30 RBIs, 77 walks, and a .254 average. His contract was purchased from Portland (PCL) for $5,000 prior to the season. He was the lone rookie in the regular lineup and hit .294 in the World Series. Traded to the New York Giants during the 1920 season,

New York sent him to the Boston Braves three years later. He was elected to the Hall of Fame in 1971.

### LHP Stan Baumgartner

*Opening Day Age: 20*
*B–L: T–L*
*6'0", 175*

He went 0–2 with a 2.42 ERA in 16 games. He did not appear in the World Series. He pitched for the Phillies from 1914 to 1916 and 1921 to 1922 and with the Philadelphia A's from 1924 to 1926. After his playing days, Baumgartner became a baseball writer for *The Philadelphia Inquirer*, covering the Phillies, including their next pennant winner, the 1950 Whiz Kids. He also wrote for *The Sporting News*.

### OF Beals Becker

*Opening Day Age: 28*
*B–L: T–L*
*5'9", 170*

During 112 games he hit 11 home runs, had 35 RBIs, and had a .246 average. Acquired in a trade with the Cincinnati Reds during the 1913 season, his 11 homers were second to Cravath's 24. He played mostly in left field and appeared in two World Series games and had no at-bats.

### C Ed Burns

*Opening Day Age: 27*
*B–R: T–R*
*5'6", 165*

During 67 games he hit zero homers and had 16 RBIs with a .241 average. The season was his third of a six-year career in

Philadelphia. He generally served as the back-up catcher. With Bill Killefer injured, he caught all five World Series games, hitting .188.

### 3B Bobby Byrne
*Opening Day Age: 30*
*B–R: T–R*
*5'7", 145*

During 105 games, he hit zero homers and had 21 RBIs with a .209 average. The veteran, who spent three years with the Cardinals and five with the Pirates before being acquired by the Phillies in August 1913, tied for the National League lead in fielding percentage among third basemen (.969). He broke a hand and was replaced by Milt Stock. Byrne played in one World Series game, going hitless in one at-bat.

### RHP George Chalmers
*Opening Day Age: 26*
*B–R: T–R*
*6'1", 189*

He went 8–9 with a 2.48 ERA in 20 starts. He was 0–1 with a 2.25 ERA in one World Series start. His contract was purchased in August 1910 from Scranton (New York State League) for $3,000. Born in Aberdeen, Scotland, his seven-year Phillies career ended after 1916.

### OF Gavvy Cravath
*Opening Day Age: 34*
*B–R: T–R*
*5'10", 186*

During 150 games he led the National League in runs (89), extra-base hits (62), homers (24), RBIs (115), walks (86), on-base percentage (.393), and slugging percentage (.510) while hitting .285. His 28 assists also led NL outfielders. He tied a club record by driving in eight runs in a game on August 8 at Cincinnati. He drove in the Phillies' first World Series run but had only one more hit in 16 total at-bats. He led the NL in home runs six times. The Phillies purchased him from Minneapolis (American Association) after the 1911 season for $9,000. He ended his Phillies career as player-manager (1919–20). His 119 career homers were a major league record until Babe Ruth broke it in 1921.

### RHP Al Demaree
*Opening Day Age: 30*
*B–L: T–R*
*6'0", 170*

During 26 starts he went 14–11 with a 3.05 ERA. Acquired from the Giants in a trade prior to the season, he did not pitch in the World Series. He won 19 games in 1916 and was traded to the Cubs in April of 1917.

### 2B Oscar Dugey
*Opening Day Age: 27*
*B–R: T–R*
*5'8", 160*

During 42 games he hit only .154 without a home run or RBI. One of two players acquired from Boston for OF Sherry Magee after the 1914 season, he was called "the luckiest kid in baseball" as he played on pennant winners in 1914 and 1915. Primarily a pinch-hitter and pinch-runner, he appeared in two World Series games for the Phillies.

### C Bill Killefer
*Opening Day Age: 27*
*B–R: T–R*
*5'10", 170*

During 105 games he hit no homers, had 24 RBIs, and had a .238 average. Considered the best defensive catcher of his era, he injured his right shoulder in early September, curtailing his playing time. He was limited to one at-bat in the World Series. He played for the Phillies from 1911 to 1917 and then was traded to the Cubs in 1917 along with Grover Cleveland Alexander. He was behind the plate for 250 of Alexander's 696 career games.

### 1B Fred Luderus

*Opening Day Age: 29*
*B–L: T–R*
*5'11", 185*

During 141 games he had 36 doubles, seven homers, 62 RBIs, and a .315 average. He was the only .300 hitter on the team. Named captain by Moran before the season started, he finished second in the NL in doubles and average. He led the team with a .438 average in the World Series. (It was a Phillies World Series record until Jayson Werth hit .444 in 2008.) His home run in Game 5 was the franchise's first. Luderus wound up with six of the team's nine RBIs. Acquired in a 1910 trade with the Cubs, he spent 11 seasons with Phillies (1910–1920). He played 1,298 games at first base, most in franchise history until Ryan Howard passed him in 2015.

### RHP Erskine Mayer

*Opening Day Age: 25*
*B–R: T–R*
*6'0", 168*

During 33 starts he went 21–15 and had a 2.36 ERA. He allowed the most home runs in the NL with nine. He was 0–1 in two World Series starts. He won 21 games the previous season, and the Phillies purchased his contract in August 1912 from Atlanta (Southern Association) for $2,500.

### RHP George McQuillan

*Opening Day Age: 29*
*B–R: T–R*
*5'11", 175*

He made eight starts in nine games and went 4–3 with a 2.12 ERA. He began the season with the Pirates (8–10) and was claimed off waivers on August 20. He did not appear in the World Series. He originally broke in with the Phillies in 1907 and went 4–0 with a 0.66 ERA in six games (five starts). He did not allow a run in his first 25 innings, which is still a club record for the start of a career.

### 2B Bert Niehoff

*Opening Day Age: 30*
*B–R: T–R*
*5'10", 170*

During 148 games he had 27 doubles, two homers, 49 RBIs, 21 stolen bases, and a .238 average. Acquired from the Reds for C Red Dooin prior to the season, he played third base for Cincinnati, but Moran moved him to second. He went 1-for-16 in the World Series. He played two more seasons for the Phillies before being traded to the Cardinals and then finished his career with the New York Giants in 1918.

### RHP Joe Oeschger

*Opening Day Age: 22*
*B–R: T–R*
*6'0", 190*

During six games he went 1–0 with a 3.42 ERA. His win came in the last game of the season. He did not appear in the World Series. He went 21–10 in 37 games at Providence (International League) in the same season. He shares the Phillies record for most innings pitched in a game with 20 in April of 1919. Pitching for the Braves in 1920, he matched a major league record by tossing 26 innings in a game. As the oldest living Phillies alumnus (91), he threw out the first ball at the Phillies first game of the 1983 World Series at Veterans Stadium.

### OF Dode Paskert

*Opening Day Age: 33*
*B–R: T–R*
*5'11", 165*

During 109 games he hit three home runs with 39 RBIs and had a .244 average. He played 73 games in center field and 20 in left. He hit .158 in the World Series. Acquired from the Reds as part of an eight-player trade after the 1910 season, he was dealt to the Cubs for OF Cy Williams, following the 1917 campaign.

### LHP Eppa Rixey

*Opening Day Age: 24*
*B–R: T–L*
*6'5", 210*

During 22 starts he went 11–12 with a 2.39 ERA. Signed out of the University of Virginia by the Phillies in 1912, he went 0–1 with a 4.05 ERA in one World Series start. In 1920 he was traded to Cincinnati for RHP Jimmy Ring and OF Greasy Neale, who later coached the Eagles in the NFL. He won 179 games with the Reds and was elected to the Baseball Hall of Fame in 1963.

### INF Milt Stock

*Opening Day Age: 21*
*B–R: T–R*
*5'8", 154*

During 69 games he hit one home run and had 15 RBIs and a .260 average. He played 55 games at third base, including four at shortstop. He went 1-for-17 in the World Series. Acquired from the Giants along with C Bert Adams and RHP Al Demaree for Hans Lobert prior to the 1915 season, the Phillies then dealt him to the Cardinals four years later. He was the third-base coach for the Brooklyn Dodgers in 1950 when Cal Abrams was thrown out at home plate, setting up Dick Sisler's pennant-winning homer in the next inning (10th).

### RHP Ben Tincup
*Opening Day Age: 22*
*B–L: T–R*
*6'1", 180*

During 10 relief appearances, he went 0–0 with a 2.03 ERA. He was 8–10 the previous season. He did not appear in the World Series. A Cherokee, he was one of the first Native Americans to play in the major leagues. He also scouted for the Phillies from 1956 to 1958.

### OF Bud Weiser
*Opening Day Age: 24*
*B–R: T–R*
*5'11", 165*

During 37 games he had zero home runs and eight RBIs while hitting .141. Born in Shamokin, Pennsylvania, Harry Budson Weiser played under the name Bud. He did not appear in the World Series. His big league career ended in 1916 after playing in four games for the Phillies.

### OF Possum Whitted
*Opening Day Age: 25*
*B–R: T–R*
*5'8", 168*

During 128 games he had one homer, 43 RBIs, a club-high 24 stolen bases, and a .281 average. He played 67 games in center field and 52 in left field. He went 1-for-15 in the World Series. Acquired from the Boston Braves as the player to be named later for Sherry Magee prior to the 1915 season, he played in 1914 World Series for Boston.

### PENNANT-CLINCHING GAME

*The Philadelphia Inquirer* on September 30, 1915, contained the following headlines on page one:

"Trail Kills Man in Wagon"

"Cyclist is Fatally Injured"

"2 Children Badly Burned Overturning Tea Kettles"

"Allies' Hard Blow Forces Germans to Reinforce Armies"

"New Orleans Hard Hit by Hurricane; Fear Vast Damage"

But the big news was a two-column headline: "PHILLIES, BEATING BRAVES, CAPTURE NATIONAL'S FLAG." (The contest, which was game No. 147, took place in Boston the day before on September 29.)

Excerpts from that *Inquirer* story:

"Winning the necessary game to assure them the championship, the Phillies, by defeating Boston by 5 to 0, captured their first National League pennant in thirty-five years.

"Wonderful pitching by Grover Cleveland Alexander, the greatest pitcher of the day, and a record-breaking home run drive by Clifford Cravath were the salient features of this wonderful game. Alexander held Boston to one hit, that being made by his former roommate, Sherry Magee, and so helpless were the Braves before the modest Nebraskan that they gave up winning long before the last inning was played. It was Alex's thirty-first victory, his thirteenth shutout and his fourth one-hit game of the present year.

"Cravath's home run was undoubtedly one of the longest ever made and it was incidentally his twenty-third of the season. He needs two more to equal baseball's record made by Buck Freeman in 1899 when he made twenty-five home runs playing with the Washington National League club. Cravath hammered out his circuit clout in the first inning

**1915 Phun Facts**

- U.S. population: 100,546,000
- Unemployment: 8.5 percent
- Average income: $1,076
- DOW average: 99.15
- New home (median price): $4,800
- New car: $500
- Gas (gallon): 8 cents
- First class stamp: 2 cents
- Bread: 7 cents
- Coffee (pound): 30 cents
- Butter (pound): 36 cents
- Eggs (dozen): 34 cents
- Milk (quart): 9 cents

with two men on base. That blow snuffed out every hope the Braves may have secretly held of winning the game.

"The Phlying Phils have now completed a record of eighteen wins out of their last twenty-two engagements, fourteen of the eighteen having been won on the road trip which critics designated as their time to 'crack.'"

Alexander struck out four and walked one. It came with two out in the first inning. He allowed only one hit—a one-out single to Sherry Magee in the fourth— during his fourth one-hitter of the season. Ironically, Magee was traded by the Phillies after the 1914 season and was Alexander's roommate.

The losing pitcher was Dick Rudolph. He and Alexander were the starting pitchers for the season opener back on April 14. Alexander also shut out Boston then 3–0.

While quotes weren't part of newspaper writing in those days, manager Pat Moran was quoted on page 1: "You can say for me that I am tickled to death and that the Phils didn't crack. Give me credit if you want to, but don't forget the boys as they worked like hell for me and deserve just as much credit as I do."

## WORLD SERIES

Philadelphia was the site of six of the first 12 World Series. Five involved the American League's Philadelphia Athletics, who lost to the Boston Braves in 1914. In 1915 the series was played for the first time in the city's National League park, Baker Bowl. The Phillies faced the Red Sox.

Although Fenway Park was the home of the Red Sox, they played their home games in the series at the newly constructed Braves Field (40,000 capacity). The Philadelphia A's offered Shibe Park to the Phillies, as its capacity (23,000) was greater than Baker Bowl (18,000), but owner William Baker declined. Instead Baker added extra seats in front of the left and center-field walls in an effort to increase the gate. Baker was criticized for the addition. A ball bouncing into the seats was ruled a ground-rule home run, and in the end, it cost the Phillies. The World Series share for the Phillies was $2,520.

### Game 1

The Phillies produced two runs in the eighth inning on two walks and a pair of infield singles by Fred Luderus and Possum Whitted to break a 1–1 tie, giving the Phillies their first World Series win by the score of 3–1. Grover Cleveland Alexander scattered eight singles in a complete-game victory. Babe Ruth, a 20-year-old left-handed pitcher who led the AL with 18 wins, was used as a pinch-hitter in his first World Series appearance and only one in this series. He grounded to first base in the ninth inning.

One of the rare artifacts from the 1915 World Series is the program sold at Phillies games at Baker Bowl. (Hunt Auctions, Inc.)

## Game 2

Woodrow Wilson became the first U. S. President to attend a World Series game and throw out the first ball. Rube Foster three-hit the Phillies and singled in the winning run in the top of the ninth inning. The Red Sox won 2–1.

## Game 3

Another three-hitter, this one by Dutch Leonard, produced another 2–1 Boston victory. Duffy Lewis' two-out single to center drove in Harry Hooper with the winning run in the last of the ninth inning. The game in Boston drew 42,300, a World Series record.

## Game 4

Ernie Shore pitched Boston's third straight 2–1 win. Luderus had three of the Phillies' seven hits, including the lone RBI in the eighth inning. The series returned to Philadelphia with Boston leading 3–1.

## Game 5

Because of an ailing right arm, Alexander was unable to start. Erskine Mayer got the nod. The Phillies scored twice in the first inning and could have had more except for a strange decision by manager Pat Moran. With the bases-loaded, no outs, and a 3–2 count on the NL home run leader, Gavvy Cravath, Moran called for a squeeze bunt. Cravath bunted into a 1–2–3 double-play. Luderus followed with an RBI double and added another run on a homer over the right-field wall in the sixth. Boston rallied and won as Foster pitched Boston's fifth straight complete game. Hooper belted two homers and Lewis had one, a ground-rule home run. Hooper's second homer was the game-winner in the top of the ninth inning, another hit that bounced into the additional seats in left field. The victory gave the Red Sox their third World Series championship. They also won in 1903 and 1912.

# 3

# Wall of Fame Legends

The tradition of honoring legends of both the Phillies and the Philadelphia Athletics began in 1978 at Veterans Stadium in a 200-level concourse display originally called the Philadelphia Baseball Hall of Fame. Former Phillies continue to be honored at Citizens Bank Park. Phillies players with five or more years of service are eligible. In addition, position players require a minimum of 700 games, while pitchers need a minimum of 180 games to be eligible. Managers and coaches need four or more years of service. All candidates must be retired for three years before they can be eligible for the 25-man ballot, though this has been waived on occasion. Consideration is given to longevity, ability, contributions to the Phillies and baseball, character, plus special achievements.

A total of 25 former A's were part of the Philadelphia Baseball Hall of Fame, starting with Connie Mack, their longtime manager/owner who was inducted posthumously in 1978. During the planning of Citizens Bank Park, the Phillies refurbished the Connie Mack statue and located it on the west side of the park. A large bronze plaque was added to the statue, listing the 25 A's legends.

Each Phillies legend is remembered with a bronze plaque in the Wall of Fame located in the Memory Lane section of Ashburn Alley. Toyota is the sponsor of Memory Lane and the Wall of Fame. This list of Phillies legends includes their Wall of Fame plaque, and the italicized paragraph is the verbatim text from the plaque at the time of induction.

## ROBIN ROBERTS
### Right-handed pitcher
### Phillies 1948–1962
### Inducted 1978

*Won 20 or more games six years in a row. First 20-win season was 1950 when he was the winning pitcher in Phillies' pennant-clinching game on the last day of the season. Was 28–7 in 1952; named Major League Player of the Year. From mid-1952 to mid-1953 completed 28 consecutive games. Pitched more than 300 innings six straight years. Selected to seven National League All-Star teams, starting a record five straight. Phillies record: 234–199. Ranks first on club's all-time list in games, complete games, innings pitched. Inducted into the Baseball Hall of Fame in 1976.*

Born: September 30, 1926, Springfield, Illinois

Died: May 6, 2010, Tampa, Florida

**Robin Evans Roberts** went to Michigan State University on a basketball scholarship but blossomed into a pitcher with the Spartans and tossed a no-hitter against rival Michigan. He signed for a $25,000 bonus with the Phillies following graduation in 1948.

He went from college to the Wilmington Blue Rocks and was called up by the Phillies after just 11 pro games (9–1 record). His major league debut came on June 18, 1948, at age 21 when he suffered a complete-game, 2–0 loss to the Pirates in Forbes Field. He was the ace of the Phillies for 14 of his 19 big league seasons and also pitched for the Orioles, Astros, and Cubs. A workhorse who didn't miss a start in the decade of the 1950s, he wound up making 609 starts and completed 305 of them and finished with 286 wins.

He's the only pitcher to beat the Braves in Boston, Milwaukee, and Atlanta.

Uniform No. 36 is retired by MSU baseball, the Blue Rocks, and Phillies. His uniform number with the Reading Phillies (No. 9) is also retired. The ballpark in his hometown is named Robin Roberts Stadium. He is a charter member (1992) of the Michigan State University Athletics Hall of Fame.

### RICHIE ASHBURN
#### Outfielder
#### Phillies 1948–1959
#### Inducted 1979

*Hit .311 during 12 seasons with Phillies. Won batting titles in 1955 (.338) and 1958 (.350). Led National League in hits three times, each time exceeding 200. Led league in stolen bases in 1948. Four-time All-Star, starting in center field twice. Holds major league record for years (four) with 500 putouts. Shares major league record for leading league in putouts most years (nine). Ranks first on Phillies all-time list in singles, second in games, at-bats, hits, third in runs scored. Hit .308 overall. Inducted into Baseball Hall of Fame in 1995. Served as Phillies broadcaster for 35 years.*

Born: March 19, 1927, Tilden, Nebraska

Died: September 9, 1997, New York, New York

**Don Richie Ashburn** grew up in the small town of Tilden, Nebraska, and was signed by the Phillies in 1945 as a catcher. Because of blinding speed, he was moved to center field that season in Utica, New York. He made his major league debut on Opening Day in 1948, the first big league game he saw. He also played for the Cubs and Mets and finished with a .308 average. After his career he became a broadcaster for the Phillies in 1963. He and Harry Kalas entertained Phillies fans from 1971 until his death in 1997. Having also written a column for *The Philadelphia Bulletin* and later the *Philadelphia Daily News*, he is regarded as the most revered athlete in Philadelphia history. Phillies fans turned Cooperstown into a sea of red when he and Mike Schmidt were enshrined in the Hall of Fame in 1995. Uniform No. 1 was retired on August 24, 1979.

### CHUCK KLEIN
Outfielder
Phillies 1928–1933, 1936–39, 1940–44
Inducted 1980

*Winner of four National League home run titles. Was MVP twice (1931, 1932). Won triple crown (.368, 28 HR, 120 RBI) in 1933. First five years in majors rank among the best for a hitter in baseball history. In 1930, when he hit .386 with 158 runs, set an NL record for left-handed batters with 170 RBI. Also, set NL record for most assists (44) in one season. Was the starting right fielder in first All-Star Game in 1933. Ranks third on Phillies all-time list in home runs, extra-base hits. Phillies stats: .316 average, 243 home runs and 1,201 RBI. Elected to Baseball Hall of Fame in 1980.*

Born: October 7, 1904, Indianapolis, Indiana

Died: March 28, 1958, Indianapolis, Indiana

**Charles Herbert Klein** was a 1923 graduate of Southport High School in Indianapolis. He worked in a steel mill for three years and started playing semi-pro baseball. Five years later his professional baseball career began in the minor leagues. During the 1928 minor league season (88 games, .331, 26 home runs), the Phillies purchased his contract from Fort Wayne for $5,500, outbidding the New York Yankees. He made his Phillies debut on July 30, 1928, as a 23-year-old. During his first five seasons, he averaged 46 doubles, nine triples, 36 homers, 138 RBIs along with a .359 average. The left-handed hitter was one of the game's premier power hitters. He was a superb defensive right fielder and also a player-coach with the Phillies from 1942 to 1945. He wore seven different numbers with the Phillies: 1, 3, 8, 26, 29, 32, and 36. He also played for the Cubs and Pirates.

## GROVER CLEVELAND ALEXANDER
### Right-handed pitcher
### Phillies 1911–1917, 1930
### Inducted 1981

*Three-time 30-game winner, earning 31, 33, 30 victories from 1915–17. ERA in those three years was 1.22, 1.55, 1.83. Broke in with Phillies with 28 wins. Set major league record in 1916 with 16 shutouts. With Phillies, led National League in innings pitched six times, working more than 300 innings every year. Led NL in wins, strikeouts, complete games, shutouts each five times. Phillies record: 190–91, club-record 61 shutouts. Ranks second in complete games, third in wins, innings pitched. Entered Baseball Hall of fame in 1939.*

Born: February 26, 1887, Elba, Nebraska

Died: November 4, 1950, St. Paul, Nebraska

One of 13 children, **Grover Cleveland Alexander** grew on up a farm and developed into one of baseball's greatest right-handed pitchers. The Phillies purchased his contract from Syracuse after the 1910 minor league season for $750. In his fourth big league season, he pitched the Phillies to their first National League pennant in 1915, posting the first of three Triple Crowns (ERA, strikeouts, and wins). He won the Phillies' first World Series game ever that fall against the Boston Red Sox. He was the first pitcher Babe Ruth faced in a World Series. In 1916 and 1917, he won both games of a doubleheader. Traded to the Chicago Cubs after the 1917 season, he pitched in three games the next year and then served in the 89th Infantry Division during World War I. He was part of the first Baseball Hall of Fame induction class. He was named after a U. S. president and portrayed by actor/future President Ronald Reagan in the 1952 motion picture, *The Winning Team*. He also played for the Cubs and Cardinals, finishing with a 373–208 record, 2.56 ERA, and 90 shutouts.

## DEL ENNIS
### Outfielder
### Phillies 1946–1956
### Inducted 1982

*Philadelphia native was National League Rookie of the Year in 1946 when he hit .313. Led league with 126 RBI in 1950 when he was main offensive power of the Whiz Kids. Drove in more than 100 runs six times with the Phillies, totaling 1,124 overall. Twice collected seven RBI in one game. Hit 25 or more home runs seven times with a career-high 31 in 1950. Hit 259 home runs with Phillies to rank second on all-time list. Ranks third in RBI and total bases in 1,630 games. Named to three NL All-Star teams, two of which he started.*

Born: June 8, 1925, Philadelphia, Pennsylvania

Died: February 8, 1996, Huntingdon Valley, Pennsylvania

**Del Ennis** is regarded as the greatest Philadelphia native to wear a Phillies uniform. He was a star in baseball and football at Olney High School. The Phillies signed him in 1943. He spent three years in the Navy during World War II. Discharged on April 5, 1946, he made his major league debut 23 days later. Eleven weeks later he became the first Phillies rookie selected to an All-Star team. At $30,000 he was the highest paid player on the 1950 National League champion Whiz Kids. After retiring he owned a bowling alley (Del Ennis Lanes) in suburban Huntingdon Valley. He wore No. 14 and also played for the Cardinals, Reds, and White Sox.

## CENTENNIAL TEAM

*In 1983 the Phillies conducted balloting for the Greatest Phillies team and Greatest Player Ever, an honor Mike Schmidt earned.*

*Bob Boone (C)*
*Pete Rose (1B)*
*Manny Trillo (2B)*
*Mike Schmidt (3B)*
*Larry Bowa (SS)*
*Richie Ashburn (OF)*
*Garry Maddox (OF)*

*Del Ennis (OF)*
*Robin Roberts (RH starter)*
*Steve Carlton (LF starter)*
*Jim Konstanty (RH reliever)*
*Tug McGraw (LH reliever)*
*Dallas Green (MGR)*

Bronze plaques are on display in the Toyota Wall of Fame, which is located in the Memory Lane section of Ashburn Alley. (Miles Kennedy)

## JIM BUNNING
### Right-handed pitcher
### Phillies 1964–1967, 1970–71
### Inducted 1984

*Pitched only perfect game in Phillies history when he beat the New York Mets in 1964. That was the first perfect game in the majors during the regular season in 42 years. Also pitched a no-hitter with Detroit in 1958. Was only the second pitcher to hurl no-hitters in each league. Won 19 games in each of first three seasons with Phillies. Started and won first game at Veterans Stadium. Won 224 games in majors, 89 with Phillies. Struck out 1,197 in 1,520.2 innings with Phillies while hurling 23 shutouts and posting 2.93 ERA. Inducted into the Baseball Hall of Fame in 1996.*

Born: October 23, 1931, Southgate, Kentucky.

**Jim Bunning** not only had a very successful big league career but excelled after he took off the baseball uniform. The slender right-handed pitcher spent 17 years in baseball, most notably with the Tigers and Phillies. He also pitched for the Pirates and Dodgers and is the first pitcher to appear in an All-Star Game in each league. When he retired, he was second on the all-time strikeout list. He dabbled as a stock broker and was a minor league manager with the Phillies for five seasons. In 1977 he was elected to the city council in Fort Thomas, Kentucky. His political path took him to the state senate, the U.S. House of Representatives, and the U.S. Senate. He retired from the Senate in 2010. The Phillies retired his No. 14 on April 6, 2001.

### ED DELAHANTY
Outfielder
Phillies 1888–1889, 1891–1901
Inducted 1985

*One of baseball's greatest hitters, his .346 lifetime average ranks fifth on the all-time major league list. Hit .348 with Phillies with 2,211 hits in 1,544 games. Phillies all-time leader in doubles (432), triples (151). Ranks second in batting average, RBI, runs, singles, extra-base hits, total bases. First Phillies player to hit four home runs in one game. Won NL batting title in 1899 with .410 average. Hit above .400 two other times (.407 in 1894, .404 in 1895). Elected to Baseball Hall of Fame in 1945. One of five brothers who played in the big leagues.*

Born: October 30, 1867, Cleveland, Ohio

Died: July 2, 1903, Niagara Falls, Ontario, Canada

**Ed (Big Ed) Delahanty** was the eldest and most talented of five brothers who played in the big leagues. During his Phillies career, he led the National League in a major offensive category 24 times. Of the four home runs he hit in one game, two were inside the park. He's the first player in baseball history to hit over .400 three times. He also played for Cleveland (Player's League) one season and two with Washington (American League). Big Ed's name appeared on the Hall of Fame ballot five times before being elected by the Veterans Committee in 1945. Death came when he was swept over Niagara Falls. One of the greatest players in Phillies history tragically died at age 35. Reports are varied as to whether he fell or jumped.

## CY WILLIAMS
### Outfielder
### Phillies 1918–1930
### Inducted 1986

*Led National League in home runs four times, three with the Phillies: 15 in 1920, 41 in 1923, and 30 in 1927. Ranks fifth on Phillies all-time list in home runs with 217. Holds club records for most RBI in May with 44 in 1923, most home runs in one month (15 in May 1923). With Phillies had .306 batting average, 1,553 hits, 237 doubles, 795 RBI, 825 runs. Hit over .300 six times with Phillies with a career-high .345 in 1926. Had career high in RBI with 114 in 1923. Finished with .292 average, 251 homers, 1,005 RBI in 19-year big league career.*

Born: December 21, 1887, Wadena, Indiana

Died: April 23, 1974, Eagle River, Wisconsin

**Frederick "Cy" Williams** majored in architecture while playing football with the fabled Knute Rockne at Notre Dame. He excelled in the high hurdles and the broad jump in track and field. After he spent six years with the Cubs, the Phillies acquired the left-handed hitting outfielder in a December 1917 trade for center fielder Dode Paskert. He led the National League in homers (41) and RBIs (114) in 1923, the most for any Phillies center fielder. He hit his 120th home run that season to break the NL record held by former Phillie Gavvy Cravath. He was the first National League player to reach 200 home runs. At age 39 he became the oldest home run leader as he hit 30 dingers in 1927. He hit 217 homers with the Phillies and 141 at Baker Bowl. He holds the club record for most pinch-hit homers in a career with nine. After retirement he worked as an architect. He died in 1974 at age 86.

## GRANNY HAMNER
### Shortstop, second baseman
### Phillies 1944–1959
### Inducted 1987

*Among youngest players ever to wear a Phillies uniform when he broke in as a 17-year-old in 1944. Spent 16 years with the club, 10 as a starter. Sparkplug of 1950 Whiz Kids. Hit .429 in the World Series. A three-time National League All-Star, he started at short-stop in 1952 and at second base two years later. Holds club record for most home runs in one season by a shortstop (17 in 1952). Hit career-high .299 in 1954. Overall Phillies average was .263 with 1,518 hits in 1,501 games.*

Born: April 16, 1927, Richmond, Virginia

Died: September 12, 1993, Philadelphia, Pennsylvania

**Granville Wilbur Hamner** made his major league debut as a shortstop for the Phillies in 1944. A brother, Garvin "Wes", 20, opened the 1945 season at second base with Granny at shortstop. He was named captain by manager Eddie Sawyer in 1952. He was regarded as a terrific clutch hitter. He was the first player in baseball history to be elected an All-Star starter at two different positions, shortstop and second base. Hamner was inducted into the Virginia Sports Hall of Fame in 1981. He played for Cleveland and Kansas City following his Phillies career and also tried pitching for the Phillies and the A's, going 0–2 with a 5.40 ERA in seven games.

## PAUL (THE POPE) OWENS
### General manager/manager
### Phillies 1972–1984
### Inducted 1988

*As General Manager, was largely responsible for putting together Phillies 1976, 1977, 1978 division champions and 1980 World Champions. Made many key trades while serving as the GM from 1972–1983. Also managed the Phillies in 1972 and 1983–84, win-ning the pennant in 1983. Managed winning 1984 NL All-Star team. Started in Phillies system as a player-manager in 1956. Managed four years in minors, then was an area scout (1959–1965) and Director of Minor League operations (1965–1972), Sr. Advisor to GM (1998–2003).*

Born: February 7, 1924, Salamanca, New York

Died: December 26, 2003, Woodbury, New Jersey

**Paul Francis Owens'** career with the Phillies in player development spanned from 1956 through 2003. He loved the grass roots of baseball, scouting and developing players. As the director of minor league operations, he had the vision to build Carpenter Field, a training complex in Clearwater. It opened in 1967. That fall he began the Florida Instructional League program. Starting in 1986, the Phillies established the Paul Owens Award, which would annually honor the best player and pitcher in the team's minor league system. He died in December 2003, three months after the closing of Veterans Stadium, home of his greatest achievements. He was 79.

### STEVE CARLTON
#### Left-handed pitcher
#### Phillies 1972–1986
#### Inducted 1989

*Second-winningest left-hander of all time; 329 wins rank behind only Warren Spahn (363). Four-time Cy Young Award winner. All-time National League strikeout leader with 4,000. Made 544 consecutive starts, an NL record. Was a 20-game winner five times with the Phillies. Best season: 1972 when he won 27 with a 1.97 ERA, 30 complete games, 310 strikeouts and a 15-game winning streak. Led NL in strikeouts and innings pitched five times; wins and complete games four times. Phillies stats: 241–161 record, 39 shutouts, 3,031 strikeouts. Ten-time All-Star. Inducted into Hall of Fame in 1994.*

Born: December 22, 1944, Miami, Florida

**Steven Norman Carlton** came to the Phillies from the St. Louis Cardinals in a controversial trade for Rick Wise during spring training of 1972. His 27 wins on a last-place team that summer earned him the nickname, "Super Steve." Lefty dominated hitters for years with a lethal slider. At one point in his career, he had the most strikeouts in baseball history. He holds Phillies career records for wins, starts, and strikeouts. No. 32 was retired by the Phillies in 1989. He pitched for the San Francisco Giants, Chicago White Sox, Cleveland Indians, and Minnesota Twins, following his brilliant Phillies career. His last game was on April 23, 1988. He was inducted into the Baseball Hall of Fame in his first year of eligibility.

### MIKE SCHMIDT
**Third baseman**
**Phillies 1972–1989**
**Inducted 1990**

*One of baseball's top home run hitters with 548. Won or tied for eight home run crowns. Three-time MVP (1980, 1981, 1986). MVP of 1980 World Series. Won 10 Gold Gloves. Selected to 12 All-Star teams. Spent entire career with Phillies, collecting 2,234 hits, 1,595 RBI, and hitting .267 in 2,404 games. All-time club leader in games, at-bats, runs, hits, RBI, home runs, total bases, extra-base hits. Set club record with 48 homers in 1980. Holds NL records for most career innings played, assists, chances, double plays by a third baseman. Inducted into baseball's Hall of Fame in 1995.*

Born: September 17, 1949, Dayton, Ohio

**Michael Jack Schmidt** was a shortstop at Ohio University when the Phillies selected him in the second round of the 1971 draft. He played his entire 18-year-career with the Phillies, establishing himself as the greatest overall third baseman in the game's history. Needless to say, he's the greatest player in Phillies history. He held 18 National League hitting records and 10 league fielding records when he retired, an indication of his all-around skills. His No. 20 was retired in 1990, and he was elected to the Baseball Hall of Fame in his first year of eligibility. Phillies fans turned Cooperstown into a sea of red during that induction, which included Richie Ashburn.

## LARRY BOWA
### Shortstop
### Phillies 1970–1981
### Inducted 1991

*As a defensive shortstop, was one of the best of all time. Holds National League record for highest career fielding percentage (.980) for a shortstop. With Phillies, he fielded .981, committing just 156 errors in 12 years. Led the NL in fielding percentage six times. Won two Gold Gloves. Switch-hitter batted .264 with Phillies. All-time club leader in games played (1,667) at shortstop. Collected 1,798 hits in 1,739 games with Phillies. Played in five All-Star games, five NLCS, one World Series in 1980 when he hit .375.*

Born: December 6, 1945, Sacramento, California

**Larry Bowa** couldn't make his high school team and wasn't among the 824 players drafted in 1965 but was signed by the Phillies because he could field, throw, and run. He was ready to quit after his first pro game in Spartanburg, striking out all four times against flame-throwing Nolan Ryan. Because of a feisty makeup, he developed into a premier shortstop and collected over 2,100 hits. Larry was the National League's all-time leader in games played at shortstop when he retired. A player, coach, manager, and coach again, Larry's worn the Phillies uniform longer than anyone in franchise history.

## CHRIS SHORT
### Left-handed pitcher
### Phillies 1959–1972
### Inducted 1992

*Ranks as one of the top left-handers in club history. Third on all-time list in games started, strikeouts; fourth in wins, games, shut-outs. Posted 132–127 record in 14 seasons with Phillies. Won 20 in 1966, 19 in 1968. Shares National League record for most opening day shutouts (three), including first game in Astrodome in 1965. Struck out 18 New York Mets in 15-innning game in 1965, tying NL record for most strikeouts in an extra-inning game by a left-hander.*

*With Phillies, he pitched in 459 games, worked 2,253 innings, struck out 1,585 and hurled 24 shutouts.*

Born: September 19, 1937, Milford, Delaware

Died: August 1, 1991, Wilmington, Delaware

**Chris Short**, the stylish left-hander, is the greatest pitcher to come out of Delaware. He made his major league debut when he was 21 years of age, two years after he signed. He was a dominant pitcher with the Phillies from 1964 to 1967, averaging 250-plus innings, 190-plus strikeouts, and 17 wins. He was a National League All-Star in 1964 and 1967 and the winning pitcher in the final game at the Polo Grounds in New York. A career .126 hitter, he once went 4-for-4 against Hall of Fame left-hander Warren Spahn. He finished his career with Milwaukee in 1973. Back problems cut his career short. He suffered a ruptured aneurysm in 1988, lapsed into a coma, never regained consciousness, and died three years later at age 53.

### CURT SIMMONS
#### Left-handed pitcher
#### Phillies 1947–1960
#### Inducted 1993

*One of baseball's earliest bonus players, signed at 18 years of age. Pitched in his first big league game and beat the New York Giants in 1947. Registered a 115–110 record with Phillies, best year coming in 1950 when he was 17–8 before being called to military duty late in the season. Won in double figures five other years. Had 193 wins overall during 20-year career. Selected for three National League All-Star teams; started 1952 game at Shibe Park. In 325 games with Phillies, hurled 109 complete games and struck out 1,052 in 1,939.2 innings.*

Born: May 19, 1929, Egypt, Pennsylvania

**Curtis Thomas Simmons** was a much sought-after pitcher at Whitehall High School where he struck out 102 in 43 innings during his senior year. On June 2, 1947, the Phillies team went to Egypt,

Pennsylvania, to face Curt and a semi-pro team in an exhibition game. He held the Phillies to seven hits while striking out 11 in a 4–4, nine-inning tie. The next day, the Phillies signed him to a $60,000 bonus, plus a promise he would be promoted to the majors in September and be given an additional $5,000. It was the largest bonus at the time. He also pitched for the St. Louis Cardinals and Chicago Cubs, and ended his career in 1967 with the California Angels. He and Robin Roberts owned and operated the Limekiln Golf Club near Ambler, Pennsylvania, following their careers.

### DICK ALLEN
**Third baseman, first baseman**
**Phillies 1963–1969, 1975–1976**
**Inducted 1994**

*National League Rookie of the Year in 1964 when he hit .318 with 201 hits, 29 home runs, 91 RBI, and led league with 13 triples, 125 runs. Known for tape-measure homers. Slammed 204 homers with Phillies while driving in 655 runs. Batted .290 in nine seasons. Hit above .300 in first four years with Phillies. Led NL in slugging percentage (.632) in 1966. Had career-high 40 home runs that year. Was MVP in American League with Chicago White Sox in 1972 when he hit .308 and led league in home runs (37) and RBI (113). Three-time All-Star with Phillies.*

Born: March 8, 1942, Wampum, Pennsylvania

**Richard Anthony Allen** was a basketball and baseball star at Wampum High School who signed a $60,000 bonus contract with the Phillies after graduation in 1960. Four years later, playing a new position (third base), he walked away with the National League Rookie of the Year award. Dick was a gifted athlete and quick and strong with great base-running instincts. While swinging a 42-ounce bat, he hit some of the longest homers in Connie Mack Stadium history. After being traded in 1969, he was brought back in 1975 to bat in the middle of the lineup that featured young sluggers Mike Schmidt and Greg Luzinski. His career ended with Oakland in 1977.

## WILLIE JONES
### Third baseman
### Phillies 1947–1959
### Inducted 1995

*Known as "Puddin' Head," was the regular third baseman for a decade starting in 1949. As a rookie, he tied a club record and Major League record with four consecutive doubles in a game. Holds National League record for most consecutive years (four) leading league's third basemen in fielding percentage. Tied NL record for most years leading in putouts (seven). Member of two All-Star teams. Hit .267 with 25 homers, 88 RBI with 1950 Whiz Kids. Was .285–22–81 the following year. Had 180 homers, 753 RBI in 1,520 Phillies games.*

Born: August 16, 1925, Dillon, South Carolina

Died: October 18, 1983, Cincinnati, Ohio

Phillies scouts discovered **Willie "Puddin' Head" Jones** playing sandlot baseball in his native South Carolina. Prior to the 1947 season, he received a $16,500 bonus to sign with the Phillies. His major league debut came that September as a 22-year old, who went hitless in one at-bat as a pinch-hitter in St. Louis. He was considered an excellent defensive third baseman. His 2,045 career putouts at third base are the most in Phillies history. He started at third base for the National League All-Stars in 1950. A right-handed hitter with power, Jones hit .258 with the Phillies and had more walks than strikeouts, 693–493. He ended his career with Cleveland (1959) and Cincinnati (1959–61) and died at age 58.

## SAM THOMPSON
### Outfielder
### Phillies 1889–1898
### Inducted 1996

*Premier 19th century long-ball hitter, won two National League home run crowns with 20 homers in 1889, 18 in 1895. Hit .407 in 1894, combining with Ed Delahanty (.407) and Billy Hamilton (.404) to form only .400-hitting outfield in major league history. Led NL with 222 hits and 37 doubles in 1893, and with 165 RBI and .654 slugging percentage in 1895. Once had eight hits in a double-header. Collected 95 homers, 272 doubles, 957 RBI in 10 seasons with Phillies while batting .335. Inducted into Baseball Hall of Fame in 1974.*

Born: March 5, 1860, Danville, Indiana

Died: November 7, 1922, Detroit, Michigan

**Samuel Luther Thompson** was an outfielder with multiple tools. A left-handed hitter, he was the first National League player to hit 20 home runs, get 200 hits, and amassed 300 total bases in a season. The 1894 outfield of Thompson-Hamilton-Delahanty became Hall of Famers. He played for Detroit in the National League (1885–88) and in the American League (1906).

During his 15-year, big-league career, Thompson drove in 100 or more runs eight times and scored over 100 runs 10 times while batting .336. His 126 home runs were second all time when he retired. For some reason it took until 1974 to induct Thompson into the Hall of Fame, which occurred 52 years after he died.

### JOHNNY CALLISON
#### Outfielder
#### Phillies 1960–1969
#### Inducted 1997

*Gained prominence for hitting three-run, ninth-inning homer that gave National League a 7–4 victory in 1964 All-Star Game. Was named MVP of the game, one of three All-Star appearances. Hit 31 homers in 1964 with 104 RBI. Was 32–101 the following year. Posted double figures in home runs eight straight years with Phillies. Led NL in triples twice, doubles once. Had career-high batting average of .300 in 1962. Hit 185 home runs in 1,432 Phillies games. Led NL right fielders in assists four straight years.*

Born: March 12, 1939, Qualls, Oklahoma

Died: October 12, 2006, Abington, Pennsylvania

Signed by the White Sox as the next Mickey Mantle, **John Wesley Callison** came to the Phillies in a trade for third baseman Gene Freese after the 1959 season. He broke in with the White Sox the year before at age 19. Gene Mauch said it best: "He can run, throw, field, and hit with power. There's nothing he can't do well on a ball field." Callison became a fan favorite and an All-Star right fielder. His All-Star Game homer was the first ever hit by a Phillies player. He also was the first player in Phillies history to hit three home runs in a game two times. The runner-up to Ken Boyer as the 1964 National League MVP, he also played for the Chicago Cubs and New York Yankees.

### GREG (THE BULL) LUZINSKI
#### Outfielder
#### Phillies 1970–1980
#### Inducted 1998

*Slammed some of the longest home runs at Veterans Stadium; eight into the upper deck in left field and two to center field. Hit more than 30 homers three times with Phillies, including a career-high 39 in 1977. Ranks fourth on club's all-time home run list with 223. Hit .281 with the Phillies with 1,299 hits, 811 RBI, 2,263 total bases in 1,289 games. Led National League in RBI with 120 in 1975. Hit .310 with five homers, 12 RBI in four NLCS with Phillies. Two-time runner up for NL MVP. Member of four All-Star teams. During 15-year career, reached double figures in home runs 12 times.*

Born: November 22, 1950, Chicago, Illinois

**Gregory Michael Luzinski** turned down a football scholarship to Kansas State to sign with the Phillies, who selected him in the first round in 1968 out of Notre Dame High School in Niles, Illinois. Originally a first baseman, he was moved to left field in 1972. He teamed with Mike Schmidt to form a powerful 1–2 power punch for nine seasons. Noted for his upper deck "Bull Blasts" at Veterans Stadium, he was the runner-up for the NL MVP in 1975 and 1977. He won the 1978 Roberto Clemente Award for community service. He has hosted Bull's BBQ ever since Citizens Bank Park opened in 2004.

## TUG MCGRAW
### Left-handed pitcher
### Phillies 1975–1984
### Inducted 1999

*Saved biggest win in Phillies history, a 4–1 decision over Kansas City in the sixth and deciding game of 1980 World Series. Saved one other game in the Series and two that year in the NLCS. Tied for National League record for most saves (five) in NLCS. Posted 49–37 record with 3.10 ERA with Phillies. Ranks third on club's all-time list in games (463), fourth in saves (94). Made two NL All-Star teams. Spent first nine years of career with New York Mets. Overall had 96–92 record with 180 saves.*

Born: August 30, 1944, Martinez, California

Died: January 5, 2004, Brentwood, Tennessee

**Frank Edwin McGraw** came to the Phillies in 1974 in a trade with the Mets, where he had preached, "You gotta believe." He brought that same enthusiasm to Philly. Six years later, he stood on the mound in Game 6 of the World Series, needing three more outs. In dramatic fashion he struck out Kansas City's Willie Wilson to give the Phillies their first World Series title. He reenacted that last pitch in the 2003 closing ceremonies of the Vet despite being weakened from a battle with a brain tumor. He died four months later at age 59.

## CLIFFORD CARLTON (GAVVY) CRAVATH
### Outfielder
### Phillies 1912–1920
### Inducted 2000

*Top National League home run hitter of the early 20th century. Led NL in homers six times between 1913–1919. His 24 homers for pennant-winning Phillies in 1915 was a major league record until broken by Babe Ruth in 1919. Was also NL record until passed by Rogers Hornsby in 1922. Hit career-high .341 in 1913 and led NL in slugging average, hits, homers, RBI. Won one other NL crown in RBI and slugging percentage. Hit .291 with Phillies with 117 home runs, 676 RBI. Tied for club records with four doubles, eight RBI in one game in 1915.*

Born: March 23, 1881, Poway, California

Died: May 23, 1963, Laguna Beach, California

**Clifford "Gavvy" Cravath** was a slugging right fielder during his Phillies career and was baseball's single-season home run leader and career homer leader until Babe Ruth came along. He led the National League in homers six seasons, the most for a Phillies player until Mike Schmidt did it seven seasons. The Phillies purchased him from Minneapolis for $9,000 after he hit a minor league record 29 home runs in 1911. He was 31 years old in his first Phillies season in 1912. His 11 homers led the club that season. Cravath served as the team's player-manager in 1919–20 and led the squad to a 91–137 record. He drove in the first World Series run for the Phillies in 1915. Following his career he was elected a judge in Laguna Beach, California, in 1927 and spent 36 years on the bench.

## GARRY MADDOX
### Outfielder
### Phillies 1975–1986
### Inducted 2001

*Called the "Secretary of Defense," was one of the top center fielders in Phillies history. Won eight Gold Gloves, a club record for an outfielder. Led National League in putouts in 1976, 1978. Placed third in NL batting races in 1973, 1976. Hit career-high .330 in 1976. Tenth-inning double drove in winning run to give Phillies NL pennant in fifth game of NLCS against Houston in 1980. During Phillies career, hit .284 with 1,333 hits in 1,328 games. Ranks among team's all-time leaders in stolen bases with 189. Had career fielding percentage of .983.*

Born: September 1, 1949, Cincinnati, Ohio

Originally a second-round selection by the Giants in the 1968 draft, **Garry Lee Maddox** spent two years (1969–1970) with the

Army in Vietnam. He resumed his minor league career in 1971 and reached the majors the following year. The Phillies acquired him on May 4, 1975, for Willie Montanez, a trade that wasn't very popular. He, though, quickly became a fan favorite in Philly with his outstanding defensive play in center field, playing on six teams that reached the postseason. He was nicknamed the "Secretary of Defense" by Harry Kalas. Garry drove in the winning run and caught the last out in the 1980 NLCS win over the Astros. Off the field, he was a leader in community charities, earning the Roberto Clemente Award in 1986. Following baseball Maddox remained in Philadelphia where he is a highly successful businessman.

## TONY TAYLOR
### Second baseman
### Phillies 1960–1971, 1974–1976
### Inducted 2002

*Played most games at second base (1,003) in Phillies history. Led National League second basemen in fielding percentage in 1963 when he made only 10 errors in 157 games. Member of 1960 NL All-Star team. Hit a career-high .301 in 1970. Ranks fourth on Phillies all-time list in games (1,669). Batted .261 during Phillies career. Had same mark in 19 big league seasons. With Phillies, he had 1,511 hits, 1,178 singles, 169 stolen bases. Phillies coach 1977–1979 and 1988–1989.*

Born: December 19, 1935, Central Alava, Cuba

**Antonio Nemesio (Sanchez) Taylor** was signed by the Giants in 1954, selected by the Cubs in the 1957 Rule 5 draft, and acquired by the Phillies early in the 1960 season for pitcher Don Cardwell and first baseman Ed Bouchee. He was the starting second baseman for 12 years and developed into an outstanding lead-off hitter. He wore the Phillies uniform for 15 seasons, becoming one of the most popular players ever. He wound up with two World Series rings with the Marlins as a coach (1997 and 2003). "TT" played the most games at second base for the Phillies until Chase Utley passed him in 2011.

## SHERRY MAGEE
### Outfielder
### Phillies 1904–1914
### Inducted 2003

*First batting champion for Phillies in the 20th century when he hit .331 in 1910. Also led National League that year in RBI (123), runs (110), total bases (263), slugging percentage (.507). Hit above .300 four other times. Led NL in RBI in 1907 and 1914. Phillies all-time stolen base leader with 387. Stole 40 or more bases five times with high of 55 in 1906. Batted .299 in 1,521 Phillies games. Ranks second on club list in triples (127), third in doubles (337). Also in top 10 in runs, hits, RBI, total bases, singles, extra-base hit. Third among Phillies outfielders in games played.*

Born: August 6, 1884, Clarendon, Pennsylvania

Died: March 23, 1929, Philadelphia, Pennsylvania

**Sherwood Robert Magee** was signed by the Phillies on June 27, 1904. The 19-year-old outfielder made his major league debut two days later. He was considered a five-tool player who could hit, run, throw, field, and hit with power. He developed into one of the greatest base stealers in Phillies history. The hot-tempered Magee flattened a National League umpire with one punch on July 10, 1911. He was fined and suspended for the rest of the season. Ironically, he became an NL umpire after his playing days were over. He died from pneumonia at age 44.

## BILLY HAMILTON
### Outfielder
### Phillies 1890–1895
### Inducted 2004

*During his Phillies career, batted over .300 each season. Was the team's first batting champion (.340 in 1891) and led National League in runs scored and walks, three times each. Playing mostly in an era when stolen bases were credited for advancing an extra base on a hit or out, "Sliding Billy" also led NL in steals, four years, and topped 100, three times. In 1894, batted a career-high .404, set major league records for runs scored in a season (196) and most consecutive games scoring runs (24); also set club record with 36-game hitting streak. Ranks as baseball's all-time leader in runs scored per game (1.06) for his 14-year career. Inducted into the Baseball Hall of Fame in 1961.*

Born: February 15, 1866, Newark, New Jersey

Died: December 15, 1940, Worcester, Massachusetts

**William Robert Hamilton** was a 5'6", left-handed hitting out-fielder with blazing speed. He trails only Ricky Henderson and Lou Brock in stolen bases. He once stole seven bases in a game for the Phillies. His 196 runs scored in 1894 is still a record. Babe Ruth came the closest with 177 in 1921. Hamilton is one of the few players to finish with more runs scored than games played. He brought more than speed to the base path, hitting .344 in his career. Hamilton was inducted posthumously into the Baseball Hall of Fame in 1961 by the Veterans Committee.

### BOB BOONE
#### Catcher
#### Phillies 1972–1981
#### Inducted 2005

*Defensive stalwart on 1976–77–78 East Division champions and 1980 World Champion Phillies. Sixth round pick as a third baseman out of Stanford University in 1969. Converted to catcher after two minor league seasons and wound up catching 1,095 games, second on Phillies all-time list to Red Dooin (1,124). Became first Phillies catcher to win a Gold Glove, 1978 and 1979. Led Phillies with a .412 average in 1980 World Series. Three-time NL All-Star, 1976, 1978, 1979. Finished Phillies career with .259 average in 1,125 games. Also played for California Angels and Kansas City Royals; caught 2,225 games in 19 big league seasons. Along with father, Ray, and sons, Bret and Aaron, the Boones were baseball's first three-generation family.*

Born: November 19, 1947, San Diego, California

**Robert Raymond Boone** was a biology major at Stanford University. He was switched to a catcher in 1971. After only 169 games behind the plate in the minors, he made his major league debut in September 1972. He was the Phillies' everyday catcher for nine years starting in 1973. An excellent defensive catcher and student of the game, he handled pitching staffs that reached the postseason five times—four with the Phillies and once with the Angels. When he retired, he had caught more games than anyone in baseball history and then saw Carlton Fisk break the record by one game. His two sons—second baseman Bret Boone and third baseman Aaron Boone—were All-Stars during their careers. Bob managed the Royals (1995–97) and Cincinnati Reds (2001–03).

## DALLAS GREEN
### Pitcher/farm director/manager
### Phillies 1960–1964, 1967, 1979–81
### Inducted 2006

*Managed the Phillies to their 1980 World Series title following a career as a pitcher and a member of the team's player development department. Posted a 169–130 record as Phillies manager, a .565 percentage, second-best in club history. Originally signed out of the University of Delaware in 1955. Spent eight years in the majors as a pitcher, six with the Phillies. Also managed in the Phillies minor league system before being named Director of Minor Leagues and Scouting in 1972. Became Phillies manager on August 31, 1979. Served as general manager/president of the Cubs, manager of Yankees and Mets. Returned to Phillies in 1998 as senior advisor to the General Manager.*

Born: August 4, 1934, Newport, Delaware

During his lengthy career with the Phillies, **Dallas Green** touched a lot of bases as a right-handed pitcher, minor league manager, director of minor leagues and scouting, and big league manager. At the request of general manager Paul Owens, Green replaced Danny Ozark as manager in 1979. Unafraid to ruffle feathers and preaching "We, Not I", he led the Phillies to his and their greatest achievement—as World Series champions in 1980. He was signed out of the University of Delaware in 1955. He was named The Sporting News Major League Executive of the Year after his Cubs reached the postseason.

## JOHN VUKOVICH
### Player/coach/staff
### Phillies 1970–1971, 1976–77, 1979–81, 1988–2004
### Inducted 2007

*One of the most respected and loyal members of the Phillies organization; spent 31 of his 41 baseball years in Philadelphia. Longest tenured coach in Phillies history, 17 seasons, 1988–2004. Coaching duties included first base, third base, the bench plus spring training coordinator. Served under six different managers. Spent 10 years in the major leagues as a player, seven with the Phillies. Excellent defensive third baseman. Member of 1980 World Champion Phillies; coach on 1993 NL pennant-winning Phillies.*

Born: July 31, 1947, Sacramento, California

Died: March 8, 2007, Philadelphia, Pennsylvania

**John Christopher Vukovich** was the longest tenured coach in Phillies history and one of the most respected persons to ever wear their uniform. A brilliant-fielding third baseman, Vuk was originally drafted by the Phillies out of Sacramento, California, in 1966. He played parts of 10 seasons with the Phillies and was a member of the 1980 World Series champions. After his playing days were over, he returned to the Phillies as a major league coach from 1988 to 2004. He was passionate about playing the game the right way and dedicated and loyal. His knowledge of the game was unmatched. He succumbed to a brain tumor at age 59.

## JUAN SAMUEL
### Second baseman
### Phillies 1983–1989
### Inducted 2008

*First Phillies second baseman to be selected to NL All-Star team as a rookie (1984). Led club in stolen bases three times, including a club-record 72 in 1984; scored over 100 runs three times. Set National League rookie record with 19 triples (1984). Led NL in triples twice and at-bats, three times. Two-time NL All-Star and winner of NL Silver Slugger Award (1987). First Phillies player to compile double figures in doubles, triples, home runs and stolen bases four consecutive seasons (1984–87). Hit .263 for the Phillies with 71 triples (9th all-time), 100 homers (first second baseman to reach 100) and 249 stolen bases (7th all-time). Played 798 games at second base, 4th on club's all-time list.*

Born: December 9, San Pedro de Macoris, Dominican Republic

**Juan Milton Samuel**, at age 22, became the Phillies regular second baseman four years after he was signed by them as an amateur free agent. He was an electrifying player with the rare combination of blinding speed and power. He reached double figures in doubles, triples, home runs, and stolen bases in each of his first four seasons, a first in Major League Baseball history. He fell one triple shy of a fifth straight year. As a rookie he led the league with 72 stolen bases, a season record and rookie record for the Phillies.

## HARRY KALAS
### Broadcaster
### 1971–2009
### Inducted 2009

*Voice of Phillies baseball on radio and TV for 39 seasons. Teamed with Richie Ashburn from 1971 until 1997. Harry was on the air for all of Mike Schmidt's 548 home runs, five Phillies no-hitters, seven National League Championship Series, three World Series, the first and final games at Veterans Stadium and the Citizens Bank Park 2004 opener. Received the prestigious Ford C. Frank Award in 2002 for "major contributions to baseball" and was inducted into the broadcasters' wing at the National Baseball Hall of Fame in Cooperstown, NY. His calls were legendary, especially his signature home run call, "Outta Heeere." On October 29, 2008, he brought the utmost joy to Phillies fans: "The 0–2 pitch, swing and a miss, struck him out, the Philadelphia Phillies are 2008 World Champions of baseball."*

Born: March 26, 1936, Naperville, Illinois

Died: April 13, 2009, Washington, D.C.

**Harry Norbert Kalas** received a lukewarm reception after replacing legendary broadcaster Bill Campbell in the Phillies booth in 1971. He quickly won the hearts of the fans. He and Richie Ashburn entertained Phillies fans for 27 years as the most beloved broadcasting team in Phillies history. In 2002 he received the Ford C. Frick Award for broadcasting excellence during Hall of Fame ceremonies in Cooperstown, New York. He threw out the first pitch on April 8, 2009, after the Phillies had received their 2008 World Series rings. It was his last game at Citizens Bank as he died five days later in the Washington Nationals' broadcasting booth preparing for another telecast. Two years later, his statue was unveiled at Citizens Bank Park near the Harry the K's restaurant.

## DARREN DAULTON
### Catcher
### Phillies 1983, 1985–1997
### Inducted 2010

*Selected in the 15th round of the 1980 draft. Developed into a three-time All-Star. One of nine players to play at least 14 seasons with the Phillies. Career .245 hitter with 134 home runs, 567 RBI in 1,109 games with the Phillies. Caught 965 games, fourth on club's all-time list. Led NL with 109 RBI in 1992, just the fourth catcher in National League history to win an RBI title. Won the Silver Slugger Award the same season. Holds Phillies single-season records for a catcher in walks (117, 1993), doubles (35, 1993) and RBI (109, 1992). Recognized as the team leader of the 1993 NL pennant-winning Phillies. Selected as the catcher on the All-Vet team, named in 2003 upon the closing of Veterans Stadium.*

Born: January 3, 1962, Arkansas City, Kansas

**Darren Arthur Daulton** was drafted as a skinny catcher out of Arkansas City High School. He was listed on scouting reports as just 150 pounds. Playing in 37 games in a rookie league that summer, he hit only .200. His 14 seasons with the Phillies are the longest tenure for a catcher in the team's modern history. He had two 100-RBI seasons, a record for a Phillies catcher. Defensively, he had the most putouts (981) in 1993 and double plays (19) in 1993 for a catcher. Darren played in 1,109 Phillies games, which was remarkable since he was on the disabled list eight times and underwent nine knee surgeries. In addition, he had a fractured right clavicle, a broken right hand, and an incomplete tear of his left rotator cuff. He ended his career with the Florida Marlins, the 1997 World Series champions.

### JOHN KRUK
#### First baseman
#### Phillies 1989–1994
#### Inducted 2011

*First Phillies player to post a career batting average of .300 or better since Richie Ashburn. Compiled a .309 average in 744 games with 790 hits. Hit over .300 in four of his six seasons with the Phillies, finishing in the NL top ten two times. Career on-base percentage of .400 ranks sixth on the Phillies all-time list. Among NL top ten in on-base percentage three times. Shares club record for most runs in a game (5). Batted .348 in the 1993 World Series. All-Star in 1991, 1992 and 1993, when he was elected the starter. Led NL first basemen with .998 fielding percentage in 1991. First baseman on the All-Vet team chosen for the closing of Veterans Stadium in 2003.*

Born: February 9, 1961, Charleston, West Virginia

**John Martin Kruk** was originally drafted in the third round of the 1981 January draft by the Pirates but didn't sign. The Padres picked him in the third round that June in the secondary phase. He made his major league debut five years later at age 25. The Phillies acquired him along with Randy Ready for Chris James in the middle of the 1989 season, one of the best trades ever for the Phillies.

He blossomed into an All-Star first baseman with the Phillies and was a key member of the 1993 National League champions.

## MIKE LIEBERTHAL
### Catcher
### Phillies 1994–2006
### Inducted 2012

*Phillies all-time leader among catchers in games caught (1,139), home runs (149) and hits (1,128). He and Jack Clements (1884–97) are the only catchers in Phillies history to surpass 1,000 hits. Wore a Phillies uniform for 13 seasons and set a club record with 10 consecutive Opening Day starts at catcher. Batted .275 in 1,174 Phillies games. Two-time All-Star (1999 and 2000). Rawlings Gold Glove winner in 1999 when he set a club record for highest fielding percentage, .997. Became sixth catcher in Major League Baseball history to hit .300 with 30 homers in a season (1999, .300, 31 HR). First Paul Owens Award winner (1992) to be inducted into the Wall of Fame.*

Born: January 18, 1972, Glendale, California

**Mike Lieberthal** was an All-American baseball player at Westlake High School, where he once hit four home runs and drove in 10 runs in one game. The Phillies selected him third overall in the first round of the 1990 draft. Since he was just 155 pounds, many were skeptical he could sustain the rigors of catching every day in the big leagues. But he wound up catching more games than anyone else in Phillies history and was an All-Star and Gold Glove winner. After playing one season with the Dodgers, "Lieby" officially retired as a Phillie on April 28, 2008.

## CURT SCHILLING
### Pitcher
### Phillies 1992–2000
### Inducted 2013

*Three-time All-Star with the Phillies; was the NL starting pitcher in 1999. Compiled a 101–78 record in nine seasons. Ranks fourth in club history in strikeouts (1,554), sixth in wins, seventh in ERA*

*(3.35) and eighth in innings pitched (1,659.1). First Phillies right-hander with 300 strikeouts in a season, setting a club record with 319 in 1997. Led the majors in strikeouts in 1997 and 1998 (300); was also the ML leader in innings (268.2) and complete games (15) in 1998. Fanned 19 in 16 innings of 1993 NLCS to be named series MVP. Shut out Toronto Blue Jays in Game 5 of the 1993 World Series, first postseason shutout by a Phillies pitcher. Selected to the All-Vet Team in 2003, the final season of Veterans Stadium.*

Born: November 14, 1966, Anchorage, Alaska

**Curtis Montague Schilling** was originally drafted in the second round of the January phase of the 1986 draft by the Boston Red Sox. Two years later he was traded to the Orioles. He would get traded four other times to the Astros (1991), Phillies (1992), Diamondbacks (2000), and back to the Red Sox (2003). Acquired by the Phillies for RHP Jason Grimsley five days before the start of the 1992 season, he was a reliever and occasional starter in his first five big league seasons before becoming a full-time starter in 1993 under Jim Fregosi and pitching coach Johnny Podres. He pitched for three World Series champions—the Diamondbacks (2001) and Red Sox (2004 and 2007). He finished with a 216–146 record, 3.46 ERA, and 3,116 strikeouts. His postseason record was a very impressive 11–2.

### CHARLIE MANUEL
**Manager**
**2005–2013**
**Inducted 2014**

*Winningest manager in Phillies history, going 780–636 in his nine seasons. Led the team to five straight division titles (2007–11), two National League pennants (2008–09) and one World Series Championship (2008). First Phillies manager with back-to-back World Series appearances. Also set a club record for most wins in a season with 102 (2011). Before the Phillies, managed the Cleveland Indians (2000–02). His final win as a manager, August 12, 2013 at Turner Field, was the 1,000th in his major league career, becoming one of 59 managers in MLB history to reach 1,000 wins.*

*Managed the 2009 and 2010 NL All-Star teams and guided the 2010 team to the first NL win in 14 years.*

Born: January 4, 1944, North Fork, West Virginia

**Charles Fuqua Manuel** is a 1963 graduate of Perry McCluer High Scholl in Buena Vista, Virginia, where he starred in baseball and basketball. His family moved to Buena Vista when he was 12 years old. He was the third of 11 children. He was offered a basketball scholarship to the University of Pennsylvania but chose baseball, signing with the Minnesota Twins for $30,000 after graduation. He spent 13 seasons (1963–75) in pro ball as an outfielder/first baseman with stops in the majors with the Twins and Los Angeles Dodgers. Most of his success on the diamond came in Japan where he played on three pennant winners and was the 1979 Pacific Coast League MVP and where he was nicknamed 'Aka-Oni" (The Red Devil) by fans and teammates. He compiled a .313 average, 189 homers, and 491 RBIs in six seasons.

## PAT BURRELL
### Left fielder
### Phillies 2000–2008
### Inducted 2015

*The first overall selection in the 1998 draft out of the University of Miami. A right-handed slugger, he hit 20 or more home runs in eight consecutive seasons. In 1,306 games with the Phillies, batted .257 with 251 home runs and 827 RBI. At the end of his Phillies career, ranked third in home runs, seventh in RBI, fourth in walks (785) and ninth in extra-base hits (518). Led National League outfielders with 18 assists in 2001. Had the last hit at Veterans Stadium, a ninth-inning single on 9/28/03. Appeared in four postseason series. Final hit in a Phillies uniform was a seventh-inning double in Game 5 of the 2008 World Series which led to the winning run as the Phils captured their second world championship.*

Born: October 10, 1976, Eureka Springs, Arkansas

**Patrick Brian Burrell** grew up in northern California, attending Bellarmine College Preparatory in San Jose, where he played

Slugging outfielder Pat Burrell is honored as the 2015 Wall of Fame inductee and the first player from the 2008 World Series championship club to receive that distinction. (Miles Kennedy)

baseball and football. A quarterback in football, he competed against Tom Brady at rival Junipero Serra High School. He concentrated on baseball during his senior year. Selected by the Boston Red Sox in the 43rd round of the 1995 summer draft, Burrell opted to attend the University of Miami as a third baseman. He won the Golden Spikes Award as the best player in college baseball (1997). Drafted by the Phillies the following summer, he reached the majors two years later. He played first base in his first big league game. He earned two World Series rings as a player, one each with the Phillies (2008) and San Francisco (2010). As a scout for the Giants, he added two more rings in 2012 and 2014.

# 4

# Phillies Potpourri

Four Phillies pitchers have won the Cy Young Award, which is voted on annually by the Baseball Writers Association of America. From 1956 to 1966, there was only one Cy Young Award winner for the major leagues. Beginning in 1967, one was selected for each league.

The award is named in honor of Denton (Cy) Young, who pitched in the majors for 22 seasons (1890–1911) with Cleveland (National League), St. Louis (National League), and Boston (American and National Leagues). The right-hander won 20 or more games 16 times, including 14 years in a row, and won more than 30 games five times. In 906 career games, he posted a 511–315 record and was inducted into the Baseball Hall of Fame in 1937.

## Steve Carlton (1972)

Carlton was a unanimous selection as the Cy Young Award winner with 120 points. Steve Blass of the Pittsburgh Pirates was second with 25. Pitching for a last-place team, Lefty had one of the most dominating seasons of any pitcher. He led the league with 27 wins (10 losses), a 1.97 ERA, 41 games, 30 complete games, 346 innings,

257 hits, and 310 strikeouts. Eight of his 27 wins were shutouts. From May 3 through August 17, he won a club-record 15 consecutive games. He set an MLB record with the percentage of team's games won, which was 45.8 percent. Lefty signed a $165,000 contract prior to the 1973 season, making him the highest paid pitcher in MLB.

### Steve Carlton (1977)

Carlton received 104 points. Tommy John, the left-hander from the Los Angeles Dodgers, was a distant runner-up with 54. Lefty led the league with 23 wins and fanned 198 in 283 innings while completing 17 of his 36 starts. He led the National League with 19 pickoffs and his 2.64 ERA ranked fourth in the league. He set a Veterans Stadium record for wins with 17.

### Steve Carlton (1980)

Carlton won the award in easy fashion again, receiving 118 points to 55 for Jerry Reuss of the Los Angeles Dodgers. In pitching the Phillies to their first World Series title, Lefty had another big season. He led the league in wins with 24 wins, 304 innings, and 286 strikeouts. On July 6 he became baseball's all-time strikeout leader for a left-handed pitcher.

### Steve Carlton (1982)

Lefty became baseball's first four-time Cy Young Award winner, earning 112 points to 29 for right-hander Steve Rogers of the Montreal Expos. He again dominated the league with 23 victories, 19 complete games, six shutouts, 295⅔ innings, 253 hits allowed, and 286 strikeouts. He was baseball's lone 20-game winner and ended up with the most wins in National League history for his age (37). He also became only the second player to win a major award 10 years apart. Willie Mays was the NL MVP in 1954 and 1965.

### John Denny (1983)

The right-hander became the second straight winner for the Phillies, earing 103 points to 61 for Cincinnati Reds right-hander Mario Soto. Denny led the league with 19 wins and a .760 winning percentage, a new Phillies record. His 2.37 ERA was second in the National League, and he won 13 of 14 decisions after the All-Star break, including seven in a row as the Phillies won the NL pennant.

### Steve Bedrosian (1987)

"Bedrock" won in the closest balloting ever with 57 points to 55 for Rick Sutcliffe of the Chicago Cubs and 54 for Rick Reuschel of the Pittsburgh Pirates/San Francisco Giants. He became the first Phillies closer to win the award. His 40 saves were tops in the majors. He set an MLB record with 13 consecutive saves (from May 25 to June 30) and he had a hand in 45 of the Phillies' 80 wins.

### Roy Halladay (2010)

A unanimous winner with 224 points, Halladay became the fifth pitcher to win the award in each league. Adam Wainwright of the St. Louis Cardinals finished second with 122 points. "Doc" finished with a 21–10 record and a 2.44 ERA. His win total was the most for a Phillies pitcher since 1982 (when Carlton went 23–11) and was the most for a Phillies right-handed pitcher since 1955 (when Robin Roberts went 23–14). He led the majors with 250⅔ innings, nine complete games, and four shutouts and walked only 30 batters. He tossed the second perfect game in Phillies history on May 29 at Miami.

### Cy Young Runners Up

1967—Jim Bunning finished second to Mike McCormick.

2011—Roy Halladay finished second to Clayton Kershaw.

## MOST VALUABLE PLAYER AWARD

The Baseball Writers Association of America first began voting for the MVP in each league in 1931. Five Phillies players have won the award in the National League. Had the MVP been in existence in 1930, Chuck Klein would have been a strong candidate to win. He collected 250 hits and drove in 170 runs, an NL record that hasn't been matched.

### Chuck Klein (1932)

Klein edged right-handed pitcher Lon Warneke of the Chicago Cubs 78–68 in points. He led the National League in games (154), runs (152), hits (226), home runs (38), slugging percentage (.646), and total bases (420). He hit .348 with 50 doubles, 38 homers, and 137 RBIs. He was the first player in the post-1920 era to lead a league in homers and steals. During his first five years with the Phillies, he averaged .359, 131.6 runs, 46.4 doubles, 36 homers, and 138.6 RBIs per season.

### Jim Konstanty (1950)

The first relief pitcher to win the award, Konstanty won by a 286–158 margin of votes over outfielder Stan Musial of the St. Louis Cardinals. Details of his award-winning season are covered in Chapter 1.

### Mike Schmidt (1986)

Getting all 24 first-place votes, Schmidt easily won over Montreal Expos catcher Gary Carter 336–193, becoming the first National League unanimous winner since St. Louis' Orlando Cepeda in 1967. Mike led the major leagues in home runs (48) while leading the NL in RBIs (121), slugging percentage (.624), and total bases (342). His home run total was a new Phillies record, surpassing his 45 of 1979. He hit .286, a career high to that point. He also led all players in All-Star voting and won his fifth straight Gold Glove.

## Mike Schmidt (1981)

He collected 321 points in winning over Montreal Expos outfielder Andre Dawson, who had 215. Schmidt became the third National League player to win back-to-back awards, joining Ernie Banks (1958–59) and Joe Morgan (1975–76). Mike led the league in runs (78), home runs (31), RBIs (91), walks (73), slugging percentage (.644), and on-base percentage (.435) in 102 games. He topped .300 for the first time. His .316 batting average was fourth-best in the NL. He also won his sixth Gold Glove, an NL record for a third baseman.

## Mike Schmidt (1983)

This represented the closest voting of Schmidt's three awards, as Schmidt garnered 287 points, and Houston Astros first baseman Glenn Davis had 231. Schmidt joined Stan Musial (1943, 1946, 1948) and Roy Campanella (1951, 1953, 1955) as the only three-time MVPs in National League history. Mike led the NL in homers (37) for the eighth time, breaking Ralph Kiner's record. He also led in RBIs (119) and slugging percentage (.547) while finishing second in walks (89) and total bases (302). Committing only six errors, Mike earned his 10th Gold Glove.

## Ryan Howard (2006)

In a battle of first basemen, Howard garnered 388 points, besting the Cardinals' Albert Pujols, who finished with 347. Ryan won the MVP award in his first full big league season, leading the majors in home runs (58), RBIs (149), and total bases (383) while hitting .313. He scored 104 runs and walked 108 times. His home run total matched Jimmie Foxx (A's) for the most by a Philadelphia player and broke Mike Schmidt's club record (48). Howard joined Cal Ripken Jr. (1982–83) as the only players to win the Rookie of the Year and MVP awards in back-to-back seasons.

## Jimmy Rollins (2007)

J-Roll became the seventh National League shortstop to win the award and did so in one of the closest races ever. Rollins pulled in 353 points to 336 for Colorado Rockies outfielder Matt Holliday. In a season in which he also won a Gold Glove and Silver Slugger, Rollins became the first major leaguer to have 200 hits, 15 triples, 25 homers, and 25 stolen bases in the same season. He led the NL in at-bats (an MLB-record 716), runs (139), triples (20), and multi-hit games (63) while hitting .296 with 212 hits, 28 doubles, 30 homers, 94 RBIs, 41 steals, and 88 extra-base hits. The runs, extra-base hits, and total bases (380) set NL records for a shortstop.

## MVP Runner-Ups

Eight times the Phillies have had a player finish second in the NL MVP voting.

1931—Chuck Klein finished second to Frankie Frisch.

1933—Chuck Klein finished second to Carl Hubbell.

1952—Robin Roberts finished second to Hank Sauer.

1964—Johnny Callison finished second to Ken Boyer.

1975—Greg Luzinski finished second to Joe Morgan.

1977—Greg Luzinski finished second to George Foster.

1993—Lenny Dykstra finished second to Barry Bonds.

2008—Ryan Howard finished second to Albert Pujols.

In 1952 Roberts lost out to the Cubs outfielder by the vote of 266–211. Robbie led the NL in wins (28–7 record), starts (37), complete games (30), and innings pitched (330). His ERA was 2.59, the lowest in his Phillies career. Sauer led the league in homers (37) and RBIs (121) while batting .270 on a fifth-place team (77–77). The Phillies finished fourth (87–67). Robbie was robbed. The Cy Young Award for pitching excellence didn't begin until 1956.

## ROOKIE OF THE YEAR AWARD

Before presenting the Phillies Rookie of the Year winners, we need to define exactly what a rookie is. According to Major League Baseball: "A player shall be considered a rookie unless, during a previous season or seasons, he has (a) exceeded 130 at-bats or 50 innings pitched in the major leagues, or (b) accumulated more than 45 days on the active roster of a major league club or clubs during the period of the 25-player limit."

So who has won this honor for the Phillies? It is a bit more complicated to answer than you would think because there have been two groups, The Sporting News (TSN) and Baseball Writers Association of America (BBWAA), who make the selection. The BBWAA is recognized as the "official" award, whether it be rookies, managers, MVPs, or Cy Youngs.

Four Phillies have won TSN awards: first baseman Ed Bouchee (1957), outfielder Lonnie Smith (1980), second baseman Juan Samuel (1984), and left-handed pitcher J.A. Happ (2009). Once upon a time, TSN selected one winner: the Major League Rookie of the Year. Two Phillies icons—outfielder Del Ennis (1946) and outfielder Richie Ashburn (1948)—won that award. The BBWAA also started out with one winner, and it was Jackie Robinson of the Brooklyn Dodgers in 1947. Two years later an award was presented to each league. Ashburn finished third that year. Here are the BBWAA winners.

### Jack Sanford (1957)

Receiving 16 total points, Sanford easily won ahead of teammate Ed Bouchee, who had four points. After posting a 1–0 record in 1956 in three games, the 28-year-old right-hander went 19–8 with a 3.08 ERA while starting 33 games the following season. He led the league with 188 strikeouts in 236⅔ innings while allowing 194 hits and 94 walks. His 12 wild pitches also led the NL. With a 10–2 record at mid-season, he was selected to the NL All-Star team.

### Dick Allen (1964)

No contest as Dick wound up with 18 votes to one each for Rico Carty (Atlanta outfielder) and Jim Ray Hart (San Francisco third baseman). Playing third base for the first time, the 22-year-old put up big numbers while playing every game. He had a .318 average, 201 hits, 125 runs, 37 doubles, 13 triples, 29 homers, 91 RBIs, 352 total bases, 67 walks, 138 strikeouts, and a .557 slugging percentage. He led the league in runs, triples, strikeouts, and total bases. In the MVP voting, he finished seventh.

### Scott Rolen (1997)

Rolen won the award with 140 points. Two runners-up had 25. He broke in with the Phillies in 1996, hitting .254 in 37 games but still qualified as a rookie the following year. Playing 156 games the 22-year-old hit .283, scored 93 runs, and drove in 92. Among his 159 hits were 35 doubles, three triples, and 21 home runs for 263 total bases. He walked 76 times and stole 16 bases. Scott led the club in games played, runs, home runs, RBIs, and total bases.

### Ryan Howard (2005)

After starting the season in Triple A, he was recalled May 3 and sent back after four games. He was recalled permanently on July 1. He garnered 109 points to finish ahead of Houston outfielder Willy Taveras, who had 78 points. In 88 games Howard hit .288 with 22 home runs and 63 RBIs. He led all National League rookies in homers and slugging percentage (.567) while finishing second in RBIs, extra-base hits (41), and on-base percentage (.356). He was selected NL Rookie of the Month for September when he hit an MLB rookie record 10 homers, which tied the club record by his predecessor Jim Thome, in 2003.

### Runners-Up

1957—Ed Bouchee finished second to Sanford.

1971—Willie Montanez finished second to Earl Williams.

## MANAGER OF YEAR AWARD

The Baseball Writers Association of America first began honoring managers in 1983. Prior to that the two wire services, Associated Press and United Press International, made yearly selections. Five Phillies managers have received Manager of the Year honors:

1950—Eddie Sawyer (AP, UPI)
1962—Gene Mauch (AP, UPI)
1964—Gene Mauch (AP)
1976—Danny Ozark (AP)
1983—Jim Fregosi (AP)
2001—Larry Bowa (BBWAA)

### BBWAA Runners-Up

1993—Jim Fregosi finished second to Dusty Baker.
2007—Charlie Manuel finished second to Bob Melvin.
2008—Charlie Manuel finished second to Lou Piniella.

It is hard to believe that Charlie won five straight National League East titles, two National League pennants, and one World Series but never won Manager of the Year. Then again, Dallas Green won the Phillies' first World Series championship in 1980 and was passed over by the AP and UPI. Houston's Bill Virdon received the AP honor. Go figure.

## POSTSEASON HONORS

Baseball has two Most Valuable Player Awards in the postseason, one for the League Championship Series and the other for the World Series. In each case the award is presented to the player "deemed to have the most impact on his team's performance in the series." A committee of reporters and officials at the game select the winners. The World Series MVP has been presented annually since 1955. The National League Championship Series MVP was first presented in 1977 with the ALCS starting in 1980.

### Manny Trillo (1980 NLCS)

Trillo was selected following the Phillies' gut-wrenching playoff win against Houston. After going 3-for-12 in the first three games, he went 5-for-9 with four RBIs over the final two games, which were both Phillies wins. In the 8–7, 10-inning clinching game, he threw out a runner at home plate in the second inning and tripled in two runs in the eighth, giving the Phillies a 7–5 lead.

### Mike Schmidt (1980 World Series)

Schmidt won the award after the Phillies won their first world championship. He batted .381 (8-for-21) with six runs scored, one double, two home runs, four walks, and a team-leading seven RBIs, while hitting safely in every game against the Kansas City Royals. He started a two-run, game-winning rally with a single in leading off the ninth in Game 5. In the 4–1, Game 6 clincher, he started the Phillies' scoring with a two-run single in the third inning.

### Gary Matthews (1983 NLCS)

"The Sarge" almost single-handedly eliminated the Los Angeles Dodgers in a four-game series. His solo homer was the lone run in a Game 2 loss that tied the series at 1–1. In Game 3 he drove in four runs on a homer and two run-producing singles. He delivered a three-run homer in the second inning of the Game 4 clincher, a game the Phillies won 7–2. He batted .429 with three homers and eight RBIs.

### Curt Schilling (1993 NLCS)

Starting Game 1 against the heavily favored Atlanta Braves, he struck out the first five batters, setting an NLCS record that still stands. The Phillies won 4–3 in 10 innings and had the same result in Game 5, which was his second start. While he was winless in two starts, he finished with a 1.69 ERA. In 16 innings he allowed 11 hits, four runs (three earned), five walks, and struck out 19.

Cole Hamels, who would go on to win World Series MVP honors, and Chase Utley (right) face the media after Game 1 of the 2008 World Series in St. Petersburg, Florida. (Miles Kennedy)

## Cole Hamels (2008 NLCS and World Series)

He became the fifth player to win both honors in the same year. If the Division Series had an MVP, he might have had a trifecta as he won the first game of the NLDS, NLCS, and World Series. With eight shutout innings (two hits, nine strikeouts), he was the winner against Milwaukee to open the NLDS. He won the NLCS Game 1 (3–2) and the clinching Game 5 (5–1) as the Phillies eliminated the Dodgers in Los Angeles. Seven days later he was a 3–2 winner in World Series Game 1 in St. Petersburg, Florida. He returned to start Game 5, working six innings before heavy rain suspended play with the score tied 2–2. In five playoff starts, he was 4–0 with a 1.80 ERA, setting club records for the most wins, innings (35), strikeouts (30), and starts in one postseason.

### Ryan Howard (2009 NLCS)

His two-run double capped a five-run fifth inning in Game 1 and pinned an 8–6 loss on Clayton Kershaw. Howard drove in three runs with a triple in Game 3 and followed with a two-run homer in the first inning of Game 4. When the Phillies closed out the NLCS with a romp in Game 5, he was hitless in two at-bats. He finished with a .333 average, five runs, five hits, eight RBIs, and six walks. His hits included a single, double, triple, and two homers.

## BROTHERS NINE

Nine pairs of brothers have worn a Phillies uniform in the long history of the ballclub. Of the 18 only three had lengthy and productive careers with the Phillies: Hall of Famer outfielder Ed Delahanty (13 seasons), infielder Granny Hamner (16 seasons), and center fielder Roy Thomas (12 seasons). Unfortunately, their brothers had careers that totaled a mere 116 games. Least productive were the Westlake brothers, who had four strikeouts in five at-bats. Only two, the Bennett and Roy brothers, were pitchers.

### Bennett, Dave RHP

As an 18-year-old, he appeared in one game with the Phillies, on June 12, 1964. His line: one inning, two hits, one run, one strikeout, one wild pitch.

### Bennett, Dennis LHP

From 1962 to 1964 with the Phillies, he was 30–28 with a 3.46 ERA in 95 games.

### Chiozza, Dino SS

He appeared in two games in 1935 on July 14 and 15, had no at-bats, and scored one run.

### Chiozza, Lou 2B-3B-LF-CF-RF

He played from 1934 to 1936 with the Phillies and had a .295 career average in 402 games. He was drafted by the Phillies in the 1933 Rule 5 Draft.

### Delahanty, Ed OF-1B

He played 13 years with the Phillies from 1888 to 1890 and 1891 to 1901. He had 2,214 hits and a .348 average. He hit over .400 three times and was inducted into the Baseball Hall of Fame in 1945.

### Delahanty, Tom 2B-3B-SS

He appeared in one game on September 18, 1884. He had a single in four at-bats and one strikeout. Three other brothers—Jim, Joe, and Frank—played in the majors.

### Hamner, Garvin 2B-SS

He appeared in 132 games in 1945 and hit for a .198 average.

### Hamner, Granny SS-2B

He made his debut on September 14, 1944, at age 17. He played 16 years with the Phillies from 1944 to 1959. He had a .262 average and hit .429 in the 1950 World Series. He was an All-Star starter at shortstop in 1952 and at second base in 1954.

### Knothe, George 2B

A University of Pennsylvania graduate, he debuted on April 25, 1932. His last game was one month later. During the six games, he had a .083 average.

### Knothe, Fritz 3B-SS

He played part of one season in 1933 and hit .150 in 41 games.

### Nix, Laynce OF
He hit .211 with five homers and 23 RBIs in 151 games from 2012 to 2013.

### Nix, Jayson 2B-SS-3B
He hit .154, one home run, and had two RBIs in 18 games in 2014.

### Roy, Charlie RHP
He had an 0–1 record and a 4.91 ERA for seven games in 1906. He also played one game at first base.

### Roy, Luther RHP
He had a 3–7 record and a 8.42 ERA in 21 games (11 starts) in 1929.

### Thomas, Bill OF-1B-2B
A native of Norristown, the University of Pennsylvania and Ursinus College alumnus hit .118 in six games with the 1902 Phillies.

### Thomas, Roy CF
He played for the Phillies from 1899 to 1908 and 1910 to 1911. He was a .295 hitter with 946 walks, 923 runs, and 228 stolen bases. He led the NL in walks seven times.

### Westlake, Jim PH
The pinch-hitter appeared in one game in 1955 and had one at-bat and one strikeout.

### Westlake, Wally OF-3B
He appeared in five games in 1956, the final season of a 10-year career. He went hitless in four at-bats with one walk and three strikeouts.

## CUP OF COFFEE

Only a small percentage of young players reach the major leagues. Some hang around for a long time. For Phillies fans their names are familiar. They are Robin Roberts, Richie Ashburn, Tony Taylor, Mike Schmidt, Larry Bowa, Steve Carlton, Jimmy Rollins, and Chase Utley, just listing a few. There are players with short careers in Philadelphia. Their names aren't as well known, and they include Joe Koppe, Ray Culp, Marvin Freeman, Solly Hemus, Karl Drews, Barry Lersch, and Aaron Rowand, to name a few. Quite a few spent only one season or a portion of a season here. The list is long. Homer Peel, Hilly Flitcraft, Lynn Lovenguth, Wally Westlake, Ted Savage, Vic Roznovsky, Eric Milton, Dave Dellucci, Sal Fasano, and many more fall into this category.

Then, there's a very small group who have their small place in Phillies history, experiencing a cup of coffee or brief stint in the majors. Nearly 2,000 players have worn a Phillies uniform. Hours of research located a total of 30 who have had said cup of coffee. Well, some careers were so short, their cup was more like an eyedropper's worth of coffee. Five played during the Veterans Stadium-Citizens Bank Park era. Fourteen were pitchers, and 16 were hitters.

### Hitters

*1.000 Club*

The 1.000 club really is exclusive. There are just two players with a perfect 1.000 batting average—one hit in one at-bat. Oddly both are Philadelphia natives. They are outfielder **Clarence "Ty" Pickup** and catcher **Bill Peterman**, who was a graduate of Olney High School. And both hits came in Philadelphia. Pickup was a defensive replacement for right fielder Gavvy Cravath, the cleanup hitter, on April 30, 1918, in a 15–0 loss to the New York Giants at Baker Bowl. His one hit was a single. On defense he recorded one putout.

On April 26, 1942, the Phillies played a doubleheader against the Brooklyn Dodgers at Connie Mack Stadium. Peterman, a catcher, entered the second game in the top of the ninth inning. He was the leadoff hitter in the bottom of the inning and singled. The Dodgers won both games 3–1 and 10–2. "Sure, I remember it," Peterman said in a 1983 Phillies Yearbook story. "I got the hit off Ed Head. It went up the middle, kind of had eyes. It happened in the first two, three weeks of the season before the Phillies went on their first western trip. I got sent down before the trip."

*Lonely Group: One Game, No At-Bats*

Another small group consists of five players who appeared in one game and never got an official at-bat. **Frank Mahar** was an amateur outfielder the Phillies added to the roster late in the 1902 season. He was in the starting lineup as the left fielder, batting seventh, on August 29 against the New York Giants at Baker Bowl. According to a SABR Bioproject, Mahar hit a ball that ricocheted off the bleachers in pregame warmups and struck him on the mouth, cutting his lip and face badly. He started the game but came out in the bottom of the first inning. It was his only professional appearance in the majors or minors.

**Joe Bennett** entered the game as a defensive sub for third baseman Frank Parkinson during a 16–12 loss to the St. Louis Cardinals at Baker Bowl on July 5, 1923. He did have one assist. Bennett was replaced by another third baseman, Russ Wrightstone. **Terry Lyons** also entered the game as a defensive sub for first baseman Don Hurst on April 19, the Phillies' second game of the 1929 season. St. Louis won 14–5 at Baker Bowl.

**Fred Van Dusen** at least reached the batter's box. He pinch hit for pitcher Lynn Lovengurth with one out in the ninth and two runners on base in the first game of a doubleheader won 9–1 by the Braves in Milwaukee's County Stadium on September 11, 1955.

The winning pitcher, Humberto Robinson, hit Van Dusen with a pitch on an 0–2 count. Van Dusen reached first base but was never seen again in a big league uniform.

**Mickey Harrington** was brought up by the Phillies on June 30, 1963, and used as a pinch-runner on July 10 but sent back to the minors five days later. Running for Roy Sievers, Harrington advanced to second on a Don Hoak single. Clay Dalrymple grounded to second for a force-out, but Harrington was picked off at third by the shortstop after making too big a turn.

*.000 Average*

This group got to bat once in the big leagues with the Phillies and didn't get a hit. It was the only game for each. **Al Froehlich** was a catcher on the 1909 club. His one at-bat came on July 2 against Boston in Baker Bowl. **Frank Fletcher** pinch hit for pitcher Ben Tincup in the second game on July 14, 1914, in Cincinnati and struck out against Rube Benton, according to the box score. **George McAvoy** pinch hit for catcher Red Dooin in St. Louis three days later. **John Cavanaugh** struck out in his one at-bat against the Cubs in Baker Bowl on July 7, 1919, which was his first game. He had entered the game as a defensive replacement.

**Cecil (Turkey) Tyson** batted once in the first game of an April 23, 1944, doubleheader in Boston and was hitless. **Jim Westlake** pinch hit for pitcher Jack Spring in the ninth inning against the Giants at the Polo Grounds on April 16, 1958, and struck out against Jim Hearn. It was the third game of the season. **Leroy Reams** pinch hit for pitcher Barry Lersch in the eighth inning against the Astros at Connie Mack Stadium and struck out against Larry Dierker. The date was May 7, 1969.

**Larry Fritz** pinch hit for Larry Christenson with two out in the last of the ninth inning against the Astros on May 30, 1975, at Veterans Stadium and flew out to left field against Doug Konieczny.

**Travis Chapman** pinch hit for third baseman Tomas Perez in the seventh inning at Turner Field in Atlanta on September 9, 2003, and was retired on a fly ball to right off Jung Bong. He remained in the game at third base but never batted again.

Drafted by the Phillies in the 17th round in 2000, Chapman climbed the baseball ladder quickly, hitting .301 with a career-high 15 homers at Reading for the Double A club in 2002. A baseball career can take some strange journeys, something Chapman learned after that season. Cleveland selected him in the Rule 5 draft and promptly sold him to Detroit, who returned him to the Phillies organization when he failed to make the Tigers roster in spring training of 2003. Back with the Phillies organization, Travis found himself in Triple A with Scranton/Wilkes-Barre.

Triple A is one step away from the big show, the ultimate goal. Following a September 2 game in Ottawa, manager Marc Bombard called Travis and two teammates, pitchers Josh Hancock and Ryan Madson, into his office and said, "Congratulations, you are going to the big leagues." It is a moment Travis will always remember. "It was pretty neat hearing those words," he recalled. "I always wanted to be a good baseball player, but at every level—high school and college—I heard, 'You are not good enough.' Even after I was drafted, there was talk that I would be an organization coach someday."

Walking into the Phillies clubhouse at Veterans Stadium on September 3, he found a locker that read, "Travis Chapman 23". On September 9 the Phillies were at Turner Field in Atlanta for a four-game series. "We were scoring a lot of runs early, and I kind of thought I might get a chance," Chapman remembered. In the seventh inning (with the Phillies leading 18–3) manager Larry Bowa let Travis know he would be pinch-hitting for Tomas Perez. "The butterflies kicked in. Jung Bong was pitching for Atlanta, and I had faced him quite a bit in the minors, actually faced him a lot,"

Chapman said, "made me feel a little more at ease. First pitch was a fastball, and I took it for a strike. I got out in front of the next pitch, a change-up, and hit a fly ball to right field."

Travis stayed in the game and played three innings at third base, where he had one fielding chance, knocking down a hot grounder inside the bag in the ninth inning but unable to make a throw. At age 25, Travis Chapman got an at-bat in the big show. It would be his only one, as he played three more seasons of minor league baseball before walking away in 2006.

But Veterans Stadium was closing. The final game was September 28 against the Braves. An emotional postgame show was going to take place, celebrating 33 years of Phillies baseball at the Vet. Being on the roster, Travis was going to be part of the closing ceremonies, one of 120 current or former Phillies who would take the field and step on home plate one last time. "Here I am a rookie," he said. "And I'm going to be part of a major history event. Seeing all the former players was awesome, brought back a lot of memories. I was taking it all in, including the reaction of the fans. I saw games at the Vet, never played there, but I got to touch home plate. I will never, ever forget that day."

How did a kid growing up in Jacksonville, Florida, get to see the Phillies play at the Vet? "My grandfather lived in Trenton, and for many summers, we went to visit him. He knew I was a huge baseball fan and would take me, my brother, and cousin to games," Travis explained. Chase Utley was the Phillies' first-round selection in the 2000 draft, the same one in which Travis was chosen. "We played on the same minor league teams for a couple of seasons and became good friends. When I was out of the game, [my wife] Julie and I visited him in Philadelphia and saw a couple of games at Citizens Bank Park."

## Pitchers

*Less Than One Inning*

Five Phillies pitchers never got out of one inning in their only major league appearance. **Tom Barry** started the second game of the 1904 season vs. Boston and lost 6–0. The date was April 15. His pitching line: two-thirds of an inning, six hits, five runs, three earned runs, one walk, one strikeout, and a 40.50 ERA. The Phillies lost 99 more games that season. Right-hander **Art Gardner** relieved starter Whitney Glazer with two out in the first inning in Pittsburgh on September 25, 1923. He faced two batters, allowed a hit and a walk, and was replaced by Jim Bishop. At least his ERA was 0.00. Left-hander **Marty Walker**, like Tom Barry, started and lost. It happened on September 30, 1928, in Brooklyn, the last game of the season. He faced five batters and allowed two hits, three walks, and four runs (two earned). He has the dubious distinction of being the losing pitcher in the 109th defeat (43 wins).

Right-hander **Anderson Garcia**'s lone appearance came on July 7, 2007, the seventh inning in Denver. He faced four batters and recorded a fly-out to deep center, a single to left, a fly-out out to deep left, and a single to right and was replaced by J. C. Romero, who allowed a run-scoring single. Thus, Garcia's career ERA rests at 13.50 for 12 pitches. Right-hander **Tyson Brummett** was the last Phillies pitcher on the mound during the 2012 season. He relieved Jonathan Papelbon in the bottom of the eighth with the Nationals winning 5–1 at home in the final game on October 3. He gave up consecutive singles and then struck out two. His big league career was: four batters, 11 pitches, and a 0.00 ERA. Of all 30 Phillies with a cup of coffee, Brummett at least had the most fans on hand for his one game.

*One Inning*
Nine pitched one inning in the majors for the Phillies, and that
was it. **Jacob Fox**, a native of Scranton, Pennsylvania, relieved in a
September 4, 1902, 12–6 win against St. Louis. In his one inning,
he allowed two hits and three runs (two earned), walked one, and
struck out one. His ERA for facing six batters was 18.00.

Left-hander **Ray Hartfanft**, born in Quakertown,
Pennsylvania, had his one inning of fame on June 16, 1913, at the
Cubs during a 13–3 loss. He faced seven batters and had three hits,
one run, one walk, and one strikeout. His career ERA was 9.00.

Right-hander **Waldo (Rusty) Yarnall** was charged with the
loss in an 11–9 decision at the Brooklyn Robins on June 30, 1916.
Facing eight batters, he gave up two runs on three hits and a walk
and owns an 18.00 ERA. Born in Chicago, Rusty graduated from
Swarthmore (Pennsylvania) High School. Left-hander **Charlie
Butler**'s claim to fame came on May 1, 1933, during a 10–0 loss
to the Pittsburgh Pirates at Baker Bowl. He owns a 9.00 ERA, after
allowing one hit, one run, and two walks against six batters. Right-
hander **Bill Webb** relieved in the ninth inning against the St. Louis
Cardinals on May 15, 1943, at Shibe Park during a 6–3 loss. He gave
up a home run to the first batter he faced, winning pitcher Mort
Cooper. He's left with a 9.00 ERA. Right-hander **Al Verdel** is one
of two Phillies to pitch one scoreless inning. It happened on April
20, 1944, the third game of the season, an 8–2 loss to the Brooklyn
Dodgers at Shibe Park. Pitching in the top of the ninth, Verdel got a
pop-up to second, a fly-out to left, and a grounder to third. Born in
Punxsutawney, Pennsylvania, Verdel graduated from Rider College.

Right-hander **Dave Bennett** appeared as an 18-year-old, June
12, 1964, in an 11–3 loss to the New York Mets at Connie Mack
Stadium. He allowed one run on two hits and a wild pitch. He
struck out one. The loser that night was his older brother, Dennis.
Right-hander **Dick Thoenen** relieved in the fourth inning against

the Los Angeles Dodgers at Connie Mack Stadium on September 16, 1967. He gave up a double and RBI single before retiring the next three batters, giving him a 9.00 career ERA.

Right-hander **Erskine Thomason** is the other pitcher with one career scoreless inning. Pitching in the ninth inning against the Chicago Cubs at the Vet on September 18, 1974, he retired all three batters, including a strikeout of the first hitter he faced. The Cubs won 5–2. Many of the 8,113 fans there that night had left before he walked in from the right-field bullpen.

Thompson, the right-handed pitcher from Laurens, South Carolina, retired the side in order but never toed a major league pitching rubber again. "I struck out my first hitter, Steve Swisher, on a 3–2 pitch," Thompson said. "I don't remember the next guy [Steve Stone], but I remember he grounded out and then I got Rick Monday on a grounder to second."

Thomason went to a local library years later and perused the *Encyclopedia of Baseball*. "There's this book with all the greats in it, and my name is there," he said. "It was a thrill then and still is a thrill." He also was the focus of a season-long video documentary by NFL Films called *Bush Leagues to Bright Lights* while pitching for the Toledo Mud Hens, whose manager was Jim Bunning. The film centered on a young prospect trying to reach the majors. Thomason was recalled when rosters expanded in September and didn't get in a game for his first eight days in the majors.

The NFL Films crew actually missed his one inning as they arrived too late, not knowing when he would pitch. So about an hour after the game, Thomason went back on the mound in an empty, darkened stadium to throw for the cameras. Now 67 years of age, Thomason laughs about that incident, although admitting "I felt kind of stupid."

His one inning in the majors still fulfilled a lifelong aspiration. "Being in the major leagues was a great experience, something I dreamed about, never thought at the time it would be that brief," Thomason said. "Looking back, there were a lot of 'what ifs'. But it was fun. And I got to be in a full length film."

In a 2004 newspaper interview with *The State*, a South Carolina newspaper, he said, "You don't dream that particular moment would be your only moment. That never crossed your mind, never even crossed your mind. I got a taste of it, which most people don't get an opportunity to do. I don't have any regrets, other than I wished it had lasted longer."

There's no record of a pitch count for his one inning under the bright lights. And the three outs were never clocked so no one knows how long he was on the mound. But everyone knows he did pitch in the majors, a dream millions of kids never experience.

## MY 50TH ANNIVERSARY TEAM

What follows are 13 Phillies profiles from 1883 to 1933. These players may be largely unknown, but each has a small place in Phillies history. Hall of Fame players and those in the Phillies Wall of Fame were ineligible for this exclusive team.

### RHP Charlie Ferguson

Charlie Ferguson was signed by the Phillies for $1,500 off the sandlots of his hometown, Charlottesville, Virginia, and never played in the minor leagues. The 6'0", 170-pounder was a gifted athlete who threw right-handed and batted from the left side. As a 21-year-old, he won his major league debut on May 1, 1884, beating the Detroit Wolverines 13–2. It was not only a complete game, but he also added a triple and two singles. He tossed a no-hitter on August 29, 1885. It was a 1–0 victory over Providence for the first no-hitter in Phillies history.

The next season Ferguson became the first pitcher in baseball history to win two games in one day. During a three-city road trip that started in Chicago that same summer, Ferguson became ill and asked manager Harry Wright if he could return to his Virginia home for proper treatment. Wright refused, but Ferguson went anyway, taking a train. After spending 10 days in bed and missing the entire trip, he rejoined the team in Philadelphia with a doctor's note in hand. Although it isn't known how many starts he missed, Ferguson finished 30–9 with a 1.98 ERA that season. Oddly, the 30 wins ranked sixth best in the NL. The ERA was the lowest. Ferguson won 12 in a row, a mark that stood in the Phillies record book until Steve Carlton's 15-game winning streak in 1972.

In 1887, Ferguson's final season, the Phillies ended up in second place, their highest finish, and set a club attendance record of 253,671. They reached second by ending the season on a 16-game winning streak (plus one tie), including 11 on the road. By comparison the club's modern winning streak is 13 consecutive games in 1977 and 1991. Ferguson played in all 17 games, going 7–0 as a pitcher and .361 as a hitter. Playing as the everyday second baseman when he didn't pitch, Ferguson led the club with 85 RBIs. He never touched a baseball again.

Many thought he may have gone down as one of the greatest baseball players ever if his life hadn't ended on April 29, 1888, from typhoid fever. Death came in Philadelphia less than two weeks after he turned 25. His four-year pitching numbers were awesome: 21–25, 26–20, 30–9, and 22–10. In 183 games on the mound, he was 99–64 with a 2.67 ERA. In 1,514⅔ innings he allowed 1,402 hits and 290 walks, while striking out 728. His 99 wins rank among the top 10 on the Phillies all-time list. When he wasn't pitching, he was used in the outfield and at second base and third base. He was a .288 career hitter, driving in 157 runs in 257 games.

## RHP/2B Kid Gleason

William (Kid) Gleason, a native of Camden, New Jersey, had two different stints with the Phillies, and they were indeed different. Gleason got the nickname because of his small 5'7", 155-pound frame. As a 21-year-old rookie starting pitcher in 1888, he finished 7–16. Two years later he won 38 games while pitching 506 innings. Keep in mind the distance from the pitching rubber to home plate was 50 feet then. Gleason compiled a 78–70 record in his first four years before being sold to the St. Louis Browns. Including the Browns, he played for four other teams the next 11 seasons. With his pitching arm having gone bad, Gleason returned to the Phillies in 1903 as the club's regular second baseman for the next four seasons. His Phillies career ended in 1908. He had a .246 average in 769 games. Out of uniform for four years, Gleason came back with the Chicago White Sox for one game in 1912.

As the White Sox manager from 1919 to 1923, he won the pennant in his first season, the year of the gambling scandal that dubbed the team the "Black Sox." Gleason's career ended as a coach with the Philadelphia Athletics from 1925 to 1931. Bedridden from a heart ailment in 1932, Gleason died a year later at age 66.

## RHP George McQuillan

As a 23-year-old in 1908, George McQuillan turned in a performance that hasn't been matched by many other Phillies rookie pitchers. He finished the season with a 23–17 record, 1.53 ERA, 48 games, 42 starts, 32 complete games, seven shutouts, and 359⅔ innings. He could have won more games as he was shut out a club-record eight times, including five 1–0 losses. No Phillies rookie has matched his ERA and complete games. Three years later Grover Cleveland Alexander won more games as a rookie (a National

League-record 28), pitched more innings (367), and matched the seven shutouts. What separates McQuillan from all Phillies pitchers actually happened in 1907 when he was 4–0 in nine games. George started his career with 25 consecutive scoreless innings from May 8 until September 29, 1907. It remains a National League record. After McQuillan went 22–22 in 1909–1910, the Phillies traded him. During the 1915 pennant-winning season, they brought him back in August. He went 4–3 with a 2.12 ERA. His 10-year big league career ended in 1918 with Cleveland. He was 54–49 with a 1.79 ERA in his Phillies career and went 85–89 in the majors. McQuillan's major league career was cut short due to his chronic alcoholism, an infection, and financial troubles. He continued to play and coach in the minor leagues and semi-pro ball. After baseball he became a manager of a furniture warehouse in Columbus, Ohio. He died of a heart attack at age 54.

### RHP Hugh Mulcahy

Mulcahy made his major league debut in 1935 as a 21-year-old and became a 200-inning workhorse from 1937 to 1940, leading the league with 56 games in 1937. Pitching on a team that lost 92, 105, 106, and 103 games, Mulcahy posted 8–18, 10–20, 9–16, and 13–22 records, earning him the unflattering nickname, "Losing Pitcher." In 1937 he lost a game after throwing one pitch, something that rarely happens.

The 1940 season was a strange one. Pitching his best, he was one of three Phillies selected to the National League All-Star team, though he didn't pitch in the July 9 game. On the last day of that month, a win boosted his record to 12–10. He then tied a club record by losing 12 consecutive games before winning his final start on September 27. He had won 13 of the team's 49 games.

Mulcahy made news off the field the following spring when, as a 27-year-old, he was the first major league player drafted into the military during World War II. The date was March 8, nine months before the bombing of Pearl Harbor. He spent 53 months in the military and earned a Bronze Star. He was discharged on August 5, 1945, joined the Phillies six days later, and pitched in five games. Two years later, his playing career ended with a 45–89 record. Mulchay spent 20 years as a White Sox minor league pitching coach/administrator. According to a SABR BioProject, Mulcahy, then 87, felt he was "a fortunate man…fortunate to break in the majors with the Phillies, fortunate to survive WWII, and fortunate to secure a job in baseball." He died at age 88 in Aliquippa, Pennsylvania.

## C Jack Clements

John J. (Jack) Clements makes the team because of a place he holds in Phillies history. The native Philadelphian caught more games than anyone for the Phillies or in baseball…for a left-handed catcher. During his 14-year career with the Phillies (1884–1897), he caught 953 games. Since then Red Dooin, Bob Boone, Darren Daulton, and Mike Lieberthal have passed him. His 14 years as a catcher was finally matched by Daulton 100 years later.

Clements' career included single seasons in the NL with St. Louis, Cleveland, and Boston. When he retired after the 1900 season, he held baseball's record for most games by a left-handed catcher with 1,073. Back then catchers stood 20 or more feet behind home plate and caught pitches on a bounce. They wore no chest protectors, masks, or shin guards. He was credited with being among the first to wear a chest protector, though details are sketchy.

Clements hit over .300 five times with the Phillies, for whom he played exactly 1,000 games. His Phillies totals were: a .289 average,

70 homers, and 636 RBIs. Clements' single-season (17 in 1893) and career home run totals (77) stood as a record for a catcher until Gabby Hartnett in the 1920s. In 1890, when manager Harry Wright was sidelined by temporary blindness, Clements managed 19 games (13–6). Clements died at age 76 in Norristown, Pennsylvania, in 1941.

## C/Manager Red Dooin

Charles (Red) Dooin was a 5'9" catcher who barely tipped the scales at 150 pounds during a 15-year career in the majors. His first 13 years were with the Phillies (1902–1914). He caught 1,124 games for the Phillies, a record that stood until broken by Mike Lieberthal on August 18, 2006, at Citizens Bank Park. Dooin still owns the club single-season record for most assists, 199, in 1909.

Dooin wasn't much of a hitter, compiling a .241 average in 1,219 games. He hit 10 home runs with six coming in 1904. Five of those six were inside the park, the most for any Phillies player in a season. On October 1, 1904, against the Pittsburgh Pirates, he became the first Phillies player to hit an inside-the-park grand slam.

A feisty, temperamental redhead, Dooin was known for blocking home plate regardless of the size of an oncoming base runner. He sustained a broken ankle and broken leg in back-to-back seasons, curtailing his playing days. Although there are different stories as to which catcher wore shin guards for the first time, some reports claim Dooin was first, wearing a pair of rattan guards during the 1906 season.

Dooin became player-manager of the Phillies in 1910. The 1913 club finished second, but he was fired following a sixth-place finish in 1914. Dooin's managerial record was 392–370, the most wins during this 50-year period. So, he's the manager of my 50th Anniversary Team. At the age of 40, Dooin's pro career came to an end in 1919 as player-manager in Reading, Pennsylvania, in the International League. The team was known as the Coal Barons. A singer-actor, Dooin spent some winters on the vaudeville circuit following his playing career. He died in Rochester, New York, on May 14, 1952, from a heart attack. He was 72 years old.

### 1B Fred Luderus

A left-handed hitter and right-handed throwing first baseman, Frederick William Luderus (lu-DARE-us) made his major league debut with the Chicago Cubs in 1909. The Phillies acquired him in a July 29, 1910, trade for left-hander Bill Foxen, who wound up pitching in only five games for the Cubs over parts of two seasons. Luderus became the Phillies' everyday first baseman for nine seasons starting in 1911. To say it was a lopsided trade is putting it mildly. Luderus left his mark on Phillies history.

- He had the most consecutive starts (nine) at first base on Opening Day.
- For 94-plus years he held the club record for most games (1,298) at his position. That mark was finally passed by Ryan Howard on May 1, 2015.
- His 1,597 putouts in 1917 remain a Phillies single-season record at his position.
- On July 15, 1911, he became the first Phillies player to hit two over-the-fence home runs in a game. He finished with 16 homers, second in the NL.
- He led the Phillies with a .438 average in their first World Series in 1915. That average was a World Series high for the Phillies until Jayson Werth hit .444 in 2008. Luderus' home run in Game 5 is the franchise's first. He wound up with six of the team's nine RBIs.

- Prior to the start of the season, manager Pat Moran named him captain. He finished second in the NL in hitting (.315) and doubles (36).
- He played 533 consecutive games from June 12, 1916, until the 1920 season opener when he couldn't play because of lumbago. In addition to earning a club record, Fred broke the MLB record of 478 games by Eddie Collins of the Chicago White Sox.

Luderus finished his Phillies career with a .278 average, 83 home runs, and 630 RBIs in 1,311 games. Including the Cubs, he appeared in 1,346 games with 1,326 at first base, the only position he ever played. Luderus died in Three Lakes, Wisconsin, from a heart attack in 1961 at age 75.

## 2B Otto Knabe

Franz Otto Knabe, nicknamed Dutch, led all Phillies in games played at second base (931) until Tony Taylor passed him in 1970. Knabe fell to third place when Chase Utley zoomed past Taylor in 2011. Born in Carrick, Pennsylvania, Knabe made his major league debut with the Phillies playing three games at third base in October, 1905, as a 21-year-old. After spending the next year in the minor leagues, Knabe became the club's everyday second baseman for seven consecutive seasons (1907–13), averaging 135 games.

He was a career .249 hitter in 946 Phillies games and walked more times (377) than he struck out (256). He was adept at playing smallball and a great fielder. Four times he led the National League in sacrifice hits. His 42 total in 1908 ranks second in Phillies history to the 43 by Kid Gleason (1905), Knabe's predecessor. Knabe's 216 career sacrifice hits are believed to be a Phillies record.

Knabe jumped to the Federal League where he was player-manager for the Baltimore Terrapins. The league folded after two seasons, and Knabe returned to the NL playing for the Pittsburgh

Pirates and Chicago Cubs in 1916, his last year. He died in Philadelphia in 1961 at 76 years of age.

## SS Mickey Doolan

For four-plus decades generations of Phillies fans have been treated to some dazzling shortstop play by a pair of natives of northern California—Larry Bowa and Jimmy Rollins. Bowa played more games at shortstop than anyone in club history (1,730) until Rollins passed him on August 14, 2012.

The original record holder was Michael (Mickey) Doolan, who was born in Ashland, Pennsylvania, a small town in the coal region. The right-handed hitter was a defensive stalwart as the Phillies regular shortstop from 1905 through 1913 or 1,298 games. According to the Elias Sports Bureau, Bowa broke Doolan's 65-year-old record on August 22, 1978.

Doolan supplanted Rudy Hulswitt, who has the dubious distinction of committing the most errors by a Phillies shortstop (81). He did so in 1903. Doolan was charged with a league-leading 66 errors in his second Phillies season when he had 395 putouts, which still stands as a record among Phillies shortstops. Mickey led NL shortstops in assists six times and five times in putouts. By comparison, Bowa topped the league in assists once and never in putouts. Rollins hasn't done either.

In 1909 Doolan was named the Phillies captain, a position he held until he jumped to the Federal League in 1914 with teammate Otto Knabe. The two played the most games at second and shortstop, respectively, for the Phillies until the Utley-Rollins era. During his Phillies career, Doolan hit .236 in 1,302 games.

Doolan attended both Bucknell College and Villanova College, earning a degree in dentistry. With his baseball career behind him, he worked as a dentist until 1947. He died four years later in Orlando, Florida, at the age of 71.

### 3B Pinky Whitney

It's hard to believe someone other than Mike Schmidt holds some records for a Phillies third baseman. Meet Arthur (Pinky) Whitney, a slightly built, 5'10", 165-pound Texan who wore a Phillies uniform from 1928 to 1933 and again from 1936 to 1939. In between he played for the Boston Braves. When the Phillies began wearing numbers on their jerseys in 1932, Whitney was No. 5. He also wore 25 (1936–37), 5 (1938), and 20 (1939). As a rookie in 1928, Whitney drove in 103 runs, which remains a club rookie record. It was the first of four seasons in which he finished with 100 or more RBIs.

It's hard to believe that Pinky Whitney, or any third baseman other than Mike Schmidt, holds some Phillies records. (National Baseball Hall of Fame and Museum)

Among the club records he holds for a third baseman:

- RBIs in a month (38 in July 1932)
- RBIs in a season (124 in 1932)
- Consecutive games with an RBI (10 in 1931)
- Hits in a season (207 in 1930), as he and Dave Cash are the only Phillies infielders with two seasons of 200 or more hits.
- Triples in a season (14 in 1929), later tied by Dick Allen in 1964
- Highest batting average in a season (.342 in 1930)
- Lifetime average (.307), which ranks 10th overall on the Phillies all-time list

Pinky was the first Phillies third baseman selected to an All-Star team, starting in 1936, the fourth season of the annual summer classic. During his 10 seasons with the Phillies, he played 1,076 games at third base, third on the club's all-time list behind Willie Jones (1,495) and Schmidt (2,212). Twice he led the NL third basemen in fielding percentage while with the Phillies. Born in San Antonio, Texas, Whitney died in Center, Texas, in 1987 at age 82.

## OF Lefty O'Doul

Francis Joseph O'Doul played only two seasons in a Phillies uniform from 1929–1930. That raises an obvious question: how in the world does he qualify for my 50th Anniversary Team? Well, he won a batting title in his first year with an astronomical .398 average. In his two seasons, he collected 456 hits and compiled a .391 average in just 294 games and struck out 40 times.

Originally a promising pitcher, arm injuries forced him to become a full-time hitter in 1928 when he was with the New York Giants. He finished an 11-year career that included five different teams and a .349 average. Born in San Francisco, Lefty suffered a stroke in November 1969 and died a short time later in the same city at age 72. O'Doul's Sports Bar remains a city landmark and popular dining spot.

## OF Roy Thomas

Doug Glanville, a center fielder with the Phillies (1998–2002, 2004), played his collegiate ball in Philadelphia at the University of Pennsylvania. Well, a long, long time ago, another Penn product, Roy Thomas, patrolled center field for the Phillies. The Norristown, Pennsylvania, native graduated from Penn in 1884 and played four years of semi-pro ball before a 12-year career with the Phillies that began in 1899. A brother, Bill, was a Phillies teammate briefly for six games in 1902.

As a rookie that year, Roy hit .325 and set career highs in games (150), runs (137), hits (178), walks (115), and on-base percentage (.457). The 137 runs remain an all-time record for a rookie in Major League Baseball. The Phillies modern rookie record for runs scored is 125 by Richie Allen in 1964. A slender 5'11", 150 pound, left-handed hitter, Thomas was considered an excellent bunter and a hitter who worked the count. In 12 years with the Phillies, he scored 923 runs, walked 946 times, and struck out just 454 times. He walked 100 or more times in seven Phillies seasons, a mark that was eventually matched by Mike Schmidt and Bobby Abreu. Six of the seven seasons, Thomas led the National League. No other Phillies player can match that.

Following his pro career, he served as a baseball coach at Penn for a while as well as Haverford College. He also was a player-manager two years in the minors. Thomas died in 1959 at his Norristown home where he lived his entire life. He was 85.

## OF John Titus

John Franklin (Silent John) Titus, a native of St. Clair, Pennsylvania, made his debut with the Phillies at age 27 in 1903, following 30 games in the minor leagues. Two years later, he became an everyday right fielder before being traded to Boston during the 1912 season. During his 10 seasons with the Phillies, Titus hit .278 in 1,219 games, which ranked 10th among Phillies outfielders until he was passed by Greg Luzinski in 1980.

A 5'9", 156-pound left-handed batter, Silent John was typical of hitters of his era. He had a keen eye at the plate and made contact. He averaged 120 hits, 21 doubles, six triples, 53 walks, and 35 strikeouts. He was hit by a pitch 78 times, which still ranks among the top five on the Phillies' all-time list. Defensively, he recorded 20 or more assists seven times.

He hit 31 home runs, nine of which were inside-the-park. Only Sherry Magee (19) had more. Titus was the first Phillies player to score five runs in game, and that happened on June 4, 1912. Six others have matched that. In a 1907 doubleheader sweep, he had a double, three triples, and seven RBIs.

Among his eccentricities were chewing toothpicks while batting and sporting a handlebar mustache long after they had gone out of fashion. Before playing baseball, he worked in the coal mines and served in the Army during the Spanish-American War. Titus died at his St. Clair home in 1943 at age 66. He was buried with full military honors.

## ON THE AIR

Broadcasters are part of a fan's life for six months a year in homes, in cars, on porches, at the beach, at picnics via radios, TVs, iPhone, iPads, and computers. It wasn't always that way. Initially, only home games were aired live. Road games were recreated by an announcer sitting in a studio in Philadelphia. The announcer would read a Western Union teletype account of the game. Using sound effects he would simulate the crack of the bat and insert prerecorded crowd noise.

The Phillies were part of the first live baseball game ever broadcast on the radio on August 5, 1921, when they played the Pirates at Forbes Field in Pittsburgh. Harold Arlin, a KDKA night-time announcer, broadcast the game from behind home plate. In 1966 the Phillies selected right-handed pitcher Steve Arlin, Harold's grandson, in the amateur draft.

Phillies games have been on radio for the entire season since Opening Day of April 14, 1936, a 4–1 win against the Boston Braves at Baker Bowl. On the air were Bill Dyer, a Philadelphia sportscaster, and Dolly Stark, an umpire, *yes, an umpire*. Home games were aired on WCAU. Dyer had a strange habit of walking around his chair before broadcasting a game. He told people that it was for good luck. He moved to Baltimore in 1940, continuing his baseball broadcasting. He broadcast the Triple A Orioles while also managing the Baltimore Bullets basketball team.

Stark umpired in the Eastern League (1927) before becoming a National League umpire (1928–35 and 1937–40). Dissatisfied with his $9,000 salary, the 38-year-old quit in 1936 and turned to broadcasting with the Phillies. "[Umpiring is] a tough, thankless job. Men in it, forced to live an isolated existence, put everything they have in it. The highest praise they receive is silence. When a man does good work under these conditions—and good umpir-ing I consider an art—I think he should command a good salary." Stark returned to umpiring again the next season and was replaced by Taylor Grant, a Philadelphian who went on to be a nationally known newscaster, first for radio and later for TV. Walt Newton and Stoney McLinn succeeded Dyer and Grant for one season in 1938.

Byrum (By) Saam, a Texan who graduated from TCU, came to Philadelphia in 1938 to do play-by-play of the Philadelphia Athletics home games. A year later Saam started doing Phillies home games. Saam had various partners for the next 10 seasons.

In 1950 the Phillies and A's decided all games would be on radio, requiring an announcer to travel with the team. Saam had to decide whether to announce the A's or Phillies. Out of loyalty to the A's, who gave him his start, he opted to remain with the American League club.

Gene Kelly, perhaps the tallest baseball broadcaster ever at 6'7", was brought in from WXLW in Indianapolis to broadcast the Phillies along with Bill Brundige. Kelly had a pro career as a pitcher cut short by an arm injury. After the A's left Philadelphia in 1955, Saam teamed with Kelly and Claude Haring on Phillies games. Kelly was let go after the 1959 season while Saam continued until he retired after the 1975 season.

Richie Ashburn became the first former player in a broadcasting booth for the Phillies, joining Saam and Bill Campbell in 1963. When the Phillies moved into Veterans Stadium in 1971, Bill Giles, the vice president, business operations, brought a young broadcaster from Houston to Philadelphia named Harry Kalas. Giles had known Kalas when both were with the Colt .45s/Astros. Kalas replaced Campbell, a very unpopular move. Campbell is the only Philadelphia broadcaster to do play-by-play of the Phillies, Eagles, and NBA's Warriors.

Over time, Kalas and Ashburn became the most beloved broadcast team ever in Philadelphia for any sport. They were on-the-air teammates for 27 seasons. The end for each came on the road. Ashburn died early Tuesday morning, September 9, 1997, in his New York hotel room after broadcasting a Phillies-Mets game. The Phillies won the game that night 1–0. Ashburn's Hall of Fame career actually began with the Phillies and ended with the Mets, and he wore No. 1.

Kalas collapsed in the visiting team's broadcast booth in Nationals Park in Washington, D.C., on April 13, 2009, about an hour before a Phillies-Nationals game. He was rushed to a hospital but died about an hour later. The Phillies won 9–8. (Ashburn died on September 9. Kalas and Ashburn last worked together on September 8.) Harry was on the air when the Phillies won their second World Series championship in 2008. He threw out the ceremonial first ball for the season opener at Citizens Bank Park on April 5, 2009. It turned out to be the last series he broadcast in Philadelphia as the Phillies went on a road trip to Denver and Washington. Kalas spent 38-plus seasons on the air for the Phillies.

Saam also broadcast baseball in Philadelphia for 38 years, but his career included both the A's and Phillies. Third on the list for longevity is Chris Wheeler, who was part of the broadcast team for 37 seasons (1977 through 2014). Ashburn is next with 35 years. Kalas, Ashburn, and "Wheels" stand alone for lengthy careers with the Phillies.

Following Saam's retirement in 1975, Andy Musser replaced him on radio, a career that continued through 2001 when Scott Graham began a career that lasted eight seasons. Meanwhile, Larry Andersen replaced Ashburn in 1998. L.A. has been on the air ever since. Tom McCarthy spent two seasons with the Phillies (2004–05), went to the New York Mets, and returned to the Phillies again in 2009. Scott Franzke, a Texan who graduated from SMU, arrived in the radio booth in 2006. He first did the pregame and postgame shows and play-by-play in the middle innings. Scott and L.A. have been a team since 2007. Jim Jackson, the Flyers' announcer, joined the radio team in 2010, handling pregame and postgame and two innings of play-by-play on home games. Another radio first for the Phillies came in 2005 when their games started to be aired in Spanish. The first Spanish broadcasting team was Bill Kulik and Danny Martinez.

Baseball's first telecast came on August 26, 1939, against Cincinnati and Brooklyn. The Phillies first televised a few home games in 1947 on WPTZ. For many years only Sunday games were telecast. In 1962 the Phillies played the Cubs in Chicago's Wrigley Field. It was the first game televised via satellite. Over-the-air TV was joined by cable TV with Prism doing the games from 1986 through 1997. Comcast SportsNet came into being in 1998. Between over-the-air TV and CSN, all Phillies games are now televised. Games can also be heard and seen on MLB.com. Saam, Ashburn, and Campbell initially worked on both radio and TV. Eventually, the Phillies had separate announcers for radio and TV, increasing the number of broadcasters. Greg Murphy was added to the TV crew in 2012 as an in-game reporter as well as for pregame and postgame interviews. Ashburn started the path for other former Phillies on the air, including Robin Roberts, Tim McCarver, Garry Maddox, Mike Schmidt, Greg Gross, Jim Fregosi, Kent Tekulve, Jay Johnstone, John Kruk, Gary Matthews, Jamie Moyer, and Matt Stairs.

Named after the former broadcaster and National League president, the Ford C. Frick Award is presented annually to a broadcaster for major contributions to baseball. It originated in 1978. Recipients are honored during the National Baseball Hall of Fame induction weekend. Honorees are permanently acknowledged in the "Scribes & Mikemen" exhibit in the Hall of Fame library.

Saam was honored in 1990; Kalas received the distinction in 2002. Two other honorees had Phillies ties. Chuck Thompson, who partnered with Saam in 1947–48 before moving on to the Baltimore Orioles, was the 1993 honoree. Tim McCarver spent 25 years on TV broadcasting Major League Baseball and received the award in 2012. His broadcasting career began in Philadelphia with Ashburn, Kalas, Musser, and Wheeler from 1980 to 1982.

## PLAYER NICKNAMES

*By Rich Westcott*

Players are remembered not only for their deeds on the field, but also for their colorful nicknames, which are as much a part of baseball as bats and balls.

The Phillies have had their share of nicknames since their inception. In the long history of the Phillies, there have been some unusual nicknames. Just sticking to one letter of the alphabet, there has been Puddin' Head, Putsy, Pretzels, and Pickles.

Perhaps one of the most unique nicknames belonged to Bob Ferguson, the Phillies' first manager in 1883. It was Death to Flying Things. Presumably, when he was a player holding down second base, Ferguson never missed a ball. Or maybe he caught all bugs that went his way. Before the 1900s there were other colorful nicknames of Phillies, including Sliding Billy (Billy Hamilton), The Tabasco Kid (Norm Elberfield), Phenomenal (John Smith), Buttermilk (Tom Dowd), Blondie (Bill Purcell), Brewery Jack (John Taylor), and Cannonball (Ledell Titcomb).

The Phillies' 2008 World Series winner had a roster that included The Flyin' Hawaiian (Shane Victorino), Chooch (Carlos Ruiz), J-Roll (Jimmy Rollins), Doc (Roy Halladay), Hollywood (Cole Hamels), the Big Piece (Ryan Howard), Lights Out (Brad Lidge), Pat the Bat (Pat Burrell), and Flash (Tom Gordon). Shortly thereafter, Polly (Placido Polanco) and Vanimal (Vance Worley) joined the team.

The club has taken the field with the Dude or Nails (Lenny Dykstra), Spike (Randy Ready), Headley (Dave Hollins), Junior (Dave Cash), Vuke (John Vukovich), and Jethro (Tommy Greene). Then, there are such favorites as Crash (Dick Allen), Sarge (Gary Matthews), Charlie Hustle (Pete Rose), Gnat (Larry Bowa), and The Secretary of Defense (Garry Maddox).

Among Phillies pitchers, who can forget Wild Thing (Mitch Williams)? To go back a little bit, you have Losing Pitcher (Hugh Mulcahy). Or even further back, you get Weeping Willie (Claude Willoughby) and Ol' Pete (Grover Cleveland Alexander). Other nicknames for pitchers include The Rock (Steve Bedrosian), Whirlybird (Bob Walk), Boom-Boom (Walter Beck), Fidgety Phil (Phil Collins), and the Curveless Wonder (Al Orth).

There have also been nicknames that were unimaginative versions of a player's name like Tugger (Tug McGraw), Schill (Curt Schilling), Eisey (Jim Eisenreich), Inky (Pete Incaviglia), Stocks (Kevin Stocker), Krukker (John Kruk), Lieby (Mike Lieberthal), and Pap (Jonathan Papelbon).

The Phillies have had scores of real, down-to-earth nicknames that tell you something about the guy himself. What do you think when you hear such gems as Horse Face (Togie Pittinger), Maje (Robert McDonnell), Sparky (George Anderson), Dutch (Darren Daulton), Earache (Benny Meyer), Puddin' Head (Willie Jones), or Putt-Putt (Richie Ashburn)? Ashburn was also known as Whitey. Other noteworthy nicknames included Shucks (Hub Pruett), Handle Hit (Milt Stock), What's the Use (Pearce Chiles), Fiddler (Frank Corridon), Dode (George Paskert), Sleuth (Tom Fleming), Stosh (Stan Lopata), Kingfish (Wes Covington), Putsy (Ralph Caballero), and Wagon Tongue (Bill Keister). There were also Schoolboy (Linwood Rowe), Nibbler (Jim Hearn), Beauty (Dave Bancroft), Frosty Bill (Bill Duggleby), Buzz (Russ Arlett), Dirty Jack (John Doyle), and Bubba (Emory Church).

Then, there's Harry the Hat (Harry Walker), Harry the Horse (Harry Anderson), and Harry the K (Harry Kalas). Initials as in L.A. (Larry Andersen) and L.C. (Larry Christenson) have also been used.

The Phillies have been especially partial to food. They've had Cookie (Octavio Rojas), Apples (Andy Lapihuska), Cod (Al Myers), Shad (Flint Rhem), Beans (Harry Keener), Peanuts (Harry

Lowrey), Pretzels (John Pezzulo), Spud (Virgil Davis), Pickles (Bill Dillhoefer), and Candy (Johnny Callison). Animals have also been well represented. Delegates included Possum (George Whitted), Reindeer Bill (Bill Killefer), Kitten (Harvey Haddix), Kitty (Jim Kaat and Bill Bransfield), Chicken (Nelson Hawks), Bear (Jim Owens), Bull (Greg Luzinski), Tiger (Don Hoak), Squirrel (Roy Sievers), Turkey (Cecil Tyson), Donkey (Frank Thomas), Rabbit (Tom Glaviano), Hawk (Ken Silvestri), Mighty Mouse (Solly Hemus), and Baby Bull (Odubel Herrera).

Reflecting their sartorial habits there has been Tight Pants (John Titus), Styles (Chris Short), Highpockets (Dick Koecher), and Bareback (Joe Oeschger). Geographic references were made by Tioga (George Burns), Bama (Carvel Rowell), Irish (Mike Ryan), Greek (Bobby DelGreco), and Chile (Jose Gomez). The Phillies have also had Cactus (Gavvy Cravath), Palm Tree (Ron Stone), Fireball (Fred Wenz), and Buckshot (Tommy Brown).

There were Lucky (Jack Lohrke) and Jinx (Jennings Poindexter), Sleepy (Bill Burns) and Nap (John Shea), Coonskin (Curt Davis), Rawhide (Jim Tabor), Stretch (Howie Schultz), Stumpy (Al Verdel), Iron Hands (Chuck Hiller), Stone Hands (Dick Stuart), Jumbo (Jim Elliott), Midget (Don Ferrarese), Shorty (Glenn Crawford), Bitsy (Elisha Mott), Runt (Jimmy Walsh), Smiling Al (Al Maul), Mad Monk (Russ Meyer), Swats (Carl Sawatski), and Swish (Bill Nicholson). And for their off-field exploits, there were Cupid (Clarence Childs) and Charmer (George Zettlein).

Managers weren't excluded. There has been Kaiser (Irving Wilhelm), Black Jack (Jack Coombs), Stud (George Myatt), The Pope (Paul Owens), Whispers (Dallas Green), Wizard of Oz (Danny Ozark), Tito (Terry Francona), Rhino (Ryne Sandberg), the Little General (Gene Mauch), and Whiskey Face (Pat Moran). Among those from the front office were Shetts (Billy Shettsline),

Ruly (Robert R.M. Carpenter III), Monty (David Montgomery), and the Squire of Kennett Square (Herb Pennock).

Over the years, the Phillies have had at least 15 Leftys, the most notable being Steve Carlton. There were a dozen or more Reds, and a number of Docs, Chiefs, Dutches, and Cys. It all goes to prove there's no name like a good nickname when it comes to baseball players.

*(Rich Westcott is a longtime writer, editor, and baseball historian who is the author of 24 books, including seven on the Phillies.)*

## PHILLIES TEAM NICKNAME

In 2014 the Phillies played their 20,000th game in Toronto against the Blue Jays. In what may classify as an insignificant note, Blue Jays was the Phillies' nickname once upon a time. Even more irrelevant, Toronto was the Phillies' Triple A affiliate from 1948 to 1950. So how and why were the Phillies once known as the Blue Jays?

A couple of months after the Carpenter family purchased the Phillies following the 1943 season, the ballclub announced it would conduct a contest for a nickname to supplement the official Phillies name. The contest would end February 27. A story from *The Philadelphia Inquirer* dated February 6, 1944, reported that "suggestions have been pouring in from fans between the ages of 12 and 82." Suggestions ranged from Aces to Zeebs. Strugglers was one of the suggestions. It came from a prisoner, who said, "I won't see any games in 1944, but I'll be out in 1945." Billy Torretti, president of the Liberty Clown Association, suggested "Rainbows" and having each player dressed in a different color.

Animals and birds dominated the suggestions, including Bobcats, Bob Whites, Bears, Beavers, Donkeys, Dragons, Eagles, Falcons, Greyhounds, Hawks, Jaguars, Lions, Owls, Quails, Ruffed Grouse, Rams, Ravens, Unicorns, Wild Cats, and Zebras. Many played off the historic prominence of Philadelphia: Bell Ringers, Centennials, Constitutionals, Federals, Flagmen, Independents, Keystones, Liberty Bells, Minute Men, Penns, Patriots, Philpenns, Quakers, Valley Forgers.

A March 4 *Evening Bulletin* story reported the Phillies received 5,064 letters and 634 suggestions. Mrs. John Crooks of Philadelphia, one of seven to suggest Blue Jays, was chosen the winner. She received a $100 war bond, but all seven received season tickets. Mrs. Crooks submitted Blue Jays because: "It reflects a new team spirit. The Blue Jay is colorful in personality and plumage. His fighting, aggressive spirit never admits defeat."

A Blue Jay appeared on the left sleeve of the uniform jerseys with Phillies in black script on the jersey front. A Blue Jay also appeared in souvenirs, publications, and club letterhead. Newspapers sometimes referred to them as the Blue Jays. The Phillies had three minor league teams—the Wilmington Blue Rocks, Elmira Blue Sox, and Bedford Blue Wings—that year.

Johns Hopkins University officials and students protested that Blue Jays had been used by the school since the 1870s. Despite the protest the Phillies used Blue Jays for 1944 and 1945. Apathy and a change in the uniforms in 1946 ended the nickname, though a Blue Jay appeared on the Phillies spring training roster/schedule as late as 1949.

# 5

# Unbreakable Records

No one ever thought Lou Gehrig's consecutive game playing streak (2,130) would ever be broken. But it was at the hands of Cal Ripken Jr., who played in 2,632 straight games. His streak came to an end in 1998, and it may stand forever.

A more infamous record belongs to Phillies pitcher John Coleman, a 5'9" right-hander out of Syracuse University, who was the ace of the first Phillies team that finished 17–81 in 1883. He won 12 of the 17 games. He led the league with 48 losses, 772 hits allowed, and 291 earned runs allowed in 61 games started. Included was a streak of losing 12 consecutive games. Three other Phillies pitchers eventually matched that record, including Russ Miller (1928), Hugh Mulcahy (1940), and Ken Reynolds (1972). Coleman's losses, hits allowed, and earned runs allowed are Major League Baseball records, records that will never be broken.

What follows are some unbreakable Phillies records since 1900. Record holders are listed alphabetically. These players hold special places in Phillies history, albeit some of the records are not proud ones.

## HITTING RECORDS

### Richie Ashburn

*Consecutive game playing streak: 730 games*
*Fewest grounded into double plays (GIDP), season: one (1948)*

The speedy center fielder began the streak on July 7, 1950. It ended when he couldn't start the 1955 season opener. He and Del Ennis collided during a spring training game in Wilmington, Delaware, that year. Ashburn injured a knee and was out of the lineup when the season started. The previous record was 533 games by first baseman Fred Luderus, and it took place from June 12, 1916, until the 1920 season opener. Ashburn's 730 games seem safe because current players just don't seem as durable.

As far as GIDP, Ashburn hit into only one in 530 plate appearances in his rookie season. The major league record is zero during 646 at-bats by Augie Galan of the Chicago Cubs in 1935. Ironically, "Whitey" actually shares the club record for most GIDP in a game with three. It occurred in San Francisco's Seals Stadium, June 28, 1959, against left-hander John Antonelli. For those of you keeping score, all were 4–6–3. Knowing Whitey, each was a sharply hit ground ball. Joe Torre holds the major league record (four) on July 21, 1975.

### Pete Childs

*Lowest slugging percentage, season: .206 (1902)*

Playing second base one season (1902) for the Phillies, Childs hit .194 in 123 games. The 30-year-old Philadelphia native had five doubles, among 78 hits, and the rest were singles. Sorry, Pete, but this is going to be your record for another century.

### Ryan Howard

*Home runs, season: 58 (2006)*

"The Big Piece," as Charlie Manuel liked to call him, put up some big numbers in his first full season in the majors, a performance

In 2006 first baseman Ryan Howard obliterated Mike Schmidt's club record for most home runs in a season. (Miles Kennedy)

that earned him the National League MVP award. His home run total smashed Mike Schmidt's club record of 48 set in 1980. It also equaled the Philadelphia baseball record for most homers set by Jimmie Foxx of the A's in 1932. Critics said Ryan had an advantage playing in hitter-friendly Citizens Bank Park. But he hit 29 there and 29 on the road, tying club records in both categories.

So will that single-season home run record ever be broken? Well, before 2006 no Phillies player ever reached 50. And Ryan became just the 23rd MLB player ever to get to that lofty number. Howard followed his 58 with seasons of 47, 48, and 45. No Phillies hitter ever had four consecutive seasons of 40 or more home runs. Chances are it will be a long time before someone matches or passes Howard's 58.

By the way, Howard hit a club-record 11 homers in spring training in 2006 and ended with four in four games during the Japanese All-Star Series in November. He won that MVP Award, too.

### Chuck Klein

*Runs, season: NL record, 158 (1930)*
*Doubles, season: 59 (1930)*
*Extra-base hits, season: NL record-tying, 107 (1930)*
*Total bases, season: 445 (1930)*
*RBIs, season: 170 (1930)*
*Highest slugging average, season: .687 (1930)*

Critics say Klein's numbers are tainted because, as a left-handed hitter, his home games were played in Baker Bowl, where the distance to the right field foul pole was 272 feet. Regardless, they are heavy numbers—all in the same season. Lenny Dykstra's 143 runs in 1993 are the closest anyone has come as far as scoring. In the doubles department, Bobby Abreu's 50 are the most for any Phillies player since Klein had 50 in 1932. Klein's 107 (1930), 103 (1932), and 94 (1929) occupy the top three places on the Phillies all-time extra-base hits list. In fourth place is Jimmy Rollins with 88 in 2007. For total bases Klein holds the top three slots again in the same sequence of seasons—445, 429, 405. Lefty O'Doul is fourth with 397 in 1929. Next is Ryan Howard with 383 in 2006. Howard's 149 RBIs in 2006 are the next highest total. Howard, again, is second with slugging percentage, recording .659 in 2006. Chuck also holds an NL record for most consecutive seasons with 200 or more hits with five and most seasons with 400 or more total bases with three. Chuck owns a lot of records that will endure forever.

### Lefty O'Doul

*Most hits, season: 254 (1929)*
*Highest batting average: .398 (1929)*

Those are lofty numbers. Chuck Klein came close the following season, getting 250 hits, which is second best. In more modern times, Richie Ashburn had 221 in 1951. It's safe to say this record will never be broken. His .398 average also will be hard to beat. The previous Phillies record was .367 by Elmer Flick in 1900. Again, Klein is second, hitting .386 in 1930. Harry Walker's .371 in 1947 ranks fourth. The major league record is .424 by St. Louis' Rogers Hornsby in 1924. Also in 1929 O'Doul set a National League record by reaching base 334 times (254 hits, 76 walks, four hit by pitches). He struck out just 19 times. Those are truly amazing numbers. Even more impressive, the season then was only 154 games long compared to the current 162 games. Lefty played in all 154.

### Connie Ryan

*Hits, game: six hits (1953)*

A 33-year-old second baseman, Ryan's big game came during a 14–12 loss to the Pirates in Pittsburgh, the Phillies' third game of the season. Four months after his record-setting performance, in which he had four singles and two doubles, the Chicago White Sox claimed him on waivers from the Phillies. He was hitting .296 in 90 games at the time, far above his .241 in 1952, his first season with the Phillies, who had acquired him in a seven-player trade with Cincinnati at the 1951 winter meetings. He spent most of his career with the Braves and was part of their organization in three cities: Boston, Milwaukee, and Atlanta. Six hits in a game is certainly attainable as two Phillies outfielders—Ed Delahanty and Sam Thompson—both accomplished that feat in 1894. The modern MLB record is Pittsburgh's Rennie Stennett, who went 7-for-7 in 1975.

### Emil Verban
*Fewest strikeouts, season: eight (1947)*

This is not a typo. A right-handed hitter, Emil (Dutch) Verban struck out just eight times in 573 plate appearances. This is a record that will never be broken. Never. That same season he had 450 putouts, a record for a Phillies second baseman. Acquired from the St. Louis Cardinals for Clyde Klutts on May 1, 1946, Verban was named to the NL All-Star team and elected a starter the next year, the Phillies' first second baseman with such honors. He batted .273 in three Phillies seasons with 31 strikeouts in 348 games. In addition to the Cardinals, Verban played for the Chicago Cubs and Boston Braves and recorded a .272 career average.

### Harry Wolverton
*Triples, game: three (1900)*

During a 23–8 Phillies rout of the Pirates in Pittsburgh, Harry "Fighting Harry" Wolverton collected three triples out of five hits. The record has been tied several times but not by anyone in a Phillies uniform. A switch-hitter, Wolverton hit .282 that season with five more triples. His eight ranked fifth on the club. He played for four other teams in his nine-year career, hitting .278, which was well below his .292 Phillies average. Wolverton managed the New York Highlanders, who became the Yankees, in 1912. After baseball he was a police officer in Oakland, California. He died at age 63 from a hit-and-run accident, the second such accident he suffered during his shift.

## PITCHING RECORDS

### Grover Cleveland Alexander

*Complete games, season: 38 (1916)*
*Innings, season: 389 (1916)*
*Wins, season: 33 (1916)*
*Shutouts, season: 16 (1916)*
*ERA, season: 1.22 (1915)*

These are out-of-the-universe numbers, numbers that have stood for a long time. So they likely will remain standing. Complete games have gone the way of the dinosaur. The closest was Robin Roberts' 33 in 1953. Since the turn of this century, the season high for a Phillies pitcher is nine by Roy Halladay in 2010. Other than Alexander's 388 innings in 1917, Roberts' 347 in 1953 are the most. Robbie also came closest to winning 30 games with 28 in 1952. As far as ERA records, Steve Carlton's 1.97 is the lone ERA under 2.00 by a Phillies pitcher since 1.86 in 1917. If you guessed 1.86 belonged to Alexander, you are correct. His 16 shutouts in a season will never, ever be matched. The most by any pitcher in the majors in 2014 was three, and that was shared by three pitchers.

### Steve Carlton

*Consecutive game winning streak: 15 (1972)*
*Consecutive games, no relief appearances, career: 499*

Acquired in an unpopular trade for Rick Wise in spring training of 1972, Steve Carlton started the season with wins in his first

One of the best to ever play, pitcher Grover Cleveland Alexander set several unbreakable records in 1915 and 1916. (National Baseball Hall of Fame and Museum)

three starts. A fifth straight loss on May 31 left him with a 5–6 record. A win over Houston on June 7 started the greatest winning streak ever by a Phillies pitcher (15 in a row) before a 2–1, 11-inning defeat to Atlanta on August 21. His ERA during the streak was 1.33 and included five shutouts. The previous club record for consecutive wins was 12 by Charlie Ferguson in 1886. If Ferguson's record lasted 85 years, chances are Lefty's will last longer. The Phillies finished that season 59–97. Lefty ended up at 27–10 with a club-record 310 strikeouts.

Lefty put up some other amazing numbers during his 15 years with the Phillies. He was as dependable a starter as there was in the modern era. He simply took the ball and didn't miss a start for a long time. His record for consecutive starts with no relief appearances will never be broken. Robin Roberts, who didn't miss a start in the decade of the 1950s, pitched in relief each of 10 consecutive seasons, starting in 1949. He held the record of 472 before Lefty. Carlton pitched one game in relief in 1971 with the St. Louis Cardinals and didn't come in from the bullpen again until 1987 in Cleveland. Out of 741 career games, Carlton relieved 32 times. He wore No. 32, too.

### Bill Duggleby
*Most runs allowed, game: 17 (1903)*

In the first game of a September 19, 1903, doubleheader in Cincinnati, the 29-year-old right-hander gave up all of the runs in a 17–7 loss. He pitched eight seasons in the majors, most of them with the Phillies. His debut came in 1898. His first major league hit was a grand slam on April 21 vs. the New York Giants. If this record was set in 1903 and hasn't been broken since, it probably won't be.

### Reggie Grabowski
*Hits allowed, inning: 11 (1934)*

A right-hander from Syracuse, New York, he had a three-year career in the majors, all with the Phillies, starting in 1932. Losing 10–4 to the New York Giants in the second game of an August 4, 1934, doubleheader at Baker Bowl, Grabowski was brought in to pitch the top of the ninth. He had one of the worst innings in Phillies history, allowing 11 runs (10 earned) on 11 hits (10 singles). It stands as a National League record. Manager Jimmie Wilson let him finish the game.

## Andy Karl

*Most innings, season, relief pitcher: 166⅔ (1945)*

This right-hander was purchased by the Phillies from the Boston Red Sox during the middle of the 1943 season. Two years later after pitching 143⅔ total innings in the majors, Karl set this Phillies record. He was in a league-leading 67 games that season, including two starts. His career lasted two more seasons, a total of 100⅓ innings. Multiple-inning relievers rarely exist anymore so this record will not be broken. Jim Konstanty came close in 1950 with 152.

## Hal Kelleher

*Most runs allowed, inning: 12 (1938)*

A native Philadelphian, Kelleher had a nightmare inning against at the Chicago Cubs on May 5, 1938. With the Phillies trailing 9–4, the right-hander entered the game in relief in the eighth inning. His line was: 10 hits, 12 runs, 12 earned, three walks, one strikeout, and a league record for most runs allowed in an inning. That season was the fourth and last for Kelleher in the majors, and all were spent with the Phillies. I never imagined that either Grabowski's or Kelleher's records would be broken. But in baseball, you should never say never. Pitching in Arizona on August 11, 2015, Phillies right-hander David Buchanan came within one of each record when he gave up 11 runs on 10 hits in the second inning.

## Bill Kirksieck

*Most home runs allowed, game: six (1939)*

Wayman William Kirksieck pitched only the 1939 season with the Phillies and actually set two records in the same game on August 13, the first of a doubleheader in the New York Giants' park. He allowed four home runs in the fourth inning, then a major league record. He gave up two more in the same game, also a MLB record at the time. He gave up 13 home runs that season in 62⅔ innings.

## Jim Konstanty

*Most innings, game, relief pitcher: 10 (1950)*
*Most wins, season, relief pitcher: 16 (1950)*

Jim Konstanty was the first relief pitcher to win an MVP Award. Though considered the closer, he was actually more than that because he often pitched more than one or two innings. As a matter of fact, he pitched 10 innings in relief on September 15, 1950. The way the game is played today with one and two-inning relievers, no one will ever work 10 innings out of the pen. His record for wins in a season will also stand forever. Ron Reed came close in 1979 with 13.

## Robin Roberts

*Consecutive complete games: 28 (1952–1953)*

This stat is another indication of how tireless a worker Robbie was. This record will never be broken. As documented in an earlier story, one of his complete games during the streak was a 17-inning outing. He did that in 1952, and no pitcher has matched him. No one will.

## Dutch Schelser

*Most hits allowed, game: 22 (1931)*

The date of this dubious record was July 11, and it was the first game of a doubleheader vs. the New York Giants at Baker Bowl. Jumbo Elliot started for the Phillies and lasted one inning and 11 batters. Schesler went the rest of the way, allowing 16 runs (14 earned) on 22 hits. The Giants won 23–5. It was the only big league season for the 31-year-old right-hander, who was born in Germany.

## Curt Simmons

*Most walks allowed, game: 12 (1948)*

Making a start in the second game of a Monday, September 6, 1948, afternoon doubleheader at Shibe Park, Simmons was tagged with a 3–0 loss to the New York Giants. The game was called after seven innings because of darkness. Simmons, a rookie, walked 12 of the 35 batters he faced in six and one-third innings. He gave up only four hits. For the season he walked 108 in 170 innings. That fell way short of the Phillies season record for most walks (164) by Earl Moore in 1911. In fairness to Curt, he actually tied the club record that was set in 1903 by 25-year-old right-hander Fred Mitchell in a July 27, 5–0 loss at Brooklyn. It's safe to say 12 walks in a game is a record that will never be broken by another Phillies pitcher. The manager would yank the pitcher before he reached that number. If he didn't, the manager might soon become an ex-manager.

## Tully Sparks, Milt Watson, and Joe Oeschger

*Most innings, game: 20*

This record will never, ever be matched or broken. Heck, pitchers have trouble going nine innings these days. Thomas (Tully) Sparks pitched all 20 innings in a 2–1 loss to the Cubs on August 24, 1905, at Baker Bowl. Scoreless after 12 innings, the Cubs scored in the 13th inning, and the Phillies matched it. Two singles and a sacrifice bunt provided the Cubs with the winning run in the 20th inning. Sparks was a 5'10", 160-pound right-hander, who spent 12 years in the majors, and the last nine were with the Phillies (95–95, 2.48 ERA in 224 games).

Milt (Mule) Watson also pitched all 20 innings and also lost a 2–1 game to the Cubs. This one was on July 17, 1918, in Chicago's

Weeghman Park. The Phillies scored their run in the fourth inning on a RBI single by right-fielder Gavvy Cravath. The Cubs scored their first run in the first inning and scored the winning run with no one out in the 21st inning. No details exist as to how the Cubs won the game. Watson gave up 19 hits, walked four, and struck out five. A right-hander, Watson pitched two years for the St. Louis Cardinals (1916–17) and two with the Phillies (1918–19). He was 21–30 with a 3.57 ERA for four years, going 7–11 while wearing a Phillies uniform.

The third Phillies pitcher to work 20 innings in a game was Joe Oeschger, and it came in a 9–9 tie against Brooklyn at Baker Bowl on April 30, 1919. Both teams scored three runs in the 19th inning. The game was called by darkness. He was traded on May 27 to the New York Giants who dealt him to the Boston Braves on August 1. Pitching for Boston on May 1, 1920, against Brooklyn, Oeschger pitched all 26 innings of a 1–1 tie called by darkness, the longest game in baseball history. Brooklyn scored in the fifth, and Boston scored in the sixth. Oeschger gave up nine hits and pitched no-hit ball over the last nine innings. "That game was one of those days when the pitchers had the hitters at their mercy. You didn't worry about them hitting the long ball over the fence. Braves Field at that time was a tremendously large field," said Oeschger in an interview with Rich Westcott in *Phillies Report* in 1983.

Oeschger spent 12 years in the majors. He pitched for the Phillies from 1914 to 1919 and again in 1924. His record with them was 29–48. One of the wins came in the last game of the 1915 season when the Phillies won the pennant. At 91 years of age and the last living member of that team, the Phillies brought Oeschger to Philadelphia to throw out the first ball for Game 3 of the World Series at Veterans Stadium in 1983. "Coming back here to Philadelphia after 68 years and being invited to participate in the World Series overwhelmed me," he told Westcott. "It was probably the greatest event in my life. Here I am, the only remaining member of the 1915 Phillies, and this invitation...I don't know how to express my thanks for the wonderful reception and the way I have been received here by the Phillies." Oeschger died on July 28, 1986 at age 94.

Hats off to Sparks, Watson and Oeschger. The closest any Phillies pitcher has come to 20 innings is by Robin Roberts, when he pitched 17 innings.

## IRON GLOVE AWARD

This chapter closes with some defensive records that will never, ever be broken. Three Phillies recorded the most errors in a season. Gloves were a lot different during the playing days of these three Phillies.

### Bob Ferguson

Ferguson allowed 88 errors as a second baseman in 1883, his only season playing for the Phillies. More amazing, he did that in 86 games. The 38-year-old started the season as the player-manager but was fired after a 4–13 start. He became the regular second baseman and, oddly, served as the club's business manager.

### Rudy Hulswitt

Hulswitt committed 81 while playing shortstop in 138 games in 1903. The 26-year-old also played in Philadelphia in 1902 and 1904 during a seven-year National League career. His three-year error total was 204. Larry Bowa had 211 errors in 2,222 big league games over 16 seasons.

### Red Dooin

The catcher committed 40 errors in 140 games in 1909. He had the dubious distinction of leading the National League in errors six times during his 15-year career, which included stints with two other NL teams.

# 6

# Spring Training Homes

Spring training is a baseball ritual that takes place every February and March. For many years spring training was designed to get players into playing shape. Typically, most baseball players could not live year-round on their baseball salaries and took on other jobs that might or might not keep them in shape. Today, players stay in shape the year round.

Spring training didn't used to be a hotbed for fans; attendance was minimal. In 2015 Major League Baseball surpassed four million in spring training attendance. Bright House Field is a major attraction for Phillies fans, and that is reflected by annual attendance totals over 100,000 since it opened in 2004. Total attendance in 1955 when Jack Russell Stadium opened was a mere 16,832. The Phillies are celebrating their 70th year in Clearwater in 2016. But for many years, they trained elsewhere, including Philadelphia from 1883 to 1901. Nine other states hosted Phillies spring training homes:

- 1902—Washington, North Carolina
- 1903—Richmond, Virginia
- 1904—Savannah, Georgia

- 1905—Augusta, Georgia
- 1906–08—Savannah, Georgia
- 1909–10—Southern Pines, North Carolina
- 1911—Birmingham, Alabama
- 1912—Hot Springs, Arkansas
- 1913—Southern Pines, North Carolina
- 1914—Wilmington, North Carolina
- 1915–18—St. Petersburg, Florida
- 1919—Charlotte, North Carolina
- 1920—Birmingham, Alabama
- 1921—Gainesville, Florida
- 1922–24—Leesburg, Florida
- 1925–27—Bradenton, Florida
- 1928–37—Winter Haven, Florida
- 1938—Biloxi, Mississippi
- 1939—New Braunfels, Texas
- 1940–42—Miami Beach, Florida
- 1943—Hershey, Pennsylvania
- 1944–45—Wilmington, Delaware
- 1946—Miami Beach, Florida
- 1947—Clearwater, Florida

### HERSHEY, PENNSYLVANIA

With the United States in World War II, the Office of Defense Transportation mandated that baseball teams hold spring training near their homes from 1943 to 1945. In order to conserve rail transportation during the war, the ODT's travel restrictions limited teams to areas north of the Potomac and Ohio Rivers and east of the Mississippi River. A Phillies team that had lost more than 100 games for five straight seasons, starting in 1938, was about to embark on a bizarre spring training and a year that ended in an equally bizarre manner.

The Phillies not only had a new manager, future Hall of Famer Bucky Harris, but also a new owner, William Cox. Gerry Nugent, who became the owner in 1932, was so financially unstable that the National League intervened, forcing Nugent to sell the team to Cox, a successful New York lumber company businessman who headed a 30-man syndicate. Cox, 33, officially assumed control as spring training began on March 15. He was known to put on the uniform and work out with the team in spring training and interfere throughout the season. He fired Harris, who went 40–53–2, after 95 games. A bitter Harris let it be known that Cox had bet on Phillies games. Following a lengthy investigation by MLB, Cox was banned from baseball. The Carpenter family of Wilmington, Delaware, purchased the Phillies that November.

Trying to find information about spring training in Hershey led to stacks of musty, old 18" x 18" scrapbooks that somehow survived moves from Connie Mack Stadium to Veterans Stadium to Citizens Bank Park. They were piled on top of files in the photo library. One of the books was labeled "1943." Browsing through the brittle and yellowed clippings revealed some interesting stories.

Harris, eight players, the traveling secretary, and the publicity director boarded a train at the Reading Terminal in Philadelphia at 10:30 AM on March 14. At 2:00 PM they arrived in Hershey. Other players went to Hershey directly from their homes. Hershey had a small, well-kept high school diamond, a training house for use in wet weather, and ample club room facilities, according to *The Philadelphia Inquirer*. Housing was split between the Community House and Community Inn. On March 30, it was noted that the entire team went through a physical exam by a physician, a first in baseball history.

Before the first workout, Harris laid out his rules: midnight curfew under penalty of $25, no horseplay, every hitter must sprint to first during batting practice, pitchers must shag fly balls, and no card playing for large stakes. He also counselled the players to cast off the defeatist complex. Eleven players, including player-coach Chuck Klein, went through the first workout on March 15. Only nine players had signed contracts. Six more players were in uniform two days later.

Because of World War II, rosters were in flux, and the Phillies were a prime example. Of the 42 players who would play for them in 1943, only 12 were in uniform the year before. Second baseman Danny Murtaugh, third baseman Pinky May, and right fielder Ron Northey were the only returning regulars. A total of 18 Phillies were in the military in 1943, an issue with which all teams dealt.

In January, Nugent traded first baseman Nick Etten to the Yankees for first baseman Ed Levy, pitcher Al Gettel, and $10,000. Levy joined the Army, and Gettel decided to stay on his farm. Cox complained, but the Yankees initially refused to correct the trade. On March 26, they finally sent catcher Tom Padden and pitcher Al Gearheauser as compensation. Another pitcher, Hilly Flitcraft, also retired to his farm. Pitcher Johnny Allen, acquired in a December 1942 trade with the Dodgers, held out and was sold back to Brooklyn on April 16. First baseman Ed Murphy was also a holdout and never made it back to the majors. Another rookie, catcher Bill Anske, was lost to the military. New players arrived almost daily. Pitcher Charlie Fuchs was acquired on waivers two days before spring training began.

Cox constantly tried to make trades or purchase players. According to one report, Cox talked on the phone with Branch Rickey of the Dodgers for 10 minutes, ringing up a $7 phone bill. Weather was a constant issue. Rain, hail, snowflakes, and the thaw of spring were problematic. Because of a muddy diamond, the Phillies were forced to work out on a football field at times. On another occasion high winds forced the Phillies indoors at the Hershey Arena.

Exhibition games took place in early April. The first was on April 5, a 5–3 loss to the Philadelphia A's in Wilmington. Two days later the Phillies won 5–3 against an Army team at New Cumberland, Pennsylvania. The game was called after six innings because of bitter wind and snowflakes. The next day the Phillies played the Indiantown Gap Army team at the Lebanon (Pennsylvania) High School field. They won a 14–0 no-hitter with the game called after seven innings, again by bad weather. On April 10 the Phillies beat the A's 2–0 at Shibe Park before a crowd of 5,000. On April 12 bad weather cancelled a game in Lancaster, Pennsylvania. The next day a game in Hagerstown, Pennsylvania, was rained out. April 15 featured a 1–1 tie in Trenton, New Jersey, played before 300 shivering fans. The final exhibition game was April 20, a 7–0 win over Yale in New Haven, Connecticut. Continuing the bad weather of the spring, the first two regular season games in Boston were rained out.

During the season, the Phillies played split doubleheaders —10:00 AM and 7:00 PM—to accommodate war workers on swing shifts. They wound up playing a club-record 43 doubleheaders, fitting for the bizarre year of 1943.

Hershey-Derry Township Historical Society librarian Carole Hite Welch was able to obtain the following firsthand report from Camilio "Mimi" Gasper, an outstanding football player who graduated from Hershey High School in 1947: "I saw the Phillies every day at spring training in Hershey and remember seeing Danny Litwhiler hit a long ball over the pine trees in left field, over the parking lot, a long fly that hit the arena wall. I also remember seeing Schoolboy (Preacher) Rowe throw. Some of the high fly balls went into Spring Creek behind the roller coaster. The young boys retrieved the balls from the creek and then ran so they could keep them."

## WILMINGTON, DELAWARE

Following the 1943 season, the Carpenter family bought the Phillies. "We had planned on returning to Hershey for spring training," explained general manager Herb Pennock. "The only reason we're moving to Wilmington, Delaware, is because Bob Carpenter owns the [minor league] Blue Rocks and the ballpark."

Wilmington Park, located at the corner of 30th Street and Governor Printz Boulevard, was where the Phillies held spring training. It was home to the University of Delaware football team from 1940 to 1952 and the Wilmington Blue Rocks of the Class B Interstate League for the same period of time. The Blue Rocks were an affiliate of the Philadelphia Athletics from 1940 to 1943 and then the Phillies from 1944 to 1952.

> **Concession Prices**
>
> • Burke's frankfurters, cheese sandwiches, and fish cakes—15 cents.
> • Orange soda, Coca-Cola, ginger ale, root beer, coffee, milk—10 cents.
> • Goldenberg's peanut chews, Wilbur-Suchard chocolate, peanuts—10 cents.
> • Chewing gum—5 cents.
> • Aristocrat ice cream—15 cents.
> • Cigars and cigarettes—ranged from 10 cents to 20 cents.

Newspaper articles differed as to the number of players who were in camp for the March 19 start. *The Philadelphia Inquirer* reported 22 players, including manager Freddie Fitzsimmons, who was still being carried on the roster as a pitcher. *The Philadelphia Record* story said 34 players were on hand.

Whatever the number of players in camp, 33 others were serving their country during the war. Every team experienced the same situation during the war years. The Hotel Dupont was the spring training headquarters. Fourteen exhibition games were listed on the schedule for Wilmington Park. The season opener was April 19 against the Brooklyn Dodgers at Shibe Park. With the Philadelphia A's owning Shibe Park, the Phillies offices were located in the

Packard Building in Center City at 15th and Chestnut. The front office consisted of eight executives. Tickets could be purchased at the team's office or Shibe Park. There were two ticket agencies in Wilmington—Adams Clothes (716 Market Street) and Humidor Smoke Shop (702 King Street).

Basketballs replaced baseballs because the first day was cancelled by snow. Fitzsimmons moved the workout indoors at the Delaware State Armory. According to clippings from *The Record*, "Freddy Fitzsimmons hustled the team to the armory at 2:00. The previous idea of working out at the rink, a building on the Carpenter estate, was given up because of the lack of transportation. Outside of a session of calisthenics and a brief game of catch, the Phillies devoted themselves to shooting basketballs at the netted hoops and heaving the leathered globules at each other in the same sort of pregame warm-ups practiced by the court quintets." The workout was stopped at 4:00. Fitzsimmons then laid out the training rules for the camp: "Midnight curfew, an 8:00 rising hour and orders for the players to be in uniform and ready for duty at 10:00 AM each day."

## CLEARWATER ATHLETIC FIELD

Clearwater Athletic Field was around way before the Phillies arrived in town. It was first occupied by the Brooklyn Robins in 1923 when they held spring training there. Ground was broken in December 1922. The cost of building the park was $25,000, and the Clearwater population was about 3,000.

Home plate was located near the intersection of Pennsylvania Avenue and Seminole Street, and left field ran parallel to Palmetto Street. Right field was parallel to what is now called N. MLK Jr. Avenue. It was 340 feet to left field and 290 to right. A wooden grandstand behind home plate originally seated 3,000, but 1,000 seats were added later. The field was surrounded by a wooden

Clearwater Athletic Field first hosted the Brooklyn Robins for spring training in 1923. Twenty-four years later it served as the Phillies' first Clearwater
home. (Rich Westcott)

fence. A wire netting was on top of the outfield fence. The North
Greenwood Recreation and Aquatic Complex now stands on the
site.

Originally called Clearwater Athletic Field, it was renamed
Ray Green Field in honor of Ray Green, the mayor of Clearwater
from 1935 to 1938 who was instrumental in upgrading the facility
during his tenure. In a 1980 interview, Eddie Moore, director of
Clearwater parks and recreation from 1938 to 1978, recalled that
the ballpark was also called "Brooklyn Field" during the Dodgers'
tenure. Whatever the name, it was eventually replaced by Jack
Russell Stadium in 1955, a block away to the east.

Various professional and minor league teams—Brooklyn twice
(1923–1932, 1936–41), the Florida State League's Clearwater
Pelicans (1924), the Independent League's Newark Bears (1933–
35), Major League Baseball's Cleveland Indians (1942 and 1946),

professional softball's Clearwater Bombers (1945–54), the Phillies (1947–54), and the Negro League's Clearwater Black Sox (1952)— trained there.

Brooklyn played the first game on March 15, 1923, against the Boston Braves who trained in St. Petersburg. Baseball commissioner Judge Kenesaw Mountain Landis threw out the first ball, and the Dodgers won 12–7 before more than 4,000 fans, according to the *St. Petersburg Times* archives. The *Times'* eight-column sports page was listed as "ATHLETIC GOSSIP AND OTHER NEWS FROM SPORT WORLD."

After a year of training in Miami Beach, the Phillies moved to Clearwater in 1947, replacing the Cleveland Indians, who relocated their spring training to Arizona. Manager Ben Chapman put pitchers and catchers through their first workout on February 24, 1947. "The ballpark is good and bad. The infield, although not tested, appears in fine shape. The outfield is a bucket of sand," reported *The Philadelphia Inquirer*. Catcher Andy Seminick was in that first spring training camp and said, "It was nothing but sand and sea shells and it was brutal. We had tough workouts, and Chapman ended every one with 50 to 75 windsprints." The players dressed in a small clubhouse on the third-base side. "It was more like a wooden shack," said Seminick, laughing. "It looked like it might fall down any minute. It was so cold the city finally agreed to install a pot-belly stove. The shower area was small, and the water was mostly cold." Cold was the weather for that spring, according to several newspaper reports. Lunch for the players consisted of one sandwich and one small milk. Players stayed at the Fort Harrison Hotel and walked to and from Athletic Field. Following spring training, the hotel closed until the following winter.

The Phillies lost their first game 13–1 on March 11 to the Detroit Tigers. Chapman exploded: "I don't intend to take any more 13–1 lickings. We're playing every game as if it counted in the standings. This is not a try-out camp, and it's not a resting place for worn out ballplayers. I've already separated the sheep from the goats, and the goats are on the way out." According to newspaper accounts, there were 1,766 paid admissions and almost that number of passes.

Although they didn't take any more "lickings", the Phillies finished a dismal 3–12 before embarking on a trip through Florida and up the country's East Coast. The exhibition season ended with two games against the Philadelphia Athletics at Shibe Park.

In March of 1948, Babe Ruth paid a visit to Athletic Field. In Robin Roberts' book, *The Whiz Kids and the 1950 Pennant*, he wrote: "Babe Ruth visited our training camp one day while I was warming up. The Babe was talking to a sportswriter, Stan Baumgartner, and it occurred to me that my mother would really appreciate an autographed ball from Ruth. So, I got a brand new ball out of the ball bag and asked to borrow a pen from Baumgartner. I asked Babe to sign the ball, and he said, 'Sure, kid' with his raspy voice. Of course, Babe's visit was in March, and he died that August of throat cancer." Putsy Caballero, an infielder, was in camp that spring and recounts Babe's visit. "I got him to sign a ball, too. When Hurricane Katrina flattened my [New Orleans] house, I lost everything, including the ball."

The Athletic Field grandstand was destroyed by fire on April 12, 1956, but the playing field remained and was sometimes used as a parking lot for games at Jack Russell Stadium. With only one field at the stadium, the Phillies often used Athletic Field as a second location, a place for rookies to practice. The field was in terrible physical shape, prompting the nickname, "Iwo Jima." The island of Iwo Jima was made of inhospitable terrain during World War II, and that was pretty much the condition of the baseball field.

Curt Simmons' first spring training there was in 1948. "I remember the clubhouse was a dinky wooden structure," he said.

"Very close quarters, nails to hang your clothing. I was a year out of high school and just thrilled to be there." As a rookie in 1950, pitcher Bob Miller went to spring training at Athletic Field. "Small clubhouse, we were always bumping into each other," he said. "It didn't matter to me. I was so proud to wear a Phillies uniform every time I stepped onto that field, which had a short right field. It was so short I hit two home runs to right-center in a game against the Cardinals. The clubhouse guys washed the uniforms every day and hung them to dry on a couple of long lines outside the clubhouse, can still see that."

**Historical Notes**

- First game—March 15, 1923.
- Phillies' first game—March 11, 1947.
- Phillies' first win—March 28, 1947, 8–7 over St. Louis on an 11th inning, walk-off home run by outfielder Johnny Wyrostek.
- Two pennant winners trained there—the 1941 Brooklyn Dodgers and 1950 Phillies.
- Clearwater Athletic Field became an official Florida Heritage Site in spring training of 2016 when a historical marker was dedicated at the site.

Dallas Green spent time on the field in 1956 for his first camp. "Rookies were sent to Iwo Jima to work out, rather than the plush field at Jack Russell," he said. "The field was as hard as rock. With right field so short, we lost a lot of baseballs during batting practice." As a rookie shortstop 11 years later, Larry Bowa put in his time there. "The infield was filled with stones," he said. "Ground balls were bouncing off my chest, arms, neck, hated that place."

With so many other major league teams holding spring training on the west coast of Florida during the era of Athletic Field, many Hall of Famers played there. Asked if any Hall of Famers had played on that field against the Phillies, Miller replied, "Yogi, Joe D, Stan Musial, Ted Williams, Al Kaline. Warren Spahn pitched there." Although specific information is sparse, it is possible Ruth played there when the Yankees trained in St. Petersburg in 1924.

During the Brooklyn years, they had numerous Hall of Famers in their camps, including shortstop Dave Bancroft, outfielder Max Carey, infielder/manager Leo Durocher, pitcher/manager Burleigh Grimes, pitcher Waite Hoyt, third baseman Freddie Lindstrom, catcher Ernie Lombardi, catcher Al Lopez, shortstop Rabbit Maranville, outfielder Joe Medwick, shortstop Pee Wee Reese, manager Wilbert Robinson, manager Casey Stengel, pitcher Dazzy Vance, outfielder Zack Wheat, and outfielder Hack Wilson. Cleveland's two years included player-manager Lou Boudreau and pitchers Bob Feller and Bob Lemon. All three are enshrined in Cooperstown, New York. Robin Roberts and Richie Ashburn are two Phillies Hall of Famers who trained and played there.

## THE MOVE TO CLEARWATER

Thanks to the Bill Veeck, Clearwater, a city on Florida's Gulf Coast, became home to the Phillies in 1947. Veeck bought the Cleveland Indians in June of 1946 and decided to move their spring training camp from Clearwater to near his Tucson, Arizona, ranch. Cleveland trained in Clearwater in 1946 and had planned on returning until Veeck stepped in. When asked by city officials to reconsider, Veeck reportedly asked for time to think about it. In the meantime city officials received responses from two big league teams, the St. Louis Browns and Phillies, and two minor league teams, Newark and Kansas City.

After the Browns decided to head for Miami, the Phillies accepted an invitation to move out of Miami Beach for Florida's west coast. "Clearwater was a small town then, mostly orange groves," Curt Simmons recalled.

A couple of days after camp opened, Veeck reportedly headed to Clearwater to negotiate sharing Athletic Field with the Phillies. His Indians were hampered with daily dust storms in Arizona. Phillies manager Ben Chapman didn't take the report too kindly:

"I'm against the proposition. We have only one park, and it's not big enough for two clubs," he said. "We want no competition here while we're training—competition for the fans, I mean, nor do we welcome any distractions." On March 7 the Phillies agreed to exclusive use of the park for nine more seasons, ending Cleveland's hope of returning.

A scrapbook from the 1940s that traveled from Connie Mack Stadium to Veterans Stadium in 1971 and to Citizens Bank Park in 2004 contained a yellowed clipping from the February 22, 1947, edition of *The Bulletin*, which read: "The Phillies bid adios to this city and its snow-covered streets this afternoon. It's major league training camp time, and the local National Leaguers boarded a B&O train for the sunny southland," Ray Kelly wrote. "The destination is Clearwater, Florida, where the Phils will hold forth for the next two months getting in shape for the baseball season."

Wives and children were permitted in camp, though that policy was off and on for a few years. "There's a grand scurry around Clearwater for flats and bungalows," reported a story from *The Bulletin*. "The prices are staggering, even to the $15,000-a-year ball player." The story added, "Frank McCormick [first baseman] found himself an apartment for $300." Players living out of the hotel were offered $5 a day for meals and $4 a day for rent. They occasionally had time to play golf at the Bellaire Golf Course. Greens fees were $1 for those associated with the Phillies; otherwise they were $2. Fishing was also in, if the players had spare time. Reportedly, a local sporting goods store sold 35 fishing rods to members of the Phillies. Shrimp was a popular bait, though one player ended up eating it. Two fishing parties for the players were scheduled one day. Seminick said Clearwater Beach was "pretty sparse." "There was a marina and a couple of places to hang out," he said.

## Historical Notes

- Phillies Hall of Famers Robin Roberts, Steve Carlton, Mike Schmidt, and Jim Bunning all played at the stadium as did many Hall of Fame players from other teams.
- Larry Bowa was a rookie there in 1967, played there as a member of the 1980 World Series champions, was a major league coach (1988–96), and managed the last game. He also holds the distinction of being the last ejection.
- Wilbur Snapp, the stadium organist (1982–86), drew national attention when he was ejected by an umpire after playing "Three Blind Mice" following a questionable call during the June 25, 1985, Clearwater minor league game.
- Baseball's first double no-hitter in 40 years occurred on August 23, 1992, courtesy of Andy Carter (Clearwater) and Scott Bakkum (Winter Haven). The Phillies won 1–0 on two walks and two sacrifice bunts in the seventh inning.
- The Clearwater Phillies won the Florida State League championship in 1993.
- Concerts included the Rolling Stones (1965) and 'N Sync (1996).
- The largest spring training attendance year was 1994 when 98,811 showed up.

## JACK RUSSELL STADIUM

Jack Russell, a former major league pitcher who had a 15-year career from 1926 to 1940 with six clubs, was a city commissioner in Clearwater and former president of the Clearwater Chamber of Commerce. He was the leading proponent for a new ballpark for the city and Phillies. Final city approval came on May 20, 1954, and a $317,563 contract was awarded to the Clearwater Construction Company the following month.

The new stadium, with a capacity of 4,744, was located east of Athletic Field. The opening game was on March 10, 1955, with Robin Roberts facing the Detroit Tigers. A two-run double by third-baseman Willie Jones gave the Phillies a 4–2 win before 4,209 fans. Among the dignitaries for the opener were MLB commissioner Ford C. Frick, National League president Warren C. Giles, American League president Will Harridge, Clearwater mayor Herbert M. Brown, city manager Francis Middleton, and four city commissioners, including Russell and Eddie Moore of the parks and recreation department. In a surprise announcement prior to the game, Mayor Brown named the new park Jack Russell Stadium. Following Russell's death in 1990, the stadium was rededicated the following spring as Jack Russell Memorial Stadium.

While some stadium adjustments and improvements over time increased and decreased the stadium seating capacity, the playing field dimensions remained 340 feet down both lines and 400 feet to dead center field. Before bleachers were added beyond first and third base in the fall in 1989, some baseball writers were known to sit in the grassy area at first base rather than the press box. The writers took off their shirts to get a suntan, prompting someone to nickname the area, "Whale Beach." When bleachers were added, writers filed a protest because their private area was gone. As a compromise the first four rows closest to home plate were reserved for the media.

In addition to the Phillies in spring training, the Clearwater Bombers, a softball team that won 10 National Amateur Softball Association titles between 1950 and 1973, played their home games there from 1955 through 1984. After the Phillies left following spring training, the field was reconfigured for softball for the Bombers' season, and that meant moving home plate much closer to the stands. Prior to the next spring training, the city would again change the field back to baseball. When the Florida State League granted Clearwater a franchise on September 26, 1984, it meant the Bombers would have to relocate, resulting in protests by the team and its fans. A new home was built for the Bombers adjacent to the Carpenter Complex. The Clearwater Phillies, under manager Ramon Aviles, played their first game against the Tampa Tarpons at the stadium on April 12, 1985.

The last spring training game was on March 28, 2003, a 2–0 win for the New York Yankees before 7,224 fans. Pat Burrell got the last hit, a ninth-inning single. (Six months later, Burrell got the last hit at Veterans Stadium.) Roberts threw out the ceremonial first ball 48 years after he threw the first pitch. All fans received a certificate of authenticity. After the games the fans were invited to stroll the bases. The very last game was on August 23, 2003. The Sarasota Red Sox defeated the Clearwater Phillies 6–2. Ryan Howard got the very last hit and made the last out. Roberts again tossed the ceremonial first ball. Much of the ballpark's main grandstand was demolished on July 21, 2007. The left and right-field bleachers, dugouts, field, batting cages, and right-field offices were retained. High schools, colleges, and other amateurs played on the field.

## CARPENTER COMPLEX AND BRIGHT HOUSE FIELD

When the Phillies big league club began training in Clearwater in 1947, their minor league camps were all over the south. Dallas Green got to experience that firsthand in 1956, his first year of spring training. He was part of a pre-camp staff of young arms brought to Clearwater to train with the big club for a short time. Dallas was sent to their Triple A camp in Plant City and later dispatched to the Class A camp in Bennettsville, South Carolina. Ten years later the Class A teams trained in Leesburg, Florida, while Double A and Triple A teams were in Dade City, Florida. Continuity of instruction didn't exist.

Paul Owens, then the director of minor leagues and scouting, had a vision of having a training facility in Clearwater for all the minor league players. His vision included a large clubhouse in the middle surrounded by four fields. Owens convinced owner Bob Carpenter and the city to build a new facility sandwiched between Old Coachman Road and Route 19. During the dedication ceremonies on March 5, 1967, Clearwater mayor Joe Turner announced the new facility would be known as Carpenter Field and be named in honor of the family who owned the Phillies since 1943. The new facility officially opened nine days after the dedication. The careers of hundreds of major leaguers got their start at Carpenter Field. Carpenter Field was financed by a no-interest $250,000 loan from the Phillies to the city of Clearwater, which was to be repaid over a 10-year period. Although the Phillies were the primary tenant, the city also used the fields for various baseball programs.

Sometime later the facility name was changed to Carpenter Complex. The one-story clubhouse structure included rooftop observation areas behind home plate of each field. Owens, scouts, and instructors would watch games from this position. The four fields were eventually named in honor of the first four Hall of Famers—Robin Roberts, Richie Ashburn, Steve Carlton, and Mike Schmidt—to have their uniform numbers retired. With a training facility now available, Owens started a Florida Instructional League program to be held every September-October. Training facilities at Jack Russell Stadium were limited so the big leaguers dressed at the complex for daily workouts until the Grapefruit League games began. With the availability of four fields, more work could get done in a shorter period of time. There was less standing around for the players.

In 1984 the Phillies placed a team in the Gulf Coast League, a short-season league for young prospects not advanced enough for higher classifications. Games are held at the complex in the afternoon on Mondays through Saturdays. Seagulls outnumber fans.

During the 1987–88 offseason, the city of Clearwater renovated the clubhouse. The original clubhouse structure was gutted and reconstructed to include a second floor. Improvements included a larger athletic training room, more offices, a large meeting room, and new lockers. The rooftop observation areas were now part of the second level. The project was completed in time for spring training in 2010. In return the Phillies extended the lease an additional eight years.

## Historical Notes

- The Phillies defeated the New York Yankees 5–1 in the first game on March 4, 2004. Marlon Byrd got the first hit, and Jimmy Rollins got the first home run.

- The Threshers' first game was a 4–1 defeat on April 8 against the nearby Dunedin Blue Jays.

- Clearwater hosted the 2005 Florida State League All-Star Game.

- On August 18, 2006, Clearwater's Julio De La Cruz pitched the first no-hitter, winning 5–0 against the Sarasota Reds.

- The Big East Tournament was first held at the park in 2006. Since then numerous other college games have taken place there.

- Tropical Storm Debby turned the playing field into a quagmire on June 24, 2012.

- Among concerts that have taken place are Willie Nelson and Bob Dylan (2005), Blue October (2006), Peter Noone and Mickey Dolenz (2007), Love & Theft (2009), and Poison (2015).

- Other events have included celebrity softball games, Boo Bash at Halloween, and high school graduations starting in 2006.

The clubhouse was named the Paul Owens Training Facility at Carpenter Complex in 2004 in honor of Owens' legacy of service to the Phillies organization. His bronze bust was unveiled and dedicated on February 22, 2012. The bust, located on the west side of the clubhouse, was commissioned as part of the Clearwater Public Art & Design Program. Stephanie Huerta was the artist and sculptor.

The crowning gem at the complex came in January 2013 with the completion of a new 20,700-square foot structure located east of the clubhouse. It houses a weight room (7,200 square feet) and six indoor batting cages and pitching mounds (13,500 square feet). It also serves as the home of the team's rehab program for injured players. The facility is heavily used in the offseason by a growing population of Phillies players who reside in the Clearwater area. Including Bright House Field, the Phillies have the finest training facility in Florida.

After 48 seasons at Jack Russell Stadium, the Phillies moved into a brand new Clearwater home in 2004 called Bright House Networks Field, and it's located adjacent to Carpenter Complex. As part of the new park, the Phillies extended their relationship with Clearwater for a minimum of another 20 years. The Phillies also opened a new home in Philadelphia—Citizens Bank Park—and became the first team with doubleheader openers in the same year. Ground was broken for the 7,000-seat ballpark in Clearwater on October 16, 2002. The outfield dimensions and configuration were modeled after Citizens Bank Park, as is the 360-degree main concourse. The grass berm beyond the outfield wall can accommodate as many as 2,000 fans.

The administration building located at the West Entry houses the Phillies clubhouse, weight room, video room, player lunch room, ticket office, Diamond Outfitters retail store, a media center, and executive offices for the Phillies and Clearwater Threshers, including several meeting rooms. Fan amenities include a group picnic area, children's play area, Tiki pavilion in left field, club suites, large video board, and multiple concession areas, many of which offer Philadelphia-flavored food. The facility covers a total of 17.5 acres previously the sight of a Home Depot store. The $31.5 million project was funded through a unique public-private partnership that included the state of Florida, Pinellas County, the City of Clearwater under mayor Brian J. Aungst, and the Phillies.

On January 20, 2004, the Phillies and Bright House Networks announced naming rights for the new ballpark, Bright House Networks Field. Six years later, the name was shortened to Bright House Field. Months prior to the opening of the new park, Hall of Famer Mike Schmidt was named manager of the Class A Clearwater team that changed its name from Phillies to Threshers. Bright House Field has become a destination for Phillies fans every year, creating numerous sellouts.

# 7

# Philadelphia Homes

### RECREATION PARK (1883–1886)

Basically, the Phillies have had five ballparks they called home. Bounded by 24th Street, 25th Street, and Columbia Avenue, Recreation Park was the Phillies' first home. About 140 million fans have flocked to Philadelphia ballparks since 1883 to see the Phillies play. "Flocked" may not be the correct term, though, as the first Phillies team drew 55,992 at Recreation Park. In 1894 a fire at the park forced the Phillies to play six games at the University of Pennsylvania field during reconstruction.

"A BIG DAY FOR BASEBALL: PHILADELPHIANS CROWD THE NEW GROUNDS" was the headline in *The New York Times* on May 1, 1887, the day after the Phillies opened their new ballpark against the New York Giants. The style of writing back then was great. Here is the game story:

"Philadelphia, April 30—The new grounds of the Philadelphia Baseball Club, at Broad-street and Lehigh-avenue, were opened this afternoon and 18,000 people were present to witness the initial game. These figures are based upon a fair and official calculation, and the crowd was undoubtedly the largest that ever witnessed a game of baseball in this city. Among the guests were Mayor Filter and hundreds of ladies. The accommodations were perfect, the playing skillful, and the occasion altogether a most enjoyable one. "Every street in Philadelphia seemed to lead to the grounds. The street cars carried great crowds. Men rode on the roof and hung to the dashboards. When the cars reached the grounds the scramble was so great that men jumped through car windows in their eagerness to get good seats. Every car on the different lines was pressed into service, and every available employee was put on to collect fares or drive the horses. Hundreds of carriages, furniture vans and huckster wagons did a thriving business, and many people walked all the way to the grounds. The Reading and Pennsylvania Railroads ran special trains. Nine trains of the Pennsylvania stopped at Germantown Junction between 2 and 4 o'clock and 14 on the Reading line at the ball grounds.

"Getting to the grounds was not half so hard a job as getting in. Men struggled and pushed and squeezed to reach the ticket windows. Still no bones were broken, and everybody who wanted to spend a quarter or a half dollar managed to get in. But it took a good many all the afternoon to accomplish their undertaking. The men who hadn't secured a tickets had to get in line at the pavilion ticket window and that line was a square long for two hours. Politicians, brokers, bankers, lawyers, merchants, gamblers and all sorts and conditions of men were jammed against each other, and the turnstile wouldn't let the people in nearly as fast as the tickets were sold. The entrance for ladies was at the corner of Fifteenth and Huntington streets. The ladies didn't have to pay, and walked up the stairs to the pavilion and over to the roped off seats at the north end of the pavilion. There were about 500 women present, and many of them were in stunning costumes.

"So far as the Phillies were concerned, it was a regular old-time batting game, in which runs were made by the use of muscular power and crafty base running. Keefe used all his skill, but it seemed impossible to pitch a ball the Philadelphia batsmen could not hit safely. Last Thursday, in the first championship game at New York, Keefe held the Phillies down to five safe hits. Today he was batted for 20, with a total of 28 bases, which included a home run and five two-basers. In the eighth inning, which was afterward cut from the score, the home team hit him for four two-basers and a single.

"Daily led the Phillies at bat for two doubles, and one of the latter was the longest hit of the game. Fogarty hit safely three times and, Wood, after making a single, lifted the ball over the right field fence, winning a suite of clothes for making the first home run on the new grounds.

"Ferguson occupied the box for the Philadelphians. It was his first championship game, and he was expected to do great work. The only one of the New-Yorkers who hit him hard was Ewing, who sent the ball over the centre field fence twice for home runs. The other eight Giants were pigmies in

**Recreation Park Phun Facts**

- 1883 National League teams: Boston Beaneaters, Buffalo Bisons, Chicago White Stockings, Cleveland Blues, Detroit Wolverines, New York Giants, Philadelphia Phillies, Providence Grays
- First game: Providence Grays 4, Phillies 3, on May 1, 1883
- Capacity: 6,500
- Playing field dimensions: 300 feet (LF), 331 feet (CF), 247 feet (RF)
- Last game: 6–1 win vs. Detroit Wolverines on October 9, 1886
- Phillies record: 102–117–5
- Attendance high: 175,623 (1886)
- Most home runs, season, Phillies: 13 (1886)
- Most home runs, career, Phillies player: Charlie Bastian (five)
- Year of Demolishing: 1890
- During the Civil War, a cavalry of the Union Army occupied the park
- 1883 Phillies lost 13 consecutive home games, a club record that still stands
- First win at home, a 20–4 vs. Detroit came in the 25th game
- Charlie Ferguson pitched the first no-hitter in Phillies history there on August 29, 1885, vs. Providence

Ferguson hands, and the six hits they made between them were widely scattered."

## BAKER BOWL (1887–1938)

Originally known as National League Park or Philadelphia Park, the name was changed to Baker Bowl in 1913 when William Baker purchased the team. It was bounded by Broad Street, Lehigh Avenue, 15th Street, and Huntingdon Avenue. The clubhouse was located on the second floor of a building in center field and included a swimming pool on the ground level. The park cost $101,000.

Baker Bowl experienced some historical moments and two disasters. Twelve fans were killed and 232 injured on August 6, 1903, after they crowded a balcony in the left-field bleachers to watch a neighborhood fire, causing the wooden structure to collapse. During the reconstruction period, the Phillies moved to Columbia Park, home of the Philadelphia Athletics of the American League, for 16 games. More troubles plagued the park in 1927 as 50 fans were injured when the first-base grandstand collapsed, forcing the Phillies to temporarily move for 12 games to Shibe Park, a home the Athletics opened in 1909. (In the middle of the 1938 season, the Phillies made Shibe Park their permanent home until the end of the 1970 season.) A bizarre incident also occurred in 1911. Sherry Magee was called out on strikes by Bill Finneran, who ejected the Phillies outfielder. Magee charged Finneran and floored him with one punch. Magee was suspended for over a month. When his career ended, Magee actually became an umpire.

Stan Baumgartner was a pitcher on the 1915 pennant-winning Phillies. After his career was over, he was a sportswriter for *The Philadelphia Inquirer.* He covered the last Baker Bowl game and wrote, "Yesterday, they said farewell to the old orchard, packed

Located in north Philadelphia, Baker Bowl cost $101,000 to build and was the Phillies' home from 1887 until 1938. (Bob Warrington collection)

their bags, and sang 'Auld Lang Syne,' and in keeping with the traditions of the Phils of recent years, took a 14–1 beating at the hands of the New York Giants." According to the Phillies' archives: "Line drives cannonaded against the rotting galvanized billboards lining the right-field fence as though fired from an artillery range. Foul balls plopped frighteningly on the pavilion roof, sending down a shower of peeling, scabrous paint and dirt. Now and then, part of the stands, weary of it all, would suddenly shriek and collapse. After 51 years the Phillies bid good-bye to the park following a game with the Giants on June 30, 1938. They left for Boston that night, their home uniforms shipped off to the laundry with a tag marked, 'Return to Shibe Park.'"

A Pennsylvania historical marker was dedicated on August 16, 2000. It reads: "The Phillies' baseball park from its opening in 1887

## Baker Bowl Phun Facts

- 1887 National League teams: Boston Beaneaters, Chicago White Stockings, Detroit Wolverines, Indianapolis Hoosiers, New York Giants, Philadelphia Phillies, Pittsburgh Alleghenys, Washington Nationals
- First game: Phillies 19, New York Giants 10 on April 30, 1887 was called after eight innings because of darkness
- Capacity: 12,500
- Playing field dimensions: 400 feet (LF), 408 feet (CF), 300 feet (RF)
- Ticket prices: 25 and 50 cents
- Player with first hit: Phillies OF Ed Andrews
- Player with first home run: Phillies OF George Wood
- Last game: 14-1 loss to New York Giants, June 30, 1938, with 1,500 in attendance
- Player with last hit: Phillies 1B Phil Weintraub
- Player with last run: Giants 3B Mel Ott
- Player with last out: Phillies C John (Cap) Clark
- Phillies record: 1,957–1,778–29
- Attendance high: 515,265 (1916)
- Most home runs, season, Phillies: 95 (1922)
- Most home runs, career, Phillies player: Chuck Klein (156)
- Most wins, season: 18–5 by Grover Cleveland Alexander in 1915
- Year of Demolishing: 1950
- Red Donahue tossed the Phillies' lone no-hitter in the park (1898)
- Won their first World Series game 3–1 over Boston there
- Babe Ruth played in his first World Series game (1915) and last game ever (1935) there
- In 1914 Honus Wagner got his 3,000[th] hit
- In 1916 Grover Cleveland Alexander recorded his 16th shutout, a record that still stands
- In 1919 Phillies pitcher Joe Oeschger set a club record by working all 20 innings of a 9–9 tie
- In 1928 Chuck Klein got his first major league hit off Alexander, who was then pitching for St. Louis
- In 1928, Fred Lindstrom, New York Giants third baseman, tied a major league by getting nine hits in a doubleheader sweep
- Lefty O'Doul went 6–8 in season-ending doubleheader in 1929 to win the batting title (.398) and set a National League record for hits (254)

until 1938. Rebuilt 1895; hailed as nation's finest stadium. Site of first World Series attended by U.S. President, 1915; Negro League World Series, 1924–26; Babe Ruth's last major league game, 1935. Razed 1950."

## SHIBE PARK/CONNIE MACK STADIUM (1909–1970)

Located at 21st Street and Lehigh Avenue (five blocks west of the Phillies' Baker Bowl), Shibe Park was opened in 1909 as the home of the Philadelphia Athletics of the American League. It cost $315,248 and took one year to build. When the park opened, the clubhouse of the A's was located on the third-base side and had room for 30 lockers and three showers. Shibe Park was named after the owner of the A's. In 1953 the name was changed to Connie Mack Stadium in honor of the longtime A's manager. The

Located at 21st Street and Lehigh Avenue, Shibe Park was opened in 1909 as a place for the American League's Philadelphia Athletics to call home. (National Baseball Hall of Fame and Museum)

## Shibe Park/Connie Mack Stadium Phun Facts

- 1938 National League teams: Boston Braves, Brooklyn Dodgers, Chicago Cubs, Cincinnati Reds, New York Giants, Philadelphia Phillies, Pittsburgh Pirates, St. Louis Cardinals
- First game: A's 8, Red Sox 1 on April 12, 1909
- Capacity: 23,000
- Playing field dimensions: 378 feet (LF), 515 feet (CF), 340 feet (RF)
- Player with first pitch: A's pitcher Eddie Plank
- Player with first hit: A's SS Simon Nicholls
- Player with first home run: A's 3B Frank Baker, who used a 52-ounce bat
- Last A's game: Yankees 4, A's 2 on September 19, 1954
- Last game: Phillies 2, Montreal 1, 10 innings on October 2, 1970
- Last winning pitcher: Dick Selma
- Player with last hit: OF Oscar Gamble
- Player with last run: C Tim McCarver
- Player with last out: Tony Taylor
- Player with last home run: Expos C John Bateman on September 29, 1970
- Last Phillies player with home run: 3B Don Money on September 25, 1970
- Phillies record: 1,205–1,340–13
- Attendance high: 1,425,891 (1964)
- Most home runs, season, Phillies: 77 (1955)
- Most home runs, career, Phillies player: Del Ennis (133)
- Most wins, season: Robin Roberts, 14–2 (1952)
- Year of Demolishing: 1976, following several fires
- First American League night game: 1939
- In 1940 the NFL's Eagles began 17 years of playing there
- In the 1940s the Negro Leagues played there
- In 1940 Jimmie Foxx, A's slugger, hit his 500th home run there
- In 1947 Jackie Robinson's first Philadelphia appearance was in a doubleheader against the Phillies
- Largest crowd: 41,660

- Hosted eight World Series, seven for A's (1910–11, 1913, 1914, 1929–1931), and one for the Phillies (1950) Hosted two All-Star Games (1943 and 1952)
- Babe Ruth hit a total of six home runs in back-to-back doubleheaders (1930)
- Lou Gehrig (1932) and Pat Seerey (1948) each hit four home runs in one game
- In 1936 Tony Lazzeri hit two grand slams and drove in 11 runs in a game
- In 1939 the Yankees hit 13 home runs in a doubleheader
- Ted Williams went 6-for-8 in a doubleheader here on the last day of the 1941 season to finish with a .406 batting average
- In 1946 the Phillies were the first team to break one million in attendance
- In 1949 the Phillies hit five home runs in one inning
- In their first postseason appearance since 1915, the Phillies fell to the Yankees 1–0 in 1950
- In 1951 Willie Mays made his debut for the Giants there
- In 1954 $1 bought a hot dog, soda, pack of cigarettes, popcorn, and a megaphone with a dime for change
- In 1956 a larger scoreboard with a large, square Longines clock on top replaced an old scoreboard
- In 1961 beer was first sold
- In 1966 Sandy Koufax made his last regular season appearance there.
- 6,047 games were played there
- Attendance totaled over 47 million
- Three U. S. presidents visited the park
- Nine Hall of Famers from the A's and three from the Phillies called it home
- Four A's pitchers tossed no-hitters there, but the Phillies had none
- Three A's—Connie Mack, Jimmy Dykes, and Eddie Joost—managed there

ballpark was home to the American League's Philadelphia Athletics from 1909 to 1954. The Phillies first played there on May 16, 1927, while repairs were being made to Baker Bowl. They moved there permanently on July 4, 1938. A grandstand ticket was $1.14 at the time. When the A's left Philadelphia for Kansas City following the 1954 season, the Phillies purchased the ballpark for $1,657,000. The original right-field fence was 12 feet high. Homeowners on 20th Street sold seats on the roofs of their houses ("rooftop bleachers") until Connie Mack raised the fence to nearly 50 feet in 1935. Numerous other changes were made over time, including additional seats. The capacity for the final year was 33,608.

William G. Weart, *Evening Telegraph* assistant sporting editor, wrote the following in the opening game program in answer as to why the park was built: "Because based ball is here to stay. Because it is now looked upon as a business as well as a pastime. Because the game has grown beyond the tough player and the other evils which surrounded it in other old days. The club owners, too, have become educated. They have come to realize that success can come only by keeping faith with the public. Shibe Park is an enduring monument to the national pastime—base ball—the greatest game ever intended for all classes of people, for all ages and for women as well as men."

Following the walk-off hit by Oscar Gamble in the final game, fans stormed the field, took clumps of sod, ripped off wood from the left-field wall, dismantled seats, and even carried out urinals and toilet seats. A once proud ballpark was an empty wreck. The plush grass playing field later became filled with tall weeds. A Connie Mack statue that stood across from the ballpark was removed, refurbished, and moved by the Phillies to Veterans Stadium. During dedication ceremonies of the statue on August 21, 1971, word came that the old park caught on fire. The city ordered the demolition of the park in 1976, but the empty lot was rat-infested and littered with debris. It remained vacant until 1990 when the Deliverance Evangelistic Church was built. Years later, Mary and Robin Roberts decided to check out the church. They walked in an open door and were confronted by a member of the church's clergy. A custodian spoke up, "I know dat man. He's okay." Robin was escorted to the area of the church were the pitcher's mound once stood. It's fitting that the last Phillie on the mound, so to speak, was the Hall of Fame pitcher. Richie Ashburn, a player and broadcaster at Connie Mack Stadium, once described it by saying, "It looked like a ballpark. It smelled like a ballpark. It had a feeling and a heartbeat, a personality that was all baseball."

A Pennsylvania historical marker was dedicated on November 1, 1997. It reads: "Early Major League baseball park opened here, 1909. Renamed, 1953. Home to the Athletics, 1909–1954; Phillies, 1938–1970. Site of three Negro League World Series; five A's World Series victories. Among first to host night games. Razed, 1976."

## VETERANS STADIUM (1971–2003)

Philadelphia voters approved $13 million in bonds to build a new multipurpose stadium in south Philadelphia to be located at the northeast corner of Broad Street and Pattison Avenue. That was May 16, 1967. Groundbreaking took place on October 2, 1967. A 1970 opening was postponed until April 1971 because of numerous changes in design, weather, cost overruns, and labor strikes. It cost $45 to $52 million, according to different sources. With an artificial playing surface of AstroTurf, the stadium would be the home of the Phillies and the NFL's Eagles. The stadium's design appeared to be circular, but it really was an "octorad" design, incorporating four arcs of a large circle and four arcs of a smaller circle to round out the corners. Other "cookie-cutter" stadiums of the era were circular or oval.

The Vet hosted its share of memorable postseason moments. The first postseason game in Philadelphia since the 1950 World

Series was a 6–3 loss to the Cincinnati Reds in the 1976 National League Championship Series. There was the infamous "Black Friday," when the Los Angeles Dodgers scored three runs in the top of the ninth after a questionable umpire call at first base in the following year's league championship series. The Phillies' first postseason win in Philadelphia since Game 1 of the 1915 World Series was a 3–1

### Veterans Stadium Phun Facts

- 1971 National League teams: Chicago Cubs, Montreal Expos, New York Mets, Philadelphia Phillies, Pittsburgh Pirates, St. Louis Cardinals, Atlanta Braves, Cincinnati Reds, Houston Astros, Los Angeles Dodgers San Diego Padres, San Francisco Giants
- First game: Phillies 4, Expos 1 on Saturday, April 10, 1971, attended by 55,352, the largest crowd ever to attend a major league game in Philadelphia
- Capacity: 56,371 (baseball), 63,358 (football)
- Playing field dimensions: 330 feet (LF), 408 feet (CF), 330 feet (RF)
- Box seats cost: $4.25
- First winning pitcher: Jim Bunning, the oldest starting pitcher in the majors at 39, won his 220th game
- First batter: Expos CF Boots Day
- Player with first hit: SS Larry Bowa
- Player with first run: Expos 2B Ron Hunt
- Player with first home run: 3B Don Money
- Last game: Braves 5, Phillies 2 on Sunday, September 28, 2003
- Last winning pitcher: Braves RHP Greg Maddux
- Player with last hit: LF Pat Burrell
- Player with last walk-off hit: 2B Chase Utley
- Player with last run: Atlanta LF Chipper Jones
- Last batter: 2B Chase Utley
- Player with last home run: 1B Jim Thome
- Phillies record: 1,415–1,199–3
- Division titles: 1976–78, 1980–81, 1983, 1993

victory against Houston in the 1980 NLCS. The greatest moment in Phillies history occurred at 11:29 PM on October 21, 1980, when Tug McGraw struck out Willie Wilson. The Phillies clinched pennants in 1983 and 1993 at home and lost the World Series there in 1983.

The final year featured season-long "Field of Memories" celebrations that included players from the 1970s, 1980s, and the 1993

- NL pennants: 1980, 1983, 1993
- World Series championship: 1980
- Attendance high: 2,775,011 (1979)
- Most home runs, season, Phillies: 101 (1977)
- Most home runs, career: Mike Schmidt (265)
- Most wins, season: Steve Carlton, 17–3 (1977)
- Most wins, career: Steve Carlton, 138–62
- Year of demolishing: March 21, 2004
- Karl Wallenda twice walked across the Vet on a high wire
- Phillie Phanatic made his debut in 1978
- 16 Old-Timers Games were held between 1970 and 1990
- Hall of Famers who played for the Phillies included Jim Bunning, Ryne Sandberg, Steve Carlton, Mike Schmidt, Joe Morgan, Tony Perez
- In 1981 Pete Rose broke Stan Musial's National League career record for hits
- In 1981 Steve Carlton recorded his 3,000th career strikeout
- In 1989 Mike Schmidt held his retirement press conference at home plate
- Ceremonies to retire uniform numbers were held for Richie Ashburn (1), Steve Carlton (32), Mike Schmidt (20), and Jim Bunning (14)
- In 1993 closer Mitch Williams got a game-winning hit at 4:40 AM
- No-hitters included Montreal's Pascual Perez (six innings in 1988) and two Phillies pitchers, Terry Mulholland (1990) and Kevin Millwood (2003)
- 66 million fans attended Phillies games

NL champions and Wacky Promotions weekends. Fans selected an All-Vet team. The final weekend was termed the "Final Innings." Harry Kalas was the master of ceremonies before the opening game in 1971. Fittingly, he performed the same duty during the emotional closing ceremonies following the last game. A total of 120 current or former Phillies were introduced, took positions on the field, and stepped on home plate one final time. In addition to 59-year-old McGraw, 79-year-old Paul Owens was able to participate in the closing ceremonies. Owens was the architect of the world champions. With Harry on the microphone, Carlton mimed one last strikeout pitch, Schmidt took one last home-run swing and trot around the bases, and McGraw, battling brain cancer, mimed his historic final pitch. It was one final memory for 33 years of Phillies baseball in Veterans Stadium.

The four Joe Brown statues (two football, two baseball) were relocated to the outer portions of the parking lot where the stadium once stood. The Phillies also built a memorial to veterans on Pattison Avenue to make sure the name Veterans Stadium will live forever. The memorial was dedicated on June 6, 2005, the anniversary of World War II's D-Day. White granite markers with a solid bronze medallion inlay were installed in the parking lot at the exact location of where home plate, the pitcher's rubber, three bases, and the two football goal posts once existed.

A Pennsylvania historical marker was dedicated on September 28, 2005. It reads: "A multi-purpose stadium opened here in 1971 and served as home to the Philadelphia Phillies and Philadelphia Eagles, 1971–2003. The stadium was the site of three World Series in 1980, 1983 and 1993; two Major League Baseball All-Star games in 1976 and 1996; two National Football Conference Championship games in 1981 and 2003; and 17 Army-Navy football games. 'The Vet' had a seating capacity of over 65,000; razed in 2004."

## CITIZENS BANK PARK (2004–)

For the first time since the Baker Bowl days, the Phillies had a ball-park of their own. Citizens Bank Park is located on the north side of Pattison Avenue, between 11th and Darien Streets, spanning a 21-acre site in the Philadelphia Sports Complex. The construction phase began on July 23, 2001. Less than three years later, an intimate state-of-the-art ballpark opened. It cost $458 million. In designing their new home, the Phillies incorporated a little flavor of Connie Mack Stadium. Rooftop bleacher seats, reminiscent of the rooftop seats residents of 20th Street once sold, are above Ashburn Alley. The Phillies also included a big square clock similar to the one that was mounted atop the CMS scoreboard. The Connie Mack statue, which was relocated from the old ballpark to Veterans Stadium, was again relocated. Now it's on the west side of Citizens Bank Park.

Jim Thome celebrates the last home run of his Phillies career—a walk-off homer at Citizens Bank Park—in dramatic fashion. (Miles Kennedy)

The Phillies already have had their share of memorable postseason moments at Citizens Bank. They won National League East division titles in 2007, 2008, 2009, and 2011 and clinched the pennant in 2009. The Phillies earned their first postseason win in 15 years with a 3–1 decision against the Brewers in 2008. Game 5 of the 2008

## Citizen Bank Park Phun Facts

- 2004 National League teams: Atlanta Braves, Florida Marlins, Montreal Expos, New York Mets, Philadelphia Phillies, Chicago Cubs, Cincinnati Reds, Houston Astros, Milwaukee Brewers, Pittsburgh Pirates, St. Louis Cardinals, Arizona Diamondbacks, Colorado Rockies, Los Angeles Dodgers, San Diego Padres, San Francisco Giants
- First game: Reds 4, Phillies 1 on Monday, April 12, 2004
- Capacity: 43,500
- Playing field dimensions: 329 feet (LF), 401 feet (CF), 330 feet (RF)
- Field box seats cost: $40 and $35
- First winning pitcher: Reds RHP Paul Wilson
- First Phillies pitcher: LHP Randy Wolf
- First batter: Reds 2B D'Angelo Jimenez
- Player with first hit: Jimenez
- Player with first run: Jimenez
- Player with first home run: Phillies RF Bobby Abreu
- First postponement: April 14
- First Phillies win: 6–4 on April 15
- First winning pitcher: LHP Rheal Cormier
- Division titles: 2007–11
- NL pennants: 2008–09
- World Series championship: 2008
- In 2004 Jim Thome hit his 400th home run
- In 2004 David Bell, whose grandfather Gus did it against the Phillies in 1951, was the first player to hit for the cycle in the new ballpark

World Series was the first game ever to be suspended by rain. The game resumed on October 29 after a 111-hour rain delay. Brad Lidge struck out Eric Hinske in the ninth to give the Phillies their second World Series championship. In his postseason debut, Roy Halladay tossed a no-hitter in beating the Cincinnati Reds in 2010.

- In 2004 the Phillies set a club record for most walks drawn in a game with 18 but lost to Baltimore in 16 innings
- In 2006 Aaron Rowand broke his nose crashing into the center-field fence
- In 2006 Mike Lieberthal broke Red Dooin's club record for most games caught with 1,125
- In 2006 Ryan Howard became the first player in team history to hit 50 home runs
- In 2009 Phillies tied a club record for most runs scored in the first inning (10) in 22–1 win against Cincinnati. Streak of 257 consecutive sellouts, longest in National League history at the time, began in July 7, 2009 and ended in August 5, 2012
- In 2011 Wilson Valdez became the first position player in team history to be a winning pitcher in a 19-inning decision
- In 2011 Cliff Lee became the third Phillies pitcher ever to toss three consecutive shutouts
- In 2011 statue of Hall of Fame broadcaster Harry Kalas was unveiled
- In 2011 a franchise attendance record of 3,600,718 was set
- In 2012 Thome's last home run as a Phillie was his 13th career walk-off blast, which set a new MLB record
- In 2013 John Mayberry Jr. became the first player in MLB history to hit two extra-inning homers, including a walk-off grand slam
- In 2014 Josh Beckett of the Dodgers tossed the first-no-hitter in the park
- In 2014 Jimmy Rollins broke Mike Schmidt's club record for most career hits

# 8

# Behind the Scenes

## PHILLIE PHANATIC

Thousands have worn a Phillies uniform in the major leagues. An equal number have worked behind the scenes throughout the years. But the most recognizable member of the Phillies organization has to be the Phillie Phanatic. When you are 6'6", 300 pounds with a 90" waist, white eyeballs, purple eyelashes, blue eyebrows, monster sized-shoes, extra long beak, extra long curled up tongue, gawking neck, and your fur is bright green, you stand out. The record shows this big, feathery creature from the Galapagos Islands made a rather quiet debut during a Phillies game at Veterans Stadium on April 24, 1978. His first TV appearance was on the Philadelphia-produced children's show *Captain Noah and His Magical Ark* along with Phillies player Tim McCarver, who was doing promotional work for the team. The Phillie Phanatic quickly evolved into the most entertaining mascot in all of sports.

A room behind home plate on the ground level of the Vet was labeled "Phanatic," but what went on behind the door wasn't known. When Citizens Bank Park opened, another room was built called "Phanatic Locker Room." It's across the hall from the umpire's room. The Phillie Phanatic can be seen popping in and out of this room. Before the door is closed, that gawking neck peeks out to make sure no one is following.

We don't know if Phillie Phanatic watches TV, has an iPod, microwave, cooler, popcorn machine, or sleeps standing up, in a bed, or a hammock. We certainly hope a shower is in order. A hot July afternoon makes players sweat profusely. Perhaps Phillie Phanatic doesn't sweat, though those who get close to him often hold their noses. Several years later its mother, Phoebe, began appearing occasionally with her son. The best guess is Phoebe also exists in the same room.

The number of Phillies from the Phanatic's Galapogos home swelled to five with the arrival of the Galapogos Gang in the summer of 2015. These four creatures help entertain fans at the ballpark. Phanatic's friends include Sid, a Galapagos sea lion. He's the oldest member of the gang. Sid had a transistor radio on the islands and listened to every Phillies game while lying on the white beaches. He's so old his favorite team is the 1950 Whiz Kids. He wears the old Phillies uniform proudly in honor of that team. Iggy is a land iguana who loves the Phanatic. If he feels the Phanatic is in trouble, he'll always come to the rescue. And like the Phanatic, he loves the Phillies and only the Phillies. Iggy loves to eat. The Phanatic has a hard time teaching Iggy how to play baseball because Iggy always eats the bat and ball. Bessie is a blue-footed booby and loves the Phanatic like a son. When the Phanatic left the islands, Bessie followed his career as the Phillies mascot and became the biggest Phillies fan in her native land. She's always proud of the fact her colorful blue feet match the same baby blue uniforms the Phillies wore in the 1970s and 1980s. Calvin is a giant tortoise and the youngest member of the gang. Growing up, Calvin was like an older brother to the Phanatic and always looked out for him when they explored the islands. The Phanatic taught Calvin the game of baseball. Calvin loves playing the game, even though he always gets thrown out at first base.

Sports' most entertaining mascot, who made his debut very quietly in 1978, stands on top of the dugout. (Phillies)

The gang worships the Phanatic, a multi-talented entertainer known for wandering throughout the stands, dumping popcorn on fans, buffing bald heads, shaking his belly, dancing on the dugout roof, leading cheers, mocking enemy players, messing with umpires, speeding onto the field in a four-wheel ATV, shooting hot dogs high into the stands, hugging fans, and posing for pictures. The Phillie Phanatic brings instant smiles everywhere every time. No athlete is as beloved. We've learned the Phanatic doesn't speak. Every year the Phillies have a pregame birthday party for the green creature, but there are no candles on the cake—perhaps indicative that he can't count either. Phanatic can write, however, as numerous Phanatic children's books have been published. There's even a "Be a Phanatic About Reading" program for students. Phillie Phanatic loves kids and vice versa. There are times when tiny toddlers cry at the appearance of this big creature. His size can be frightening.

Phanatic merchandise is very popular. Among the vast inventory are pins, stuffed green look-a-like dolls of all sizes, dangle hats, big nosed sunglasses, shirts, bibs, bottles, pacifiers, puppets, bobbleheads, watches, pennants, key chains, garden mascots, bleacher masks, and pillows. Somehow, Phillie Phanatic appears at multiple events when there is no Phillies game. Often he can be found at a minor league game. Fans flock to see him entertain. It's a big deal when Phillie Phanatic comes to town. Local mascots will perform but fail to match the Phanatic's gig.

We also know Phillie Phanatic loves worldwide traveling, having gone to Japan three times, Australia twice plus Mexico, Canada, Venezuela, Puerto Rico, and the Galapagos Islands. He has rubbed elbows with celebrities including Michael Jordan, Kelsey Grammer, Chubby Checker, Elton John, Billy Joel, Jonathan Silverman, Hootie & the Blowfish, Meat Loaf, Grace Kelly, Ethel Kennedy, Chevy Chase, Lily Tomlin, Marlo Thomas, Phil Donahue, Joe Piscopo, Bill Cosby, David Brenner, Bruce Springsteen, Arnold Palmer, U.S. attorney general John Ashcroft, President George W. Bush, and many, many more. The Phanatic has appeared in closing credits of the film *Rocky* and in TV shows *Jon & Kate Plus 8*, *The Simpsons*, *30 Rock*, *The Late Show with David Letterman*, *TODAY*, *Good Morning America*, and *The Rosie O'Donnell Show*. An ESPN *SportsCenter* fixture, the Phanatic has also starred in that network's as well as Fox Network's commercials. Derek Jeter even got to co-star with the Phanatic on an ESPN spot. The Phanatic has starred in his own videos, too: *Phillie Phanatic Goes Hollywood*, *Time Travelin' Phanatic*, *Channel Surfin' Phanatic*, and the latest, which came out in September of 2015, *The Phillie Phanatic's One-Man Band*.

The Phillie Phanatic was voted the most beloved Philadelphian in *Philadelphia Magazine*'s "Best of Philly" issue; top mascot in sports, according to *Forbes*; and the best mascot ever by *Sports Illustrated for Kids*. The Phanatic is a charter member of the Mascot Hall of Fame. The greatest honor that can be bestowed upon a ballplayer is to be inducted into the National Baseball Hall of Fame and Museum in Cooperstown, New York. Phillie Phanatic was so honored on July 27, 2002. His costume is on permanent display.

All of this pales in comparison to leading a World Series parade down Broad Street. Phillie Phanatic's done that twice. When asked if that is its favorite gig, the big green head nodded affirmatively. When asked for a bucket list, Phillie Phanatic scribbled on a piece of paper. It wants another World Series.

## DIRECTOR, ENTERTAINMENT

A *field general* is generally a term given to a quarterback in football, the guy who calls and directs the next play. Borrowing that label the Phillies have their own field general, a lady who directs all the pregame festivities at Citizens Bank Park. Her name is Chris Long, and her official title is director, entertainment. Her career with the Phillies didn't start out that way as she was hired as a secretary to Frank Sullivan, the club's director of promotions. During the day she worked with Frank, but during games she was an elevator operator at Veterans Stadium. The year was 1971, the first season of the Vet. Eventually she escaped elevator duty to be the escort for the national anthem singers, bands, and other guests who were performing or being introduced on the field.

Her role evolved into more hands-on for the pregame festivities. Out of nowhere in April 1978, a big green furry creature appeared at a Phillies home game, a quiet debut for Phillie Phanatic. Within weeks requests for the Phanatic began to pour in. Chris became the creature's first booking agent. That began to occupy so much of her day time that the responsibility was shifted to another employee. A good chunk of Chris' time is scheduling anthem singers, people throwing out the ceremonial first pitches, color guards, and musical groups. About five years ago, Theresa

Leydan was hired as an assistant with the idea that she would someday succeed Chris. Starting during the 2015 season, Chris began easing out of the position that required working all 81 home games.

So how does one get to sing the national anthem at a Phillies game? "Individuals and groups submit tapes," she began explaining. "Some of the home dates are immediately filled with choirs or choruses as part of our corporate/community nights. We prefer groups as we have had some difficult experiences with solo singers." Almost year-round she can be found playing tapes while working on the computer on other projects. Years ago a neighboring employee exclaimed, "Hey Chrissy, that's the 14th anthem today." Now Theresa's neighbors can respond as she's assumed that friendly chore. And there is often more than one person throwing out the first pitch. "Most we had was nine all throwing at the same time," she laughed.

She and the Phanatic work hand-in-hand in scheduling fifth-inning skits on the field and seventh-inning dancing on the first-base dugout roof. During the conflicts in Afghanistan and Iraq, the Phillies kept getting calls asking for help in saluting the military being deployed or returning. "As you can imagine, some of the calls were very emotional. [Head groundskeeper] Mike Boekholder came up with the idea of having a military member change the bases after the third inning," she said. "We don't do it every game, but the reaction from fans is phenomenal every time." On occasion first responders are saluted this way.

After 9/11 Major League Baseball directed all teams to have a performance of "God Bless America" as part of the game experience. "We do it Opening Day, Sunday, and on the summer holidays: Memorial Day, Flag Day, 4th of July," Chris added. On those holidays the Phillies annually salute veterans by choosing them as singers. Working with veterans groups, Chris will have representatives from various wars and conflicts on the field along with a large American flag. The Phillies have always believed honoring veterans is very important.

When the team is on the road, her hours are pretty normal—9:00 AM to 5:00 or 5:30 PM. Much of her day is planning the pregame show for each of the games on the next homestand. For home games she has a long day, working from 9:00 AM until after the end of each game. Once the game has started, she has time for dinner in the press dining room before heading for the field and the Phanatic's fifth-inning gig.

Chris prepares a detailed game log broken down minute by minute. That log is distributed to both clubhouses, the umpires, baseball administration, public relations, Boekholder, and public address announcer Dan Baker, who also receives a script from her. For a 7:05 night game, the show begins at 6:36 with a welcome by Baker. One minute is allotted for each first pitch, two minutes for the anthem, and three for the announcement of the starting lineups. Chris can be seen on the field, toting a clipboard and wearing a headset to communicate with the PhanaVision control room. She can also be heard, saying, "Let's go, hurry up. Where's the Phanatic?" There's a lot to be squeezed into festivities that need to end so the game can begin precisely at 7:05. If there is a delay, she will hear it from the Phillies dugout. Their starting pitcher is ready to go, and any delay can upset his mental and physical preparation. Who gave her the most guff? Chris responded, "John Vukovich, Dallas Green, and Jim Fregosi. I can still hear Vuk, 'Hey Crissy, get that dog and pony show out of here,'" she said laughing.

When Bill Giles came aboard, he felt it was important to entertain the fans. For years Opening Day meant some sort of an act—Kiteman, Benny the Bomb, Cannon Man, Rocketman, and parachute acts, to name a few. Other pregame fun ranged from ostrich races to performing elephants, the highest jumping Easter

Bunny, players blindfolded trying to smash watermelons with a bat, cash scrambles, wheelbarrow races, and cow-milking contests. Toss in two walks across the Vet on a tightrope by the Great Wallenda. "Been there, done that," she laughed again. "But I wasn't in charge when the ostrich race bombed."

The Phillies' first national exposure came in 1976 when they hosted the All-Star Game. That began a run of postseason appearances through 1981 except in 1979. During those days the host team pretty much ran the show. MLB drafted Chris to run the All-Star Game shows in 1981 (Cleveland) and 1984 (San Francisco) because of her and the Phillies' reputation. During the 2007–2011 postseason runs, MLB was in charge during the League Championship Series and World Series. "The clubs are pretty much on their own for the Division Series," Chris says. "Early in the day for each LCS and WS game, there's a production meeting run by MLB. I attend as every pregame had to be timed to the second, not just the minute. MLB determines the singers and presentations while the home team schedules the color guard and ceremonial first balls for the World Series."

Chris has been in the middle of some bizarre pregame incidents. Asked for her top three, she lowered her head and began doodling with a pencil. Using the David Letterman reverse order, here's her list. No. 3: "We scheduled a duck race one time home to first. We quickly learned they don't race let alone walk in a straight line." No. 2: "We had a dog act that was going to perform with the Phanatic on the field between innings. When the dog saw the first baseman roll the ball to the second baseman, the dog took off trying to get the ball. Back and forth he went. I yelled for the trainer, 'Go get your dog!' She replied, 'No one told me a ball would be on the field.' Finally another employee and I ran out there to grab the dog." No. 1: "The Ringling Brothers Circus was performing across the street at the Spectrum. To help promote the shows, the circus agreed to bring some elephants to the Vet field pregame. They entered from right field followed by three pooper scoopers dressed as clowns. All of a sudden, the elephants stopped and urinated into the dugout...our dugout."

### PUBLIC ADDRESS ANNOUNCER

His voice is his most recognizable trait. But in many ways, he's one of the many faces of the Phillies. Say hello to Dan Baker, the Phillies' public address (PA) announcer since 1972. Although he is heard more than he is seen, Baker can be spotted on the field before every Phillies home game. The best-dressed man on the field, a virtual walking advertisement for Brooks Brothers, he's easy to spot. The tie he's wearing hangs loose when he arrives at Citizens Bank Park a couple of hours prior to game time. After tying that tie, he heads to the glass-enclosed area located behind Section 212 in the Hall of Fame Club, home of the Phanavision control room and his place of work 81 times a season.

Six people are seated in front-row stations on the left side of the climate-controlled studio. Anywhere from 17 to 19 work in the control room, which is equipped with 136 television monitors. Dan occupies the second seat from the right. Sitting to his right is a spotter, a person who helps keep Dan informed of potential changes on the field. That person also charts the time between innings. MLB's rule is the first batter of a half-inning needs to be announced one minute, 40 seconds before the first pitch. In front of Baker resting on a table is a microphone on a stand and a control box with a red button. Those are his working tools. Press the red button, and his recognizable voice blares throughout the ballpark: *Batting first for the Philadelphia Phillies, No. 37, center fielder Odubel Herrera.*

Before he gets to do that, there's homework. He checks every name in the starting lineups. Next he goes over the pregame script several times. "The cardinal sin for a PA announcer is to mispronounce a name," he cautions. With a blue felt tip pen, he makes note of names that need checking on the 5"x7" index cards he numbers in sequence. To verify player enunciations, he'll ask the public relations staffs, radio/TV announcers, or even the player himself. If there's an uncertain name that's part of the pregame festivities, he'll seek the proper pronunciation when he arrives on the field around 45 minutes prior to game time.

A control room production meeting is usually held one and a half hours before the first pitch. A detailed schedule of the pregame events timed down to the second is available to the entire control room staff. It is the topic of the meeting. Once that meeting is adjourned, Baker and the entire crew head for the press dining room for a pregame meal. "I learned from my parents a long time ago the importance of enunciating every syllable," he says while munching on a pork chop. "That is the key to being a PA announcer. If you speak too fast, the fans won't understand what you are saying."

About 25 minutes prior to game time, he'll stand behind a microphone on the field with the script in hand: *Ladies and gentlemen. Welcome to Citizens Bank Park for tonight's National League game between the Pittsburgh Pirates and Phillies.* That's the first indication that a game is soon to begin.

Dave Abramson, chief technical engineer and a member of the control room staff, will pinch hit when needed. When a bathroom break is needed during the game, Baker will dash out of the room to a nearby restroom and try to be back in time for the first batter of the next inning. When Major League Baseball initiated new rules to speed up the pace of the game between innings last season, the dash had to be quicker.

Baker is a lifelong Phillies fan who takes defeats hard. In one particular game, Cole Hamels was in a jam, with runners on first and second and one out. "[Pirates catcher Russell] Martin can hit into double plays, and we need one," he mutters to anyone within ear shot. Then he presses the red button: "Now batting, No. 55, catcher Russell Martin." Martin doubles into the left-field corner, driving in one run. "Oh, well," he mutters again to those in the box, not over the microphone.

On occasion, he's gotten feedback from Phillies players. Baker said, "One time Rob Ducey, a really nice person, approached me. 'Dan, bench players don't seem to get the same enthusiastic announcement. I know we aren't the big names, but we should get equal treatment.' I really didn't think I did it but was appreciative of the feedback. I rededicated myself to make sure I didn't snub any player." His favorite name to enunciate? Baker paused, "I guess it would be MICK-eee Mor-an-DIN-i."

Baker is as good as it gets in the business, but like anyone he's had his slipups. "I practice and practice, and it isn't very often I make a mistake, but I remember a game back in the mid-1970s when the Phillies hosted the Giants," Baker said. "The Giants had Willie McCovey, No. 44, on the roster. The Phillies had a player by the name of Willie Montanez, No. 27. Montanez came to the plate, and I announced, 'Now batting for the Phillies, No. 27, Willie McCovey.' I was embarrassed. Next day, Montanez walks up behind me on the field, taps me on the shoulder, and with that big smile of his, says 'Montanez, Montanez.'"

Since joining the Phillies gameday staff over four decades ago, Baker estimates that he has missed a total of about 15 games. So he's no threat to Cal Ripken's consecutive game streak. But in the world of PA announcers, two are recognized as legends: Pat Piper, who worked 59 years for the Cubs, and Bob Sheppard, a 57-year employee of the Yankees. Someday Baker will reach that level of legendary longevity. But to many Phillies fans, who correlate Baker's voice with a day at the ballpark, Baker is already a legend.

## BULL'S BBQ

He was known for "Bull Blasts" at Veterans Stadium, including a home run that hit the Liberty Bell some 500 feet away in center field. He was among the first Phillies players to treat underprivileged kids to free seats, doing so through his "Bull Ring," which earned him the 1978 Roberto Clemente Award. Ever since Citizens Bank Park opened, he's been in the lineup every day in the outfield. But Greg Luzinski's place isn't in left field anymore. It's behind Section 104, manning Bull's BBQ. Instead of playing, "the Bull" is greeting fans and filling their bellies. He's there for all home games, tucked in the corner right next to the big green structure that identifies Bull's BBQ. Baseball's largest grill is located up front next to a large smoker. Smoke billows from the grill at times filling the air with the aroma of ribs. "In all the years we've been here, we've only had one complaint from a fan about the smoke," he acknowledged.

During the design process of Citizens Bank Park, the Phillies and their concessionaire, Aramark, put a lot of thought into developing an outfield food court, an area that would eventually be called Ashburn Alley. Among the many amenities in Baltimore's Camden Yards was Boog's BBQ. Smoke revealed its right-field location. The Orioles had a burly first baseman named Boog Powell, and he was there every game. Since it was very successful, the Phillies decided to imitate that eatery with Bull's BBQ at the east end anchor to Ashburn Alley. "Boog and I used to work for Miller Lite so I got to know him. Fans will stop by my place to chat and talk about Boog's BBQ. I tell them, 'Next time you see Boog, let him know I have a better menu, more variety. We're better,'" he said, laughing.

Ribs, pulled pork, and half chickens were the original menu. Calling himself "a spicy guy," Greg, with help from Aramark, came up with his own BBQ sauce. "It has a little bite to it, but that's the way I like it. It's actually produced in 55-gallon drums in North Carolina and shipped up here to Hatfield's in gallon bottles. We use a lot of it," he said. At one time smoked turkey legs were added to the menu. "We had to stop serving them because fans thought the legs weren't cooked thoroughly, but when you smoke chicken or turkey, it is red looking, giving the wrong impression. [Radio station] WIP learned about the turkey legs being removed, started a campaign on the radio to have them put back on the menu. They've been there ever since," Luzinski explained. Another menu addition is a "Bull Dog," which is a foot-long kielbasa. Apparently, the only item on the menu not labeled "Bull" are the baked beans. "Not so sure 'Bull Beans' would sell," Luzinski said. Cole slaw, bags of Herr's potato chips, bottled water, soda, and a variety of beer are also available. The most popular items are (in order): pulled pork, Bull Dog, and then ribs.

Fans file through two lines to load up their trays and then munch while sitting on metal picnic tables, which are, of course, colored Phillies red.

The Bull arrives around 5:30 PM when the gates to Ashburn Alley open. He used to play all nine innings, but now he'll depart after the seventh. Aramark has a small souvenir area adjacent to the food area with caps of all sorts, color pictures of Greg as a player, his game jerseys, and light blue Phillies T-shirts with his name and 19 on the back in white. The BBQ staff all wear burgundy "Luzinski 19" shirts. Gail Pellicane is the supervisor. She's spent 23 years working for Aramark, first at Veterans Stadium and now with Bull. "She's great. When a fan comes up with a complaint about the food or whatever, I send them to Gail," he said, laughing. "I played here for a long time and really didn't realize that south

Philly was really like a small town within a city. Everybody knows each other, and a lot of them work here."

Bull's station is a booth that resembles a place you would buy tickets. There's a TV to his right that is housed in a wooden dog-house-like structure. That's his connection to the game. He can hear the crowd roar, but he is way too far from right-center field. "I can't even see the scoreboard," he said, "but the sunsets can be gorgeous." He's armed with an assortment of pens. Signing autographs, taking pictures with fans, talking baseball, hugging children or elderly ladies, it's all part of his gameday routine. The Phillies have had cruises for fans in January and trips to different cities during the season. Greg and his wife, Jean, are part of the traveling party. Quite often, those fans will stop by Bull's BBQ to relive the good times they shared on the trips. Bull proudly wears the 1980 World Series ring on his right hand and the one from 2008 on his left hand. Fans of all ages ask to see them, touch them, and take pictures with cell phones. Does 81 home games mean eating barbecue 81 times? "I don't eat. I taste, not just this but other food in the Alley."

During the season Luzinski and Phillies PA announcer Dan Baker co-host a one-hour radio show on Levittown, Pennsylvania's WBWB. Shows take place at various restaurants—yet another opportunity for the Bull to connect with the fans. As everyone knows, the Phillies had a five-year run of domination. "This place was always packed and filled with energy. It was something I'll always remember. There were so many fans [near the back of section 104] that they blocked the concourse." With the Phillies in a rebuilding mode, success on the field has dwindled as has attendance. Yet Bull's BBQ keeps busy. "[In 2015] I thought the fans were great," said Luzinski. "When they started playing better in the second half, you could feel energy in the park again. They liked seeing the young kids play. They wanted to talk about them, wanted to know what's coming in the minors."

## DIRECTOR, LANDSCAPING AND SITE WORK OPERATIONS

This title belongs to Pam Hall, a University of Pennsylvania post-graduate with a master's degree in landscape architecture. Her job is to keep Citizens Bank Park beautiful. She first joined the Phillies organization in 2001 as the vision of a new ballpark was becoming a reality. She was the site-work manager for John Stranix, the ballpark project manager. Pam worked out of the Maggio Building on Darien Street and still has her office there. When Citizens Bank Park opened, she made a point to Phillies management, "You need someone to manage the landscaping." Having a degree in that area meant she was the right person.

A baseball season lasts six months with more tacked on if the team is in the postseason. A Pam Hall season matches that and much more. A baseball field of green grass is not part of her territory. Her responsibilities include landscaping the perimeter of the ballpark and the parking lots west and northwest of Citizens Bank Park. "It's 100 acres in size and more like a park," she explains.

Pam's staff includes one year-round employee and three who are on the job all year except six weeks. Supplementing the staff are a batch of summer interns. They usually are four college students who are majoring in some form of landscaping and six to eight students from the W. B. Saul High School of Agricultural Sciences. The college kids begin in April while the high school students have a seven-week session once school is out. Multiple hands are needed as Pam's inventory includes over 2,000 trees, hundreds of shrubs, and many annuals and perennials. All require pruning, fertilizing, and watering.

Her season actually begins in January. "I attend nursery shows to meet vendors and get an idea of the latest in plants. That's followed by making arrangements with area nurseries," Pam said. "In March we begin cleaning out the beds and plant cool weather flowers such as pansies. That'll take us through the first week of May." Then it's good-bye pansies, hello summer flowers. That planting will take her through the baseball season. "When we're in the postseason," she said, "we'll have a third planting."

Inside the park includes trees, the shrubbery, and ivy and a long row of flower boxes on top of the left-field wall and two in the bullpen areas. Liriope, which is also called monkey grass and lantana, comprise the summer planting in the left-field boxes. "Lantana will bloom all summer and can handle heat," Pam offered. Above the bullpen a pansy mix is planted in the spring followed by cascading geraniums that will bloom till the end of October or first frost. Once the planting is done in the flower boxes, detailed maintenance is required. "Plants in both places may be damaged or diseased so we constantly monitor the two areas. Fans can be so anxious to get a ball that lands in the left-field boxes that they dig up the flowers. No big deal, we replace the flowers plus fertilize and water," she continued. Trees need attention, too. "We've replaced many trees since the park opened," she said. "Some were damaged or diseased. We learned the cherry trees inside the first-base gate weren't the right fit. We replaced them with maples and hornbeams. They fit much better."

There's an irrigation system that takes care of all the landscaping that surrounds the park. Trees not in that footprint are watered by gator bags, which fit around the trees and are filled with water. Small holes at the bottom provide water at a slow rate. Water elsewhere on the 100 acres is provided by two tanks, a 500-gallon one that fits on a pickup truck and a 300-gallon tank that sits on the back of a gator utility vehicle. "During the hot and humid months like July and August, we do a lot of watering," she explained.

What's there to do in December? Pam smiles and said, "Holiday decorations." Every holiday season, the Phillies like to decorate the Pattison Avenue side of Citizens Bank Park. "We have a 24-foot tree that goes outside the third-base gates, large wreaths, small potted trees, and other decorations," she said. "Everything has been converted into LED lights." Inside the offices poinsettias and artificially decorated trees are located on each floor, the Hall of Fame Club, and Diamond Club. The latter two locations are available for events through the team's ballpark enterprises department. It takes Pam's crew two to three weeks to decorate the place and about 10 days to remove everything. Lending a big hand are the ballpark's electricians and carpenters.

When the team is on the road, that's when the major work is done, such as replacing trees. "For fan safety digging holes and leaving them uncovered can only be done at a time when there is a stretch of no games," she said while grabbing her smart phone. "Through technology I can turn the irrigation off and on from this. I don't need to be at the park."

When asked what fans might notice when they go to Citizens Bank Park, Pam, without looking at a piece of paper, rattled off: "Impatiens; pansies; petunias; geraniums; lantana; coleus; verbena; sweet potato vines; elephant ears —yes, I said 'elephant ears'—serve as a centerpiece in the large pots, perennials like black-eye-susan; liriope; hostas; allium; phlox; and roses, to name a few, shrubs— hydrangea; spirea; barberry; red; and yellowtwig dogwood; Virginia sweetspire; spice bush; mugo pines; azalea; winter berry; and more. And along with a few varieties of ornamental grasses, we have a variety of trees—maples, zelkovas, oaks, witch hazel, dogwoods, red bud, Kentucky coffee tree, arborvitae, and more."

## DIRECTOR, FIELD OPERATIONS

The smell of hot dogs on the grill, the sound of vendors hawking scorecards, and the sight of a plush green playing field are what fans experience upon walking through the Citizens Bank Park gates. Credit for the green field rests with Mike Boekholder, director, field operations, and his merry crew of five full-time groundskeepers and an additional 12 to 14 game-day troops.

Having spent five years doing the same job at Victory Field, home of the Indianapolis Indians of the International League, Mike's phone rang early in the 2003 season. The call was from the Phillies wanting to employ the Washington state native as the head groundskeeper for their new home. He joined the Phillies that July 1 and oversaw the installation of the park's first sod in late October and the installation of state-of-the-art drainage and irrigation systems.

On non-gamedays, Boekholder arrives at his job around 9:00 AM and will be there "as long as needed to get the job done," he says. Gamedays he arrives at 10:00 AM and stays about an hour after the game has ended. "A lot depends on the weather, meaning we may have to cover the field after a game or before leaving when we have no game," Mike explained. Laughing, he said, "Come to think, weather can affect us a lot."

During the All-Star Game break, he and his crew often replace sod behind home plate, an area that gets worn out because of batting practice. "We'll seed with rye and again early the next spring, but from June until September, the field is strictly Bermuda grass," he added. Fertilizing is usually done when the team is on the road, and he mows the grass every day the team is at home. He uses a riding mower to give the crisscross pattern that is very noticeable on the field. Does that qualify as a unique skill or talent? "Probably neither," he said smiling.

He lives on the field for nine months of the year but also spends time in an office located in the right-field corner. Next time you are at the park, look for the window in foul territory on the green outfield wall. He's the one at the desk, which includes a radar monitor and a laptop on his right. A larger screen and keyboard sits on top of a work station on his left. "That controls the irrigation system, but I can also control it on my cell phone," he explained. The room also includes a sofa ("perfect for a short nap"), file drawers, a large framed photo of the park's first game, and a small glass-doored refrigerator filled with Coca-Colas. He can watch the game on a large wall-mounted TV or spin around in his chair and peek out the window.

Next to his office is the field entrance for his crew and their equipment. Tucked under Section 108 is the batting cage, which gets pulled out pregame and then stored until the next day. There's also a large room labeled "Field Equipment Storage" under the same section of seats. It's a cross between a John Deere showroom and the garden section of Lowes. It has John Deere gators, tractors, and riding mowers, walk-behind mowers of all sizes, plus wheelbarrows, edgers, hoses, field rakes, shovels, brooms, fertilizer spreaders, rollers, fuel, and stacks of fertilizer.

Boekholder won't spend the entire game in his right-field office. Under the Diamond Club seats by the third-base dugout field entrance is a room labeled Field Maintenance but more commonly known as the "Ready Room." That's where he and the grounds crew are stationed ready for in-game work and tarp duty in case of rain. The room is home to three blue leather couches, a large TV, radar monitor, and refrigerator. There are field rakes, normal rakes, shovels, brooms, hoses, tampers, extra bases, large squeegees, chalk, and red wooden forms for lining the batter's boxes and foul lines. There are bags of clay conditioner in case the mound needs in-game work, bags of field conditioner to spread on the dirt if needed after rain, and various types of devices to hand-drag the infield. Mike can be spotted on the field during threatening weather informing the umpire crew chief of the situation. "They're great guys. I was once in a small umpiring school run by a couple of umps, and I knew many others from the minor leagues," he said.

He and his crew get the field ready about 30 minutes prior to game time. The routine includes hand dragging the infield, smoothing dirt at home plate and on the mound, watering the dirt portions, and chalking the foul lines and batter's boxes. Postgame also has a routine but a longer one. Sixteen members of his crew invade the field about two minutes after the last out. All the activity sort of resembles an anthill with bodies moving all over the place. Two lonesome souls wander to the bullpens to do their thing. Tools include field rakes, hand-held blowers, wheelbarrows, tampers, shovels, brooms, and hoses. The mound, both batter's boxes, and the area where the home-plate umpire operates are refurbished with clay and water. The foul lines in the infield and batter's boxes are removed, one person drags the infield riding a John Deere bunker rake, another chap removes the three bases and hand-rakes those areas, two guys armed with blowers on their backs blow dirt from grass areas back onto the dirt, and one person is assigned to the warning track in front of each dugout smoothing the dirt with hand rakes. Yet another crewmember fertilizes various grass areas following an obvious pattern and never colliding with a fellow worker. There's also a person in left field with a broom and shovel. "You gotta get rid of sunflower seed shells. A broom and shovel is the best way," he explained. Watering the infield and covering the mound and home plate with round tarps ends the day.

How often is the home plate and pitching rubber changed? "There's no set schedule. After Josh Beckett's no-hitter in 2014, he wanted the pitching rubber. So we dug it up after the game and replaced it. We also replaced if after Aaron Nola's first game [in 2015]," Boekholder says.

December is down time for Mike and his full-time crew. "We generally can work on the field up until Thanksgiving." In January there are conferences and MLB groundskeepers' meetings to attend. February is the time to order supplies, purchase equipment, hire his gameday staff of 25 people who work on rotations during the season, order uniforms for everyone, and finalize the maintenance plan for the season. Weather permitting, they are back on the field in March getting ready for another season. Does he do the gardening at his home? "Nope, my wife does that," he said. "She's better at it."

## GENERAL MANAGER, FACILITIES, SPECTRA

In planning their new home, the Phillies had the opportunity to take on more responsibilities when it came to concessions, maintenance, and overall operation. By partnering with Aramark, the Phillies share input on merchandise, food/beverage varieties, quality, and pricing. Being able to maintain the playing field and landscaping could be done in-house. When it came to overall upkeep of Citizens Bank Park, they contracted with Spectra, a company that specializes in facility maintenance.

Occupying an office on the Suite Level of Citizens Bank Park is Carolyn DiGiuseppe, general manager, Spectra. Her responsibility is to keep Citizens Bank Park safe, clean, and operable. As the operations coordinator for Global Spectrum, the previous company name, she has been part of the Phillies home since 2003, the year before it opened. Carolyn moved into the head position in 2014. "Our role has multiple facets: cleanliness of the park, safety such as making sure elevators and escalators are always operable, the fire alarm system, field pump system, lighting including the light towers, generators, trash removal, recycling, fixing leaks, HVAC control systems, PECO power services, bird netting—pretty much hands on everything," she explained. She oversees a full-time management staff of ten. Spectra's roster also includes full-time union trades, electricians (four), carpenters (fives), plumbers (two), steam fitters (three), and painter (one). Each has its own workshop on the service level, the same level as the clubhouses. Behind her desk is a large file drawer with contact information for more than 100 contractors or vendors needed to keep the park in tip-top shape.

The baseball season is one of continuous maintenance. If an elevator goes down, there is an immediate need to get it functioning again. Safety is the No. 1 concern. If there's a problem with the field pump system, that is critical when the team is home. "This area was a swamp at one time, and without the pump system, the field wouldn't be playable," Carolyn said. Winter means putting the park into hibernation mode, so to speak. Water in the restrooms and suites needs to be turned off. From concession stands vents to the concrete, massive cleaning is required. Snow and ice removal come under her umbrella, keeping the perimeter clean. While the team is in spring training, her team is into spring cleaning and reversing the winterization.

There are seven entrances to Citizens Bank Park, and Carolyn is a stickler for keeping those areas clean. "It is so important to have a positive first impression. If you are entering a facility or building with piled-up trash, dirty windows, dirty concrete, or floors, but once you enter, the place is neat and clean, you'll only remember what you saw initially and won't go back," she explained. "I'm really fussy about keeping windows clean."

For a night game, the Phillies front office staff hours begin at 9:00 AM. The manager, coaches, and players begin arriving as early as noon. Carolyn gets to her office daily around 6:00 AM and departs around 9:00 PM or the seventh inning. Other management staffers will have staggered hours. "I just like to get in early, gives me a chance to read the maintenance issues that arose the day before. There are the never-ending emails to review and respond. I check today's work project schedule. Plus, I file a report to corporate headquarters weekly," Carolyn said. "We also work closely with the Phillies and [architect] Ewing Cole on capital improvements. It is vital to plan ahead and avoid major issues."

Although she has an office, the entire ballpark is her world. She's on the go more than she sits, armed with a BlackBerry and two walkie-talkies so she can communicate with everyone on the staff. When the team is on the road, she gets to leave as early as 4:30 PM. The workload isn't necessarily easier. "Major project work can be done then. Cleaning continues [as] special events or trade shows may be scheduled for the ballpark. Plus we have concerts every summer that require the union trades," Carolyn explained.

After the game one of the management staffers is in charge of the cleaning detail. The first shift of workers begins around 10:00 PM. The "pickers" basically pick up all the loose trash. They are followed an hour later by workers with air blowers. Next a shift armed with power washers cleans seats and concrete in the seating bowl and concourses. In the morning another power washing crew continues the process.

Every other Tuesday morning throughout the year, the Phillies conduct a weekly business staff meeting of multiple departments in the boardroom just down the hall from Carolyn's office. She is included. What follows is a small sample of her reports, which paint a picture of what facility management really entails.

- Terminix will be back on-site this week to continue the work on the bird netting in the TV truck bay and at the suite patio.
- The electricians and carpenters will be assisting with the W.B. Mason Trade Show setup. In addition our cleaning staff is working with Aramark on clearing the concourse for the setup starting today.
- The steamfitters are working with Johnson Controls on upgrades to the HVAC controls system in the ballpark.
- PECO is working on one of the two power services that power the ballpark. We will be operating on one service until the work is completed Wednesday.

- The trades are working with Aramark on cleaning the exhaust hoods in Harry the K's kitchens as well as the concessions on the upper terrace and pavilion level.
- The plumbers are working in concession stands with an outside contractor on grease trap cleaning.
- The plumbers will also be working in the west merchandise warehouse on repairs to an iron pipe. Corrosion resulted in leaks due to soda.
- Pat Dolan is working with our safety consultant on the employee training for June. Focus will be on fall protection and confined space training for those affected.
- Newly power-coated metal recycle units were added to the perimeter of the building. These units were previously trash units.
- Our cleaning staff is focused on the concourse this week in preparation for the W.B. Mason and Season Ticket Holder events this week.
- Carpet cleaners will be in the administration building this Saturday.

Almost anything can happen in a ballpark. When asked for an example of a bizarre incident or two, she pondered for a short while before responding, "We have a hawk who visits us every season, a season nest holder, if you will," she said laughing. "Our electricians climbed light tower six to change some large bulbs and were attacked by the hawk. We called in the Pennsylvania Fish & Wild Life Commission seeking answers on how to handle the situation. We learned to live with unity. We also had a game in 2015 involving a squirrel. He or she came down the wires holding up the home-plate screen, ran across the top of the screen onto another guide wire, and jumped into the Phillies dugout. [It] scared Chase Utley half to death. The squirrel got a lot of national attention on television. We were able to trap the squirrel the next day and take it to a wooded area, its natural habitat."

## DIRECTOR, TEAM TRAVEL AND CLUBHOUSE SERVICES

As a 10-year-old, Frank Coppenbarger helped out in the clubhouse of his hometown team, the Decatur (Illinois) Giants of the Midwest League. It was the start of a clubhouse/equipment manager path that carried him through the minor leagues to the big leagues in 1981 with the St. Louis Cardinals. He was brought to Philadelphia in 1989 by general manager Lee Thomas to take over the Phillies clubhouse. Ten years later he also assumed the traveling secretary duties. "There are a lot of little details that become big ones if you forget one," said Coppenbarger, the director of team travel and clubhouse services.

Frank's office is the first door on the right once you walk through the double-door entrance to the large clubhouse area. His desk resembles any other work area, but his room is decorated with numerous framed photos of all sizes and occasions, a large bat rack, miniature models of each major league stadium, a small cooler, caps from the postseason years, and a *really* giant baseball glove. It's like a mini-museum. Being a huge University of Illinois fan, there's also an orange football helmet and a Fighting Illini folding metal chair.

For a home night game, Frank usually wanders in around noon and leaves about an hour after the game. Up until 2014, he made every road trip. Now he misses a couple per season. If there is a day off at home, Frank has a day off. The clubhouse services portion of his role is to oversee three managers: Phil Sheridan (home clubhouse), Dan O'Rourke (equipment and umpire services), and Kevin Steinhour (visiting clubhouse). There's also Joe Swanhart who works for the Phillies from February through the end of the season.

"Swanny" prepares and organizes all food, beverages, and snacks for the clubhouse in spring training and the season. Made-to-order breakfast from Lenny's Restaurant is available at Bright House Field every morning followed by lunch and snacks and a postgame spread. At Citizens Bank Park, Swanny will prepare lunch and a full postgame meal for the players, manager, and coaches and breakfast for day games. Snacks are available all the time. He'll also have some of Philadelphia's finest restaurants cater pregame and postgame meals instead of wearing a chef's hat in the clubhouse kitchen. Tables and chairs are in a dining area next to the kitchen. "Swanny will also make one road trip per season," Coppenbarger said. "He'll help with the equipment but also observe how other clubs handle meals, nothing like seeing it firsthand." Cost for the food and beverages and certain equipment is covered by a monthly fee the players and coaches pay Coppenbarger and his staff.

The team travel portion is his biggest and most time-consuming duty. He's basically a one-man travel agency, scheduling buses, trucks, trains, airplanes, and hotels for a traveling party that normally includes 55 persons. For the postseason that number swells from 120 to 130 as players' wives, ownership, and club executives will travel with the team. "I usually get the first draft of next year's schedule in June," he explained. "Game times are missing, and slight adjustments can be made, but I will know where and when we will be on the road. The first priority is selecting hotels in each city. Changing hotels may require a trip there after the season. I need to see everything firsthand and meet people face-to-face. Bids for charter flights are handled early in the postseason. We need a 737, 800-series aircraft with the exception of the West Coast when we will use a larger plane. Once all the game times have been set, which can be as late as December, I'll reach out to the bus and truck companies and provide them with a detailed schedule." That schedule will include departure times to and from the ballpark or hotel or airport. That includes a "spot time." "We need to have them on the spot 30 minutes prior to departure. They sit and wait, but that's better than having them arrive late because of one reason or another," Frank explained. In most cities Frank will arrange for the bus to shuttle from the hotel to the ballpark and back again for a second trip. There's only one bus after the game, and no bus is needed in San Diego as the ballpark is across the street from the hotel.

Travel to New York from Philadelphia and back takes place via a bus. Trips to Baltimore and Washington are on Amtrak charter trains. Equipment is trucked to those cities. Dress code for trips is determined by the manager. For most recent seasons, sport coats, dress slacks, and collared shirt are required until Memorial Day at which time sport coats become optional. Sneakers are allowed except on flights.

When the Phillies are leaving for a road trip, Frank will post a sign in the clubhouse of the bus departure time (usually one hour after the last out). Two days prior he calls the bus and truck companies to review the times and locations needed. Hotels receive a rooming list. United Airlines, the 2015 charter provider, lets Frank know if the airplane has landed and is waiting at the Philadelphia airport. On the rare occasion when the aircraft is late getting to an airport—mostly because of weather issues—Frank will delay the bus departure from the ballpark until he has heard from the airline. Security checks are generally done at the ballpark through TSA. "I really don't know how traveling secretaries did this job before cell phones," he said shaking his head.

Glitches do occur. "One time the equipment truck went to the wrong airport in Houston. Another time we were playing in Oakland but staying in San Francisco. We flew into San Francisco, but the equipment truck was waiting for us at the Oakland airport.

Buses have always been in the right place at the right time, knock on wood."

Although rooms are booked well in advance, and hotels are very cooperative in providing additional rooms at the last minute, Frank's experienced three hotel nightmares. "We were rained out in Boston on get-away day, and the Red Sox decided to hold us over to play the next day. We had checked out of the hotel and couldn't get back in because they were sold out. Players were in the clubhouse anxious to get back to the hotel. I had to scramble to get rooms. A similar thing happened in New York twice. Once the United Nations general assembly was in session, and rooms were nowhere to be found. I finally came up with three different hotels, which meant adjusting the bus schedules. In the postseason that's the biggest worry, enough to keep me awake at night. It happened to the Rays in 2008 when the game here was suspended. They wound up getting rooms in Wilmington because Philadelphia hotels were booked solid," he said.

Then, there was Pope Francis' visit to Philadelphia late in 2015. The Phillies finished their last road series in Washington, D.C., on Sunday, September 27. Travel plans called for an Amtrak charter train that evening for the traveling party of 60. Frank had to change plans as the parking lots in and around the sports complex were being used for tourist buses. Some streets in Center City were closed, and it was questionable that Frank's buses could meet the team at 30th Street Station. "If you live in outlying suburbs, you can get home on your own Sunday night," Coppenbarger told Jim Salisbury of CSNPhilly.com. "One of our athletic trainers lives in West Chester, so I think he'll head home after the game. But the Pope's not going to be in West Chester." Many of the rookies on the team were staying in a Center City hotel. Getting there could be an issue because of traffic and street closings. "Some of our guys haven't been here that long and they only know one way home,"

Frank added. "The GPS doesn't factor in the Pope." Instead, official team travel didn't happen until Monday. Instead of 30th Street Station, the Phillies got off the train in Wilmington and bused to Citizens Bank Park.

Tickets are another Coppenbarger chore. Players are entitled to four complimentary tickets for family and two for friends. They are taxed for the tickets. All tickets in the postseason must be paid for as there are no comps. Each clubhouse is equipped with two computers for the players to request tickets. Computers are turned off two hours prior to game time. A ticket list and tickets are delivered to Frank from the ticket office. He places tickets in envelopes, putting all families in the same section. The envelopes are returned to the ticket office and placed at the will call window.

Coppenbarger has an office refrigerator full of Budweiser, Coca-Cola, and a bottle of champagne. "We needed it when Charlie [Manuel] won his 500th game as our manager and when Doc [Roy Halladay] pitched his no-hitter in the playoffs. You never know when something special may happen," Frank explained. He went on to tell the story of Cole Hamels' 2015 no-hitter in Chicago last season. "After the sixth inning, I asked Mike Burkhardt [Cubs' visiting clubhouse manager] if he had any champagne. He was busy working, didn't realize what was going on, and asked why. I told him I didn't want to jinx anyone, but Cole is pitching a no-hitter. Burkhardt said he would send a clubhouse worker to a nearby liquor store to get a bottle." Within minutes of the final out, the Baseball Hall of Fame emailed Frank, asking for Cole's hat and a ball from the game. Cole wanted the pitching rubber and/or home plate as souvenirs, and Frank began the process of requesting both from the Cubs.

When the Phillies call up a player from the minor leagues, Frank will get a hotel room in Philadelphia if the player doesn't have a friend on the team who will allow him to move in. When a new player comes to the Phillies via a trade, Frank is responsible for arranging transportation and a hotel room. The other team will provide the same for the player leaving the Phillies. Uniform numbers come under Frank's jurisdiction. After Jimmy Rollins was traded, Coppenbarger decided not to issue No. 11 for a while. He followed the same procedure for No. 35 (Hamels) and No. 26 (Chase Utley). Eventually the numbers will be worn again. The Phillies' policy on retiring uniform numbers is limited to their Hall of Fame icons.

Baseball annually holds meetings in December. Hotel accommodations for the Phillies group is handled by Frank. Different segments of the game will hold individual meetings, including equipment managers and traveling secretaries. November and January are less demanding months as far as time at the ballpark for him. February means the start of spring training. At the end of the season, the Phillies are responsible for providing transportation to a player's home. The same applies for getting to Clearwater. Hotel needs don't exist in spring training, but two buses are needed for each road trip. And tickets kick in again. Following the last game, an airplane awaits at the Tampa International Airport ready to take the Phillies to their season-opening destination. Rest assured, Frank will call to confirm the details.

## MANAGER, VISITING CLUBHOUSE

Once a young bat boy in the minor leagues, Kevin Steinhour now takes care of the big boys in the major leagues as Phillies' manager of the visiting clubhouse, a position he has held since 1990. Growing up in Springfield, Illinois, Steinhour served as the bat boy of the St. Louis Cardinals' Triple A team in that city. He was 12 years old. His path to the majors continued during his high school days as he worked both the home and visiting clubhouses in Springfield. After graduation he spent two years with the Triple A Louisville Redbirds before being brought to Philadelphia by Frank

Coppenbarger, a fellow Springfield native and clubhouse employee in the minors and with the Cardinals. Coppenbarger was hired by Phillies general manager Lee Thomas just before the 1989 season. Steinhour finished his tour in Louisville before joining the Phillies organization. Steinhour worked at Veterans Stadium for 14 years before the opening of Citizens Bank Park in 2004. "The facilities in the visiting clubhouse are among the best in the game," Steinhour said. "I heard that from the players this first season and still hear it."

Those facilities include a clubhouse of 47 lockers, coaches' room, manager's office, training room, weight room, players' lounge/kitchen, laundry room, storage area, video room, and a small office for the traveling secretary. Oh, and harkening back to Kevin's roots, there is one more room: a small dressing room for the bat boy. With MLB adding instant replay in 2014, replay equipment was also placed in the video room. Steinhour's staff includes four young men, two of whom double as chefs, and a bat boy, who is normally college-aged. Steinhour is the lone full-time Phillies employee.

The National League schedule determines his life for six months. Home games at Citizens Bank Park are a must, but road games are different. That time is spent working in the vacant Phillies clubhouse, placing his food orders for the next homestand and grabbing a day off here and there. But he will also make road trips as the Phillies' equipment manager. For a six-game homestand that starts on a Friday night against the Marlins and ends with a Wednesday day game against the Braves, Steinhour's work begins on Thursday night when the Marlins' equipment truck arrives after their night game in Atlanta. "We know the Marlins travel itinerary and will be at the park around the time their plane lands," said Steinhour. "It'll take us about two hours to unload the truck and fill the lockers," he explains. "If we also have to wash and dry dirty uniforms and undergarments, it could take a little longer." The laundry room contains two large washers and five dryers.

For 7:05 night games, he'll get to the clubhouse around 11:30 AM each day and be there until approximately two hours after the game has ended. While paying a visit to the clubhouse around noon of a night game, he was found in the kitchen slicing a watermelon. For a 1:35 PM Sunday game, he arrives around 7:30 AM. Teams usually leave town about an hour after the last out of the final game of a series, so Steinhour and his crew always have a lot of packing to do. They actually have to begin the packing process as soon as the first pitch is thrown. "Each team has two large hampers, one for uniforms and one for sweatshirts, shorts, T-shirts, socks, jocks, and things like that," he explained. "After the game the dirty stuff gets tossed in the hampers. Those hampers will go on a truck and head for Shea Stadium where the Marlins next play." After the Marlins have departed, the remainder of his Sunday is spent waiting for the Braves equipment truck to arrive from their afternoon game in Cincinnati. There are more dirty uniforms to launder. Then it's time to go home. Two night games and a 1:05 afternoon game end the homestand. The routine is the same.

While visiting teams always have a bus to take them to Citizens Bank Park from the hotel, many players arrive on their own early, sometimes as early as 1:00 PM for a 7:05 night game. The manager and coaches often are early birds, too. Men need nutrition. "Pregame we cook burgers, tacos, grilled chicken, and turkey burgers for those who prefer something healthier. There's also a sandwich bar and different beverages but not beer. For day games we have a full breakfast. Postgame meals are catered," Steinhour says.

What's the most popular pregame food order? "That's easy, cheesesteaks," he said smiling. "Players have said, 'I've been waiting three weeks for a cheesesteak.'" As the players file out of the clubhouse after the final game of a series, they give a check or cash to

Steinhour for his clubhouse services, which includes the pregame and postgame food spreads. Does Steinhour have a favorite player, coach, or manager? He pauses before saying, "Bobby Cox and Joe Torre. Bobby is probably my favorite, a really great person, sort of like an uncle. He'd talk anything—baseball, family, Illinois football. Torre was a regular guy. When he walked into a room, you could feel his presence."

Once in a while a circumstance will arise that requires quick attention. If a team acquires a new player or brings up a minor leaguer, Steinhour may be called upon to quickly put a name and number on the back of a jersey. He and Coppenbarger use a business about 10 minutes from the ballpark to do the sewing. "I sort of wish I could do the sewing, but this way is easier," Steinhour said.

When Manny Ramirez was with the Dodgers, he forgot to pack his blue spikes one time. "His size was 13. Oftentimes we'll ask his teammates if they have an extra pair. But nobody had his size. I went online and reached out to sporting goods companies that weren't too far from the park. I was able to find a pair at Dick's Sporting Goods. I said, 'Don't sell them. I'll send someone right over.'"

His most unusual experience happened during the 2008 World Series against Tampa Bay, specifically Game 5, which was suspended by rain after five and a half innings, a World Series first. "After the game, the Rays were going back to St. Petersburg either way, Game 6 or no game," Kevin said. "So we had everything pretty well packed. But now [with the suspended game], we had to unpack. On top of that, they had checked out of their Philadelphia hotel and couldn't get rooms in the city. They wound up going to the Hotel DuPont in Wilmington. Players were asking, 'Where can we eat in Wilmington?' I said, 'I'm sure the hotel has first-class dining.' The weather was still bad the next day, and the game couldn't be resumed. Several players came to the park to hit in the cages. Pitchers threw in the cages. The game finally resumed the next day. Normally, it takes us four innings to pack, and we start when the game starts. Well, this time the game resumed in the sixth inning, meaning we had to move really quickly. During the season we generally peek at the TVs but don't really focus on the score. But this is the World Series, a potential clinching game, a chance for the Phillies to win the championship. We wanted to watch but couldn't. There's no cheering in a clubhouse so when the game ended, we hustled into the laundry room, closed the door, and quickly celebrated, then back to a somber clubhouse. We had to hide our emotions. After the Rays left, we popped some champagne."

## MANAGER, EQUIPMENT AND UMPIRE SERVICES

Veterans Stadium is where Dan O'Rourke began his career first as a bat boy in 1985 before moving into the clubhouse. "I was 22, and Frank [Coppenbarger] kidded me, 'You're old for a bat boy. How about joining the staff in the clubhouse?'" That was 1989. A year later he fled Philly for Houston, where he was manager of the Astros' home clubhouse. Coppenbarger brought him back home in 2001 as assistant clubhouse manager. Now he wears two hats, so to speak.

Gameday at Citizens Bank Park finds Dan running back and forth between the Phillies clubhouse and the umpire's room and lounge, which is located on the service level, the same level as both clubhouses. The short trips are multiple. His job is to equip the Phillies players and oversee the umpire's facility. Equipment for the players is everything from undergarments to uniforms to bats, balls, and sunflower seeds. Every spring training Majestic, manufacturer of the uniforms, visits Bright House Field to measure all players in camp plus the manager and his staff. Each player will be provided with two sets of uniforms, which are home pinstriped, home alternate, and road gray. Pitchers and catchers each get a third set. Opening the season at home in 2015, the new uniforms arrived at Citizens Bank Park a week before the first game. In addition to the uniforms with names and numbers, there are extra blank jerseys and pants. You see, pants have a tendency to tear when a player slides. Once upon a time, Dan would have been armed with a needle and thread to repair the tears. Not anymore.

Gloves and shoes are provided by various manufacturers through individual contracts with the players. The Phillies are responsible for the rest. There are nearly 900 bats and 48,000 baseballs each season. Chase Utley used the most bats. "He's very selective about the wood and will go through a lot of bats over the course of a season," Dan said. Baseballs are manufactured by Rawlings Sporting Goods Company. There are as many as 30 bat companies. "We buy from 10," Dan volunteered.

For a night game, Dan arrives at the clubhouse around noon. "Players and coaches begin filing in shortly, and we're there for any equipment they may need that's not in their lockers," he explained. He heads home around midnight. During day games he has an 8:00 AM arrival and stays until an hour or two after the game.

Before entering the Phillies clubhouse, there's a room on the left that houses three large washers, two large and two smaller dryers. Some laundry is hung to dry on multiple racks. "When the team gets back from a road trip, we unpack the truck and bags and wash the undergarments right away because they will be needed the next day," Dan said. "We do the road uniforms the next day because we won't be using them until the next trip. After a home game, it's the opposite, except on get-away day."

In mid-afternoon of the first day of a series, Dan unpacks four trunks for the umpires with each weighing about 100 pounds. There's laundry to be done in time for that day's game. Each umpire has his own shin guards, chest protector, mask, and shoes for when he works home plate. The umps get to the park around two hours prior to game time. "We have cheesesteaks for them from the visiting clubhouse kitchen as a pregame meal. For day games we have breakfast, pancakes, eggs, the whole works. The home-plate umpire will have something lighter. They are also entitled to tickets for the game, and that needs to be done as soon as they arrive," Dan continued. After the game food is provided again through the visiting clubhouse.

Umpires work only one series and then move on. They travel as a four-man crew. "The crew chief will decide which flight or train they will take after the final game of a series. The other three have specific travel duties, depending upon seniority. One makes transportation reservations, another the hotel accommodations, and the fourth car rental for when they arrive in the next city," Dan explained. For postgame food on get-away day, he packs a bag for each to take with them—sort of like sending your child off to school with a brown bag lunch. DHL handles transporting their trunks to the next city. Dan will call DHL and request a time for the driver and truck to arrive at Citizens Bank Park, usually targeting an hour after the anticipated end of a game. If there is a rain delay or extra innings, the driver sits by patiently watching the game on TV with Dan.

The umpire facilities include a dressing area. Around the corner is a lounge that has a cooler for beverages, a sofa and matching chairs, table and chairs, and a table for snacks, including bubble gum. A laptop sits on a work station next to the cooler. "The home-plate umpire is required to check after every game the calls made on each pitch," Dan said. On the opposite side of the room is a large monitor mounted on the wall, a VCR/DVR, and keyboard. "I tape every game, and the crew will review unusual plays in the game. When they eject someone, they have to file a

Chase Utley, who is the 34th player in World Series history to hit a home run in his first at-bat, used more bats during the course of the season than any other Phillie. (Miles Kennedy)

written report with complete details down to the inning, outs, balls, strikes."

Once in a rare moon, an umpire will be without his equipment because of a shipping problem or an umpire being called up from the minors at the last minute. "Major League Baseball supplies a trunk of umpire equipment—everything but black socks and shoes. I then need to call New York for the combination of the lock, and we can have him in official gear," Dan said.

Another one of his early afternoon chores is rubbing 12 dozen baseballs for the game. A special mud from a New Jersey creek is used to remove the shine and slickness of the balls. For washing and drying the umpire's gear, Dan uses the Phillies' laundry room. Asked if he lugs a big laundry basket, "Nope. I have a blue laundry cart, the last piece of equipment from Veterans Stadium that's still in use."

## MANAGER, HOME CLUBHOUSE

Phil Sheridan, a 1992 graduate of Notre Dame University, where he was the senior student equipment manager of the football team that played in three consecutive bowls, is the manager of the home clubhouse. Counting spring training and the regular season, one year he figured out he did more than 3,000 loads of laundry for the Phillies. When he's home with his family, his wife, Jenn, is happy to pass on the laundry chore to her husband. "She told me you're much better at it," said Phil, chuckling. With six young ones, there's plenty of laundry but well short of 3,000 loads. But from February through late October (longer if the Phillies are in the postseason) he spends more time in ballparks than his home.

After helping pack equipment in January to be trucked to spring training in Clearwater, Florida, Phil will abandon Philly for Bright House Field about a week before the truck arrives. "We usually load the truck on a Friday so that it gets to Clearwater by Sunday," he explained. "Dan [O'Rourke], Kevin [Steinhour], and some of our clubhouse staff will complete the loading. Dan and Kevin then fly to Clearwater. We unload on a Sunday and begin unpacking right away."

Once the season begins, he arrives at Citizens Bank Park around 11:45 AM for a 7:05 night game. "Kevin will make two road trips. Dan and I split the rest," Phil said. Dan spends time in the clubhouse but also oversees the umpire's room. Phil, along with five seasonal clubhouse assistants, begins his day stocking the player lockers with their game uniforms and undergarments. "Everything a player wears is numbered, so we can easily sort it. We have so many red T-shirts. If a player was missing one, we'd have to search 40 lockers. We don't have time. That's why we number everything right from the beginning. When Aaron Nola came up, first thing Dan did was unpack his bag and start numbering

No. 27. Nola also needed new T-shirts, jackets, hoodies, shorts, socks, and athletic supporters. Each was numbered before Dan put everything in Aaron's locker."

Every player has two complete uniforms while pitchers and catchers will have extra jerseys. Uniforms and undergarments worn for batting practice get washed as soon as the game starts. Some players will shower before a game, creating a laundry load of towels. Once the game starts, Phil and a couple of assistants head for the laundry room where a flat-screen TV is mounted on the wall. "It helps us follow the game," Phil explained. "If a catcher's mask breaks, we can see that and quickly replace it. Plus, we're fans and like to know what is going on."

Once the game has ended, Phil and his troops go around and pick up dirty uniforms. Undergarments are tossed into carts back to the laundry room. Uniforms are washed and hung to dry overnight. Undergarments get the dryer treatment. "We have various chemicals to remove grass stains, dirt stains, and pine tar that gets on uniforms. I'm popular with Little League moms if I'm at one of their games," he said, laughing. Every player showers after games, creating as many as five loads of towels.

Once all the athletes have left and the clubhouse is free of clutter, Phil and his crew leave. That's usually one and a half hours after the game has ended. There's a different postgame routine on getaway games. "While BP is going on, we'll put each player's equipment bag in front of his locker," he said. "Once they come off the field, the players will begin packing undergarments, an extra baseball glove, sunglasses, toiletries, extra shoes, batting gloves, and the like. Depending on where we are going and the weather, we pack light or heavy jackets and sweatshirts. The bat boy's job after each game is to clean the players' shoes and put them in the lockers. On getaway games he packs them in each player's bag. Each hitter also has a bat bag to pack. Players will finish packing after they showered and shaved." The gray road uniforms were packed in red trunks earlier that day. Medical equipment and trunks of video equipment are part of the traveling party.

Following security screenings the players board buses for a trip to the airport. Phil will ride in the equipment truck and will oversee the loading of luggage and all equipment on the United Airlines charter aircraft. He then climbs the steps, finds his seat, and relaxes for a while. Weight of all the luggage and equipment is anywhere from 5,000 to 6,000 pounds. Phil's back down the steps to oversee the unloading after the aircraft has reached its destination city. "I'll peek in the aircraft luggage departments to make sure nothing was left in there. Sometimes it offends the crew, but I need to make sure." Two trucks will be there, one for the luggage that will be taken to the hotel and one for the equipment bags and trunks that will head for the ballpark where the visiting team's clubhouse staff is waiting to unpack everything. Phil rides in the luggage truck to the hotel and then follows through with the bellmen to make sure the luggage is taken to the rooms of the traveling party. There was a time he, Kevin, or Dan would go with the equipment truck to the ballpark. "That was in the prehistoric days of no cell phones," Phil said. "If the visiting clubhouse manager has a question, he'll call or send a photo of a trunk with which he's not familiar." The Phillies are one of the few teams that wears red shoes. "We carry a bag of red shoes of assorted sizes in case we get a new player on the trip."

When not traveling, Phil or Kevin or Dan get weekends off. During the week they "usually wander in the clubhouse about 9 to 10 in the morning and stay until 4 to 4:30. If the team is on the West Coast, it could be as late as 5 to 5:30 in case we get a call that something is needed from our clubhouse. The latest UPS pickup is 6:00 PM." Once the season has ended and the players have cleared out their lockers, which can take five to seven days, Phil and Dan will begin cleaning up and taking inventory of each piece of equipment and undergarment. Equipment managers attend baseball's winter meetings for a meeting of their own and visit displays by vendors. Ordering gear for next year is an offseason ritual, except for clothing provider Majestic that "will ask for an estimate of T-shirts, sweatshirts, jackets, and hoodies by the end of July during the season," Phil explained.

Packing and unpacking over the course of a baseball marathon season can create some unusual circumstances. "In a period of three days in 2006, we got Jamie Moyer, Jeff Conine, and Jose Hernandez," he recalled. "They wore the same size shoe. We only had one pair in their size. They passed them along to the next guy as their new shoe orders arrived. At one point each wore the same pair on their first day. Luckily, it was only one new player per day. We got to Yankee Stadium for a workout before the first game there in the 2009 World Series, and Raul [Ibanez] comes up to me, 'Phil, you won't believe this, but I forgot to pack my glove.' He borrowed one for that day. Fortunately, a Phillies employee was coming to the game the next day, and he brought the glove. We acquired Hunter Pence from Houston in late July of 2011. Players sign contracts with the various shoe companies to wear their brands. He was under contract with Reebok and wore black shoes in Houston. We had Nike and Under Armour, but he couldn't wear them. We had to spray his black shoes red for a couple of days until Reebok could get red ones for the start of a road trip in Denver," he revealed.

## DIRECTOR, VIDEO PRODUCTION

"You're our new video guy. Welcome aboard." That's the message a young Dan Stephenson got from Bill Giles after the 1981 Phillies season. While tending bar at Downey's restaurant, Stephenson met broadcaster Chris Wheeler, also a member of the team's public relations department. "Wheels" mentioned the Phillies' need for a video person after learning Stephenson had a small video business. Three weeks later Giles and his partners who had purchased the Phillies were having dinner at Downey's. Asked to tend bar, Stephenson first said no. "Then I remembered my chat with Wheels, and I changed my mind. I was a huge, hard-core fan, met the Pope [Paul Owens], one of the most memorable characters I've known. First time I met Giles, too."

His first assignment was to report to Clearwater, Florida, for spring training. Stephenson's job was to videotape Phillies hitters and pitchers. "I set up a camera behind home plate, using VHS tapes," said Stephenson, who became known to everyone at the Phillies as "Video Dan" or just "Vid." When the Phillies decided to send spring training interviews to TV stations back north, Vid was the cameraman responsible for sending the material. In the beginning he would have to hand-deliver a tape to the Tampa airport for a late-afternoon flight to Philadelphia. Hopefully, a flight attendant would take it off the flight and leave it at the check-in counter for a TV rep to pick up. In later years the interviews could be sent via satellite from the Home Shopping Network that is based in Clearwater. "Today it's all done by computer, which would have saved me from getting this gray hair," he said, laughing.

During the season he'd film hitters and pitchers at Veterans Stadium. Road games were taped at his home and broken down by him so that the players could check their at-bats or pitches when the team returned home. "When Mike Schmidt was in a slump, he'd take the tapes home to study, was always trying to figure out what was wrong. Joe Morgan looked at every pitch," Stephenson said. "Pete Rose and Lefty [Steve Carlton] never looked at video."

As technology changed over the years, so did Stephenson's job. His creative video skills were being used by the organization in other ways. "[In 1987] Schmidt was going to reach 500 home runs, needed five at the start of the season," Video Dan explained. "Mike Tollin, who had a video company in New York at the time and was a friend of the Phillies, thought there was a story there as Mike chased 500. Tollin needed a camera person for behind-the-scenes access and felt I was the right person. Starting late in spring training, I literally followed Schmidt everywhere at the ballpark. Up until then filming in the clubhouse was prohibited. I had to gain the trust of the players that this would be alright. I also knew there were boundaries not to be crossed."

The following year Tollin wanted to produce a video yearbook capturing the entire season. Video Dan again manned the camera while Tollin wrote the script. The result was *The Game's Easy, Harry,* narrated by Richie Ashburn and Harry Kalas. When Tollin moved on to producing movies in Hollywood, it opened a big door for Video Dan. "I went to David Montgomery in 1991 and asked if there was any way I could go from a part-time employee to full-time and take on the complete video yearbook production," he said. "David said, 'Go for it.'" Vid's been a one-man production crew ever since. "The story line on every season is different. I'd think of ideas as early as spring training and begin filming but wouldn't begin a storyboard, write, or edit the video until the season ended. Merchandising wanted the videos in time for the Christmas shopping season, which basically gave me two months." That resulted in very long days and sleepless nights. Admittedly, "Some days I wasn't the most pleasant person," he said. "The most enjoyable one was the 1993 Video Yearbook, *Whatever It Takes, Dude.* There were so many characters and misfits on that team. Major League Baseball Productions was producing video yearbooks for each team at the time. They wanted to do ours, but we said no...Although we lost the World Series, we were the most loved losing team and still very popular today. MLB said we would probably sell 5,000 if we lost and perhaps 20,000 if we won. Well, we sold 50,000."

The most pressure-packed video production happened in 2008. "The World Series went until October 29. Brad Lidge was the most logical [voice] since he was riding an unbroken streak of saves. I didn't want to ask for fear of jinxing him. My opening came after he struck out the last batter to win the series. At first he was hesitant, felt someone like Pat Burrell, who had been there longer was a better choice. I finally convinced him, but time was pressing. Instead of flying him to Philly to tape the narration, we arranged for him to go to a studio near his Denver home. I was able to listen on the phone. He did a great job, very few retakes," Vid said.

Kevin Camiscioli was brought aboard as the manager of video coaching in 1996, which had become a full-time job at home and on the road. It freed Video Dan to use his creative talents in other areas. His ideas and video skills were being folded into the Phillies advertising world. In addition to the season-long video yearbook, he began to produce documentaries. *Flashback: A Century of Phillies Baseball* won a Mid-Atlantic Emmy Award in 1999. He was nominated for others after that.

In-game features for PhanaVision at Veterans Stadium and Citizens Bank Park came under his umbrella. If a player or executive was being honored and a video tribute was requested, he did it. Young Richard Ashburn showed up one day with box full of 16 mm film his dad had taken in spring training and during the season. It sparked the idea for a documentary on the Hall of Famer from Tilden, Nebraska, called *Richie Ashburn—A Baseball Life*. Vid and Richard even went to Tilden to film the little town Ashburn so often mentioned. "Whitey was the most beloved sports figure in this town. Capturing his life was a no-brainer," Video Dan said. "One video I still want to do is the life of Mike Schmidt. I've got some great interviews over time in the can." More recently, he produced a video on the Philadelphia Stars of the old Negro League days. He's also the creative point man for the many Phillie Phanatic videos.

Video Dan has earned the respect and trust of the players, creating special relationships. His reputation was passed on to new players. That relationship was both an advantage and disadvantage. Players would cooperate with him, but occasionally, fellow employees believed the players would do anything for him on video. Vid did little things for the players that went a long way to build the relationship. The day Carlton was released, Video Dan was emotionally upset. "Few people knew the real Steve Carlton. He was witty, funny, and laughed a lot, except on the day he was going to pitch. He was on a different planet then. After his last game, I decided to tape comments from his teammates and send the video to him," Video Dan said. "So many alumni mention how appreciative they are to have the video to show to their kids who were very young when they played here."

His work station at the Vet was near the Phillies clubhouse. Players would drift in and out before, during, and after games. "Terry Mulholland is pitching a no-hitter [in 1990]. There's a superstition in baseball that no one mentions that there is a no-hitter going on. Come the eighth inning, I grabbed my camera to head for the dugout. I don't remember which players were in my office, but they barked, 'What are you doing?' I went to the dugout and stood way behind Nick Leyva. Nick, the coaches, and the players all glared at me, like, hey, get the hell out of here. I wanted to film the last out and was praying that it would happen. When Charlie Hayes caught the last out, I was never so happy."

When it came time to commemorate the 10th anniversary of the 1993 bunch, Video Dan came through with yet another video. "We had so much unused behind-the-scenes video from the clubhouse and trainer's room where they all went after games. Larry

Andersen and Kruk, two different birds, were the perfect pair to tell the story," he beamed.

Scott Palmer hosts a weekly pregame TV show during the season, *Behind the Pinstripes*. When video became part of www. phillies-com, the show was also posted on the website as well as other videos. Vid has experienced the 2008 World Series championships and parade, the beginnings and endings of Phillies legends, the closing of the Vet, and the opening of Citizens Bank Park plus a similar ballpark scenario in Clearwater. Two of his most emotional memories didn't involve bats and baseballs. "9/11 was such an emotional shock to everyone in this country. I felt incredibly helpless. When it was determined baseball would resume on September 17, I realized we were going to be one of the first games played," he said. "We decided a somber pregame event was needed. I quickly realized this could not be a Phillies-centered video. It needed to be about this game that is ingrained in this country. Ignoring copyright issues, I used video segments from the Ken Burns documentary, *Baseball*. For music Lee Greenwood's 'Proud to Be an American' fit perfectly. The game was on TBS nationally so a lot of people were tuned in. I can still see the tears flowing down Larry Bowa's cheeks that night."

The other involved Harry Kalas. "It was only fitting that Harry's memorial service be held at the ballpark. He loved the game, the players, and the fans. Very touching that the players and some of us got to lift his casket into the hearse. Harry left the ballpark for the last time, a lifetime Kodak moment." "High Hopes" was Harry's favorite song. After every Citizens Bank Park win, a video of Harry singing is played. Video Dan originally taped that after the Phillies won the National League East in 1993.

Video Dan's work station is a mess. "Organized chaos" is the way he described it. "One time I went to Clearwater for a few days in September to film the kids we had in the Florida Instructional

League. While I was gone, Kent Tekulve and Steve Bedrosian cleaned up my office. I couldn't find anything for a year," he said. There's a room on the service level at Citizens Bank Park labeled "Audio/Video" and located adjacent to the Media Room. It's the video services production room, originally designed to accommodate two employees, but it's now occupied by seven. To the rear tucked in a corner is a small separate room—Video's Dan office. There are three monitors, an audio mixer, walls decorated with framed photos of his heroes, and a tall beige file drawer. There are piles and stacks of VHS cassettes of all formats and CDs. "Yes, but I know where everything is...almost everything," Dan said. "Do me a favor, don't let Tekulve and Bedrosian in here. They'll mess up everything."

## MANAGER, VIDEO COACHING SYSTEM

When asked how many pitches he sees in a season, Kevin Camiscioli laughed. "I'm not sure I really want to know," said the manager, video coaching system. He watches every pitch on a monitor through the entire Phillies' 162-game season. It is all part of a video coaching system that is used by the players, the manager, and coaches.

When Kevin joined the Phillies in 1996, the system used VHS tapes. "If the pitching coach came to me and asked to see every curveball a certain pitcher threw, I'd say, 'Okay, but it will take a week to get it to you,'" Camiscioli said. In the late 1990s, digital video came along and so did a program called BATS, a real gamechanger. "It really enabled us to generate a lot more scouting reports, spray charts, pitch tendencies, you name it," he explained. "Chase [Utley] was a student of the game. He'd come in the video room around two to three in the afternoon and look at video of that night's pitcher, his at-bats against him in the past, and the pitcher's other starts, not necessarily against the Phillies. Other players use it, too, but Chase spent the most time. [Roy] Halladay was big on video studies, too."

Every room at Citizens Bank Park has a home-plate-shaped sign mounted next to the door. "Video Coaching" identifies the room located about 20 feet behind the Phillies dugout. It is Kevin's home away from home. He sits at a console of monitors and keyboards. A large monitor is mounted on the wall, one of four in the room. Directly in front of him is the Major League Baseball replay monitor. With his right hand on a pen pad, he charts the type of pitch, location, velocity, and result. His left hand manipulates a keyboard to the MLB replay system. Audio comes from Phillies telecasts or broadcasts.

Elsewhere in the room are seven individual computer monitors, where players can hunker down and check their at-bats or pitches or the enemy. Catchers Carlos Ruiz and Cameron Rupp will view video of the enemy hitters they will be facing. Coaches also use the facilities, checking the time an enemy pitcher takes to deliver a pitch—important base-stealing information. They also view video of enemy outfielders for arm strength and accuracy. "We can also download video to iPads so players and coaches can study at their lockers, in hotels, on buses, and at home," Camiscioli added.

Kevin normally gets to the park around noon to 1:00 PM for a night game. Marc Sigismondo, coordinator, video coaching starts setting up for the day as early as 9:00 AM. "There's three of us involved, Marc, myself, and Brett Gross [video coaching representative, minor league operations]," Kevin said. "It's not a one-man operation anymore." Once a game has ended, there's about another hour of work, including maintenance before heading home.

Camiscioli also travels with the team. In addition to bats, gloves, uniforms, and the like, four red trunks of video equipment go with the team, which contain, among other items: 10 laptops, a large external hard drive, and plenty of cables. Not every visiting clubhouse has a separate room, so he'll sometimes set up in the middle of the clubhouse. During games, both at home and on the road, hitters often check out video of their last at-bat. Pitchers usually watch the video from their outing after the game or the next day, according to Kevin.

In 2014 Major League Baseball began instant replay, which Kevin calls another "gamechanger." When manager Pete Mackanin wants to question an umpire's call, Larry Bowa will get on a telephone in the dugout. He's calling Kevin. "Every team has a system called Hawkeye," he explains. "It provides 15 different camera angles. It is like a huge DVR, forward, backward, zoom in, zoom out, pause, overlays, and split screens." Kevin relays what he sees to Bowa, who lets Mackanin know.

Kevin last saw a game from the stands at Veterans Stadium in 1993. Three years later he became glued to a monitor. For personal reasons he's missed a few games but not many. One wondered what he does when nature calls. "You have to be quick, real quick," he said. "ESPN and FOX have longer breaks between innings. That makes it a little easier."

For years all major league teams had an advance scout, someone who scouted the next team on the schedule. It was a lonely job and one of endless ballparks, airports, hotels. Three games in Los Angeles followed by two games in San Francisco, and four in San Diego, for example. Craig Colbert was the most recent Phillies scout assigned to that duty. In 2014, as a supplement, Kevin and Marc began sending Colbert videos of every Dodgers game that season when he was about to begin a three-game series in Los Angeles. It enabled Colbert to file more detailed reports because he was seeing multiple games instead of three. The next year the Phillies joined a growing list of clubs who do all their advance scouting through video. They no longer send a scout on the road.

This is the third gamechanger. The fourth is the video coaching in the Phillies' minor league system, a project Gross oversees. Each minor league ballpark in the Phillies system is equipped with four stationary cameras. Lehigh Valley and Reading may have more camera angles as Triple A and Double A will have some games on television. All four fields at Carpenter Complex are also equipped with four cameras. It's another tool for minor league managers and coaches to use in instructing and developing players. The Phillies have roving instructors who visit different teams. The video is highly beneficial to them. The system allows the Phillies to build a complete video library of every minor league player. And it allows Mackanin and his players to see a pitcher they are facing for the first time who was just brought up from the minor leagues. Before the major league manager would call the Triple A manager to see if his team faced this certain pitcher. A verbal report was the best-case scenario.

For the record Kevin saw 47,565 pitches in 2014...unless he blinked.

## RADIO BROADCASTER

A sports buff, Scott Franzke enrolled at Southern Methodist University in his hometown following high school graduation. "Initially, I had visions of being a writer but became more interested in broadcasting and switched my major," he said. "We didn't have a baseball team, so I did the play-by-play of basketball and football." After graduating in 1994, Scott began his radio career as a talk show host on Prime Sports Radio. Three years later, he was a part-time pregame and postgame host for the Texas Rangers. "I really wanted to do radio play-by-play of baseball, but all I had as a demo tape was a couple innings from a high school game. Eric Nadel [Rangers broadcaster] told me I needed to get some experience and suggested I go to the minor leagues. I received an offer

Scott Franzke joined the Phillies broadcasting team in 2006 after starting his big league career with the Texas Rangers in 1997. (Miles Kennedy)

from the club in Eugene, Oregon, but it was a short-season rookie league. I decided to go to the winter meetings in Nashville and look for a minor league job, not much luck."

He eventually landed a broadcasting job with the Kane County [Illinois] Cougars, a Class A team  in the Midwest League in 1999. After three seasons there, he returned to the Rangers as their full-time studio host of the same pregame and postgame shows and occasional fill-in play-by-play announcer. Now armed with a much better demo tape, Franzke began searching for play-by-play opportunities. "There's a website, Call of the Game, which posts job opportunities and other news in broadcasting. It was there that I learned the Phillies were looking for an announcer because Tom McCarthy left to go to the Mets. But before that I interviewed with the Astros and never heard back from them. I was doing news briefs early in the morning when a friend called, 'Sorry to learn you didn't get the Houston job.' I was crushed. I thought it was the perfect job being that I'm from Texas."

Franzke sent Rob Brooks, Phillies manager of broadcasting, a demo tape and was interviewed after the 2005 baseball season. "I had a job with Triple A Albuquerque and had an airline ticket to fly to Pawtucket for an interview for another Triple A play-by-play job. The Phillies job included pregame and postgame shows and the middle three innings of play-by-play." Scott said good-bye to Texas and a year later was the Phillies' main radio play-by-play guy, working with Larry Andersen. Broadcasting 162 regular season games provides the opportunity to fill the air while not being overly talkative. Preparation is vital, and Scott spent hours filling notebooks. "I had a binder for every club," he says. "For a three-city road trip, it meant carrying four, one for the Phillies and one each for the teams on the trip. At home it was easier."

Nearly six years ago, he came across a computer program on the Internet called OneNote. It has simplified his daily game preparation and provided a convenient source for everything he needs while he is on the air. "Day-by-day stats of every Phillies player, a section for each team, and room for notes, clips, you name it," Scott added, "it eliminated the hard copy." Everything is loaded in a Microsoft Surface Pro 3 tablet. "Before I would have a page for every Braves pitcher, for example, and most of their players. I'd write whatever notes I could find about a particular player, things I couldn't find elsewhere or stories I had heard about them. If a player got traded in the offseason, I'd simply move him from one binder to another. If it happened during the season and I was on the road, his page was back home. Now, I can move players on OneNote anytime," he continued.

Finding, copying, and pasting information is year-round for Scott. "I can browse the Internet all winter, find notes and stories about our players and visiting players in magazines, newspapers, websites. Once I see something of interest, I simply send it to OneNote. I may have found a story in December and won't need it or use it until June, but it's there. I can also send emails during the season that relate to a player right to OneNote. When the moment comes where I have some time to talk about players, I have all the information right in front of me electronically, not reams of paper." During the season he'll prepare for that night's game at home before heading to the ballpark. "I don't camp at my desk for hours, just 10 to 12 minutes here and there," he said. "On the road I have a lot more time because I'm not involved in errands, paying bills, lining up babysitters, and a 'honey-do' list for around the house."

For a 7:05 night game at Citizens Bank Park, he usually arrives by 3:30 PM. He'll spend time in the dugout, listening to the manager's media session, tape a pregame show with the manager, and then head for the broadcasters' workroom, which is located about 20 feet from the Phillies broadcast booth. Each team provides pages of notes that he'll review plus a packet that includes every possible statistical breakdown except how well a player hits when there is a full moon. There's also banter between the Phillies broadcasters who are in the workroom. Some of it is informational, some of it is needling, and some of it may be playing a prank on a broadcaster who is not present. If he needs more information on a visiting player, he'll chat with their broadcasters.

Scott's workstation during home games is the Richie Ashburn broadcast booth located directly behind home plate and adjacent to the Phillies' TV booth. Looking out at the field, Scott sits on the right side, and Andersen sits on the left. The engineer is stationed at an elevated table directly behind Scott. When the clock strikes seven, he opens his tablet and is ready for work: *From Citizens*

*Bank Park where the Phillies today play the Milwaukee Brewers in the final game of a three-game series. Welcome everybody on a beautiful night for baseball.*

When a rookie, Taylor Jungmann, is starting for the Brewers, it is the first time the Phillies or Franzke has seen the tall right-hander. Scott clicks on Jungmann's page, which contains basic information and stats but also multiple notes. Written in red ink in the upper right-hand corner are the types of pitches Jungmann throws and their speeds. It was posted by Scott earlier that day. He also highlights some notes by touching the screen: Jungmann graduated from Georgetown High School in Georgetown, Texas, he pitched for the University of Texas, and his batterymate was Cameron Rupp. Later in the same game, Corey Knebel relieves Jungmann. "L.A., did you know that Knebel went to the exact same high school and was on the same staff at Texas with Jungmann?" Scott reveals.

Franzke keeps tabs on every major league game and will post notes. "There may be an interesting play or situation in a White Sox-Tigers game that is different. There are times that the same situation arises in a Phillies game and I can use the information to further explain it to the fans...and L.A. (Andersen)," he said wryly. Franzke and Andersen have formed an entertaining on-the-air duo.

When Scott was asked if he knew much about L.A. before coming to Philadelphia, he smiled, "I remember seeing a picture of him with sunflower seeds pasted on his face. A very good friend of mine is a big, big Red Sox fan, so I was well aware L.A. was traded to the Sox for Jeff Bagwell. L.A. is viewed by many as a funny guy, a clown. But he's developed into an exceptional analyst on radio and a very good friend. You never know what to expect in a baseball game. It's the same working with L.A."

## MINOR LEAGUE MANAGER

Dusty Wathan has been with the Phillies minor league managing/coaching ranks for eight seasons. He started in Williamsport in 2008 and now manages the Double A Reading Fightin' Phils. He's been around the game since he was a youngster as his dad, John, was a big league catcher for 10 seasons with Kansas City and a manager in the majors for six seasons. Dusty followed his dad's career, spending 14 years in pro ball as a catcher, including a three-game stint with the Royals in 2002 and then turning to managing in the minors. Dusty was seven years old when the Phillies defeated the Royals and his dad in the 1980 World Series. Dusty has vague memories of the series. "I remember watching the games on TV," he said. Pausing and chuckling, "What I remember most about that fall was the TV show, *Family Feud*, between the Royals and Phillies. Dad got all 209 points on the bonus round. People still talk about that."

Dusty, his wife Heidi, and their four children reside in suburban Charlotte, North Carolina. "Reside" is limited to September through February for Dusty. His offseasons have consisted at various times of working for UPS, giving private catching lessons, and participating in baseball clinics in Brazil. Each minor league team provides living quarters and a car for its manager. Heidi and the kids are able to join Dusty during the summer months. Each person in player development is given three days off during the season by the Phillies. In 2015 Huck, his oldest son at 12, played in a youth baseball tournament in Cooperstown, New York, and Dusty's days off were spent in Cooperstown watching Huck play.

Dusty usually leaves his Wyomissing apartment for FirstEnergy Stadium around noon for a 7:05 night game. He has a small office in the clubhouse area with a desk and chair, blue metal locker, red file drawer, black leather couch, and refrigerator. A laptop and printer take center stage on the desk and are heavily used. On the side of the file drawer is the Reading schedule. A black magic marker crosses off each game. His three coaches, Mickey Morandini, Frank Caccitore, and Dave Lundquist, have a dressing area right around the corner. The athletic trainer is Aaron Scott,

## Wathan's Daily Pregame Schedule

2:00 PM    Jerome Williams (on a rehab assignment), Tom Windle, and Mark Leiter are on the mound participating in pitcher's fielding practice, commonly known as PFP. Lundquist stands at home plate with a bag of baseballs and hits various types of ground balls to each pitcher. Aaron (athletic trainer) is a stationary first baseman. After catching the ball, he flips each near the coaches' box. When the drill is finished, each pitcher picks up the balls and puts them back in the bag. Williams is a big leaguer, but he doesn't act that way. "He's been terrific with the guys," Dusty said. "First day here we had a morning game, he did his work and stuck around."

2:24 PM    Pitchers gather in right field with Justin (conditioning coach) for a little fun, Frisbee tossing.

2:30 PM    Players do calisthenics.

2:40 PM    A black sliding mat is laid out in the first-base coaches' box. One-by-one each pitcher runs from right field and practices sliding. Ethan Martin gets up and grabs his right knee, "Got a sliding burn." Before sliding mats, it would have been a grass burn.

2:51 PM    All pitchers run the bases. Starting at home plate, one pitcher will run straight through the first-base bag. Another, about five feet behind, will circle the bases. Later, there are drills on scoring from second base.

2:58 PM    Everybody goes back to right field for long tossing, which is followed by bullpen side work for Ben Lively (35 tosses), Joely Rodriquez (15 tosses), Tyler Knigge just off the disabled list (12 tosses), and Colton Murray (12 tosses).

3:06 PM    Third baseman Harold Martinez and two second basemen, KC Serna and Brodie Greene, work on turning double plays with Mickey as the hitter/instructor. Before the next drill, Dusty chats with Dave and hits tennis ball pop-ups to his son, Huck. Check that. He tries to hit tennis ball pop-ups. The success rate was low.

and the conditioning coach is Justin Miloszewski. When Reading plays another National League team, Dusty will stay in the dugout, and Mickey coaches third. If they are playing an American League team, Dusty is at third and Mickey at first. Frank charts hitters, and Dave handles the pitching staff.

3:30 PM    The rest of the position players take the field. They begin various run-the-bases drills, followed by long toss. During long toss, Dusty, a former catcher, stations J.P. Crawford at second base while two catchers, Andrew Knapp and Rene Garcia, practice throwing to second. Knapp is two years removed from Tommy John surgery on his right arm and works daily to build up arm strength.

4:00 PM    Batting practice starts. Well, this is when it is supposed to start. On this hot and humid July day in Reading, the skies begin pouring, and 25 male and female Reading employees roll out the tarp. There's no BP, but each team, Reading and Portland, in this case, will hit in their respective indoor batting cages. Dusty will throw a round of BP daily, sometimes twice but not today. There's also a weight room in the right-field corner of the stadium, which is used by both teams during the rain.

Dusty returns to his office for another cup of coffee, a bite to eat, and more administrative work. A major league manager is subject to the friendly world of media interviews for both pregame and postgame, but it's different in Double A ball. For Dusty his pregame media sessions at home will often take place in the dugout and the postgame in his office, depending upon the volume of reporters. On the road, media numbers are greatly reduced; it's sometimes zero. Eric Scarcella, Reading's public relations director, will schedule pregame interviews during the time the visiting team takes BP. It could involve Dusty or a player or two. With a small clubhouse, Eric has player interviews take place in the concourse outside the clubhouse. Forty-five minutes prior to game time, players are left to prepare mentally for the game.

Following each game, Aaron will email an injury report to Dusty and others in baseball development. Dusty will check with Aaron each pregame for an update. He'll also meet with Dave about the pitchers who are available. Once that's done Dusty prints the batting order on an 8"x13" lineup card. Copies are posted in the clubhouse and dugout. The next printing job includes three smaller lineup cards—one for his back pocket, one for the umpires, and one for the visiting manager.

He puts on a gray Fightin' Phils T-shirt with "62" on the back in big white numerals. Charcoal gym shorts and a powder blue cap with a yellow script "B" is the team's pregame uniform. (B is for "Baseballtown," what Reading is known as.) In the minor leagues, especially when a team is at home, there is extra work done on the field every day. Chatting on a cell phone, Dusty will observe from a seat in the stands behind home plate before migrating to the field.

After each game each minor league manager and pitching coach will file two reports. One is emailed to the Philadelphia office, where it gets distributed the following morning to all executives and everyone in baseball development and scouting. The other is a verbal report, which is recorded and accessible by those traveling.

In addition to the basic game information—runs by inning, totals, weather conditions, etc.—Dusty will add comments on the performance of the catcher (dropped balls, passed balls, wild pitches, stolen base attempts, speed of throws to second, etc.). Every batter has three columns: hitting, defense, and base running. Comments are always supplied in the hitting column. For example, on left fielder Cam Perkins it reads: "line drive single to right, RBI double to right-center, robbed on a 5–3 play". Regarding defense on Crawford, it reads: "464 dp good turn; one of the best double plays I have ever seen to end the game." And for base running of Brock Stassi, it reads: "bad jump on contact with SS half way." Dusty's part of the report ends with this game summary: "Great job by the pitching staff on a bullpen day. O'Sullivan came in with runners on 1st/2nd 1 out and gave up a broken-bat single for a run before preserving the lead by getting two ground balls in the 8th and then with the help of his defense threw up a zero in the 9th for the save. RBI double by Perkins and a good situational at-bat by Serna ended up being all we needed; good team win. Great end to the ball game with an unbelievable double play Serna to Crawford to Stassi with tying run on third."

The length of Lundquist's reports depends upon the number of pitchers used in the game. At the top he lists the scheduled starters for the next five games. That is followed by the pregame side work, which was covered earlier. And plenty of details, including the pitcher's line for the night, number of pitches per inning, release times, types of pitches thrown (fastball, curve, slider, split, change, other). Each pitch is broken down by grade, number of balls and strikes, command, quality movement, mph (low, high, average), swings/misses, swings/misses percentages, and a comment on each pitcher. For Reinier Roibal, the starter, it reads: "got stronger as he went. fb showed good late life with angle. slider stayed up in zone early, tightened up later. cb had good tilt. got into a good rhythm in 2nd inning and maintained into 4th. looked good tonight."

Following a shower, Dusty exits his office, generally an hour and a half after the last out. He either goes back home to the apartment or boards a bus. Asked about the most rewarding part of being a manager, he smiled and said, "Sending a kid to the next level or the big leagues and seeing their dreams come true." How about the opposite end of the spectrum? "Releasing a kid. You spend a lot of time with them. They become like sons. It is the worst part of job." Pausing, he added part two: "Long bus rides. We had three trips to Portland [Maine] this season. Once we left after a night game here, we got there at 7:30/8 the next morning and played at six that night." There's a Reading tradition of playing one 9:35 AM game every season. "I like those. We're 4–0. Besides, I was mostly a back-up catcher in the minors. I got to play on day games," he said, laughing.

The life of a minor league manager includes a revolving roster. The season opening roster won't be the same for the last game. Players come and go, but adjustments must be made. "The goal is send them up and keep winning," Wathan said. The 2015 roster certainly continued to change. Elvis Araujo, Aaron Nola, Aaron Altherr, and Adam Loewen began with him and eventually wound up in the majors. Jesse Biddle, Kelly Dugan, Gabriel Lino, and Brian Pointer advanced to Triple A. Joely Rodriquez, the lone player on the Phillies 40-man roster, took the opposite route. KC Serna went Double A, Triple A, and then back to Double A; he began as the shortstop and ended at second base. Carlos Alonzo, the incumbent second baseman, played 12 games and missed the rest of the season because of a knee injury. Roman Quinn, the switch-hitting center-field speedster, was injured on June 12 and never returned. He was replaced by Destin Hood, a minor league acquisition. Zach Eflin spent two weeks with Team USA in the Pan Am Games. J.P. Crawford, Andrew Knapp, Brodie Greene, Reinier Roibal, Edubray Ramos, Angelo Mora, and Dylan Cozens began the season in Clearwater. Starting pitcher Tom Windle moved to the bullpen on June 30. Ethan Martin came out of the organization's rehab program and pitched once at Clearwater before moving up to Reading on July 20. Jake Thompson, Nick Pivetta, Jimmy Cordero, and Nick Williams came over to the Phillies organization in July trades. First baseman Brock Stassi and left fielder Perkins were the only players who were at the same positions on Opening Day and the last championship playoff game.

## MID-ATLANTIC REGIONAL SUPERVISOR

A first baseman at Villanova University, Gene Schall was selected by the Phillies in the fourth round in 1991. He spent from 1991 to 2002 in the minors, where he hit. 285, and parts of two seasons in the majors with the Phillies, where he hit .252 in 52 total games from 1995 to 1996. Traded to the White Sox for Mike Robertson on January 31, 1997, he later returned to the Phillies organization, ending his playing days with Scranton/Wilkes-Barre in 2002.

Following that 12-year pro career, Schall returned to Villanova to complete a bachelor's degree in business with a minor in psychology. He needed an internship, and there was only one opening...in the IT department. "Not knowing anything about computers, I took it, got assigned to the help desk. You can imagine how much help I was," he said, laughing. Mike Arbuckle (assistant general manager/scouting and player development) reached out to Gene to see if he was interested in getting back into the game. "I was but told Mike I didn't want to be in uniform as I had enough of that and I didn't want an office job. Mike replied, 'That makes you a scout.'"

In 2008 a new career was launched as an area scout for the Phillies, looking at amateur talent in Pennsylvania, Ohio, New York, and South Jersey. The next year Gene was promoted to regional supervisor. His territory was the eastern part of the country from Florida to Canada. He assumed the title of Mid-Atlantic regional supervisor in 2014, overseeing three area scouts. There are four regional supervisors, two scouting coordinators, and the director of amateur scouting administration. The staff includes 16 area scouts, 18 independent contractors (who receive a stipend and expenses), and a bushel barrel of associate scouts also referred to as "bird dogs." That group consists of coaches, umpires, and friends who will let the area scout know if there is a player who is a candidate to follow.

Yet another phase of the team's amateur scouting world is international scouting, headed by Sal Agostinelli. Scouts and independent contractors cover Venezuela, Panama, Dominican Republic, Antilles, Mexico, Aruba, Colombia, Korea, Italy, and the Pacific Rim. The signing period in the Latin American countries begins in early summer. Players in these areas are not subject to the annual summer draft. The Major League Baseball season generally begins in April and ends in October. With the exception of a few weeks of down time, Schall's life, and that of a scout, is January through December. He explains: "In the middle of January, Johnny [Almaraz] will have a three-day meeting at Citizens Bank Park with the coordinators, area supervisors, and baseball administration staff. It is the first step in preparing for the draft. We zero in on the top 10 to 20 kids we will want to follow. Around the third week of January, junior colleges and high schools in Florida, the Southwest, and far west begin playing. Division I college programs start in February. It cranks up even more as we get into March."

Airplanes, car rentals, hotels, games, and players consume Gene's schedule. In April of 2015, a meeting with Almaraz, coordinators, and area supervisors took place in Dallas. "We reviewed the top players that might be available when we select 10th in the first round and 48th in the second round," Gene said. "Through the area scouts, we learn of players who have gone backward or new players to consider." That same group begins to double-check the top prospects no matter where they are located in the country. They'll double back again on these players in early May before they set up shop in the draft room at Citizens Bank Park about 10 days before the draft begins. "Johnny believes the more eyes, reports, angles, and information will help us in slotting the players," Gene said.

While the naked eye is still No.1 in judging a player, technology has provided additional tools in judging players. "The information that is available today is mind-boggling—10 times more than was there five to seven years ago. The radar gun helps, but Louisville Sluggers let you know how hard the kid is throwing," he said. "We have video of almost every player. Colleges and even high schools have multiple video cameras on the fields, providing various views. Every high school league and college conference has all kinds of statistics. Through analytics we can digest all this information and learn that a certain player may not play up to his stats. Analytics helps us paint a total picture."

Technology is a gigantic tool to help scouts and their schedules. "I don't know how scouts did it 20 to 30 years ago," Schall says. "One scout told me he'd be heading for a game, would pull off the road when he saw a pay phone, and call his voicemail to see if the game to which he's heading is still on or cancelled. Today we have the Internet, smartphones, iPads, and GPS. Communication is 24/7, real easy to stay in touch with each other. A text lets me know if the game is still on. My GPS takes me right to the field. No more paper maps," he said.

Baseball's summer draft in 2015 began June 8. Commissioner Rob Manfred stepped to the microphone: "With the 10th selection in the draft, the Phillies select Cornelius Randolph from Griffin High School, Griffin, Georgia." Randolph is from Schall's territory, which is specifically that of scout Aaron Jersild, whose area, in addition to Georgia, includes South Carolina, northern Florida, and Latin America. Gene explained, "Cornelius had been on our radar for two years of high school baseball and summer leagues. Aaron pegged him as a high pick right from the beginning. All of us saw him play multiple times. I probably saw him 25 to 30 times. We all agreed he was the most comfortable high school hitter in the country. Many high school players are question marks when it comes to hitting, inconsistency. This guy hit everywhere we saw him. As Johnny said on draft day, Cornelius is a ballplayer and he loves to play. We can see talent, but we need to learn what makes a kid tick. Getting to know the parents and teammates is extremely important. Aaron spent a lot of time with the family. Some kids view being drafted as sort of a novelty. Others want to play. You need to learn if a kid is willing to spend time developing his skills in the minor leagues riding buses and failing. Baseball is a game of failure. Being a great athlete, Cornelius was a shortstop/pitcher. We're looking to change his position. Is it left field? Third base? It will take some time to learn, but we believe his make-up will allow him to do this."

After the draft it's not exactly time for Schall to hit the beaches of Cape Cod. Instead, various high school showcase events are held across the country in the summer, keeping him busy. There will be tryouts for the USA Jr. Team (high schoolers) and Team USA (college players) in North Carolina. The Phillies scout all the college summer leagues. Gene will spend two weeks in Cape Cod... scouting. "Players eligible for 2016 and 2017 can be seen," he said. "It's the beginning for the next draft."

Late August turns into a short downtime for Gene and the amateur scouts before college programs reboot in September. Some high schools have fall ball. According to Gene, late October is the unofficial end of the scouting season. Pro scouting is a separate wing of Phillies baseball operations. Fifteen scouts cover the professional leagues strictly. Gene will dabble in pro scouting by spending some November and December time in the Venezuela and Dominican Winter Leagues.

The greatest joy of his job is finding future major leaguers. "Watching them go through the difficult development process and make it to the top," he said. All the travel doesn't get to him. "It's much easier than being a player riding buses and then having to play a game," Schall explained, though there are complications. "Sometimes I wake up in a hotel and don't know where I am. I've returned car rentals to the wrong company. Many times I arrive at an airport with tickets for three different destinations. It depends if a certain player is going to play, pitching rotations, and weather conditions. The airline people think I'm crazy. There have been times when I'm seated, the airplane doors close, and my destination needs to be changed. Something like seven to eight times the plane went back to the gate to let me off after I pleaded my case."

## PROFESSIONAL COVERAGE SCOUT

Always searching for baseball talent, Del Unser, one of the many 1980 World Champion heroes, is in the lineup among professional coverage scouts for the Phillies. Residing in Scottsdale, Arizona, he's been doing this since he was hired by then-general manager Ed Wade in 1998. Del started in pro baseball in 1966 when he was a first-round pick by the Washington Senators. He was a player in the minors for his first two seasons and a big leaguer from 1968 through 1982, spending two stints with the Phillies. He was a big weapon off the bench in the 1980 postseason with five hits, including three doubles and three RBIs. Following a year out of the game, he returned to the Phillies, first as a minor league hitting instructor, then as a big league coach, and finally as the farm director. His father, Al Unser, had a similar career as a player, manager, and scout.

Mike Ondo is the Phillies' director of professional scouting and is based in Citizens Bank Park. He oversees Del and six others as professional coverage scouts, including Sonny Bowers, Steve Jongeward, Jesse Levis, Jon Mercurio, Roy Tanner, and Dan Wright. But that's not all for Ondo as Ed Wade (special assignment baseball operations), Howie Freiling, Dave Hollins, and Craig Colbert (special assignment scouts) are also part of the professional coverage lineup. But, wait, there's more. Gordon Lakey (director major league scouting) and Charley Kerfeld and Bart Braun (special assistants to the general manager) have assignments that include big league and minor league coverage. "Ed asked me if I was interested in pro scouting after I left my front-office career," Unser said. "I was, but I was interested in moving out west to be near our daughters. We were a bit thin in pro scouting in California at the time so it worked out. After a while [my wife] Dale and I relocated to Scottsdale, which is a perfectly centralized location for my territory."

Del's teams include the Angels, Dodgers, Diamondbacks, and Padres (major league level); three Triple A teams, Salt Lake (Angels), Oklahoma City (Dodgers), and El Paso (Padres); four Double A teams, Mobile (Diamondbacks), Birmingham (White Sox), Biloxi (Brewers), Montgomery (Rays), and Mississippi (Braves); and five high Single A clubs, Rancho Cucamongo (Dodgers), High Desert Rangers (Rangers), Lake Elsinore (Padres), Lancaster (Astros), and Inland Empire (Angels). Toss in the mid-season California-Carolina League All-Star Game and coverage of the Arizona Fall League, which is held annually in his backyard.

Every Wednesday morning at 11, there's a conference call involving all the pro coverage scouts with baseball operations. "It's very valuable and informational," Unser said. "We discuss our needs at the time and are asked to offer opinions on players we have seen. The GM wants as much information as possible so he can make a decision. Not every scout sees a player the same way. We each have a snapshot of a player not a picture album. There are often strong disagreements, and that is healthy."

An avid golfer, Unser kidded when asked what his Januarys are like. He joked, "My handicap gets lower. There are some days blacked out for my family that month." Every major league team has a rehabilitation program for its injured players. "I'll spend time going to the various training sites in my area, looking at these players work out. Reports are filed in a database," he said. "Spring training begins in mid-February, and Ondo will assign certain teams in the Phoenix area to me. Early focus is on players who have no options. Lakey spends his spring in the area, and Kerfeld and Braun may come to Arizona to scout players we might be interested in. I'll provide Ondo with my schedule of minor league teams to see if it fits the overall schedule. We welcome other opinions, but it isn't beneficial to have two or three of us sitting in the stands scouting the same team at the same time."

Getting to the ballparks early to watch both teams take batting practice is something all pro scouts are instructed to do. "The first couple rounds of batting practice are the best. You get to see the hitters at their best. After that they get into long ball contests. That's a pet peeve of mine," Unser admitted. Unser's minor league schedule is lumped together depending upon his team's schedules. "The Southern League plays five-game series, which gives me a chance to see each of their starting pitchers. In 11 days I can see four different Southern League teams. I work it out in the California League by staying in an Oceanside hotel. That way I can see three teams in 12 days without changing hotels," he said.

When the major league All-Star Game comes around in mid-July, all Phillies pro scouts must have their reports in to Ondo in preparation for the July 31 trade deadline. "It's an exciting time for a scout. We're available for a phone call at any time and we're on alert to go here or there to get additional scouting views of players. During last year's Hamels trade discussions, I was assigned to Fresno, Houston's Triple A team."

Deals can still be made after the deadline as the Phillies did in 2015, sending Chase Utley, who cleared waivers, to the Dodgers for two prospects, Darnell Sweeney and John Richy. Both played for Dodgers minor league teams on Unser's coverage. "Sweeney's a versatile player with some speed, has a little alley pop, hits from both sides. His swing can be long, but in BP I've seen a shorter stroke, like him better as an outfielder," Unser said. "Richy has pitch-ability and could develop into a fourth or fifth starter, 88 to 90 on the gun, curveball has some bite, throws a slider and a cutter." Unser explained that radar guns are a valuable tool. "But they don't paint the entire picture on a pitcher," he said. "Does his fastball move? Does he have heart? Can he bear down with the game on the line? How does he handle adversity? How does he mix with his teammates?" After seeing pitchers, Dell will write his reports right after breakfast the next day.

August means getting back to a combination of his major and minor league teams again. The minors traditionally end in early September so it's one last chance to see those players. September's focus is on his four big league clubs. "Rosters expand in September, providing a chance to see some minor leaguers in the bigs," Unser said. Baseball has the Arizona Fall League in which the best prospects from each of the 30 organizations participate. Six teams of 35 players each begin a 32-game schedule in mid-October. That means more backyard baseball for Del. "Ondo will assign one of us to one team providing maximum coverage," Unser explained. In October of 2015, the Phillies baseball administration department, executives, major league manager and staff, player development, scouting, and trainers/conditioning coaches convened in Clearwater, Florida, for a four-day organization meeting.

Acknowledging that it is a total team effort in acquiring players, Unser admitted he was one who recommended Jeff Francoeur: "I saw him in El Paso in 2014. He still drove the ball as a hitter and had a good arm, talked with him at the Reno airport one time. I was impressed with his personality and thought he might be a fit for us as a right-handed hitter in the outfield, something we were lacking." Ondo's pro coverage scouts deserve the credit for coming up with Odubel Herrera, a minor leaguer with the Texas Rangers, who had never played above Double A ball. They liked his ability enough to select him in the Rule 5 draft in 2014. He turned in an impressive rookie season in 2015. Another find was left-handed reliever Elvis Araujo, who was signed as a minor league free agent on November 13, 2014. Like Odubel, Elvis had never pitched higher than Double A. Both are considered building blocks for the future.

## CLEARWATER BULLPEN GUARD

The Clearwater Threshers employ about 500 gameday employees at Bright House Field for spring training and their Florida State League season. One is Rand Stollmack, whose assignment is bullpen security during spring games. During the FSL season, he's an usher since a bullpen security person isn't necessary. Rand is a Clearwater native who went straight from high school to the Army as a paratrooper for 15 years. The construction world was next when he opted to make a career change in 1994 by becoming a groundskeeper for the Blue Jays in Dunedin, Florida, and followed that by joining the Rays in St. Petersburg before joining his good friend, Opie Cheek, with the Clearwater Threshers when Bright House Field opened in 2004. Opie is the award-winning field supervisor at Bright House and Carpenter Complex. Five knee surgeries for Rand ended a full-time career of long hours. So he became a game-day employee in 2012, assigned to the bullpens, which was one of his chores while on the grounds crew.

Wearing beige shorts, a navy blue BHF golf shirt, sneakers, and a red Phillies hat, Rand arrives at the ballpark around 9:30 AM for a 1:00 PM afternoon game. "I wipe down all the seats and railings in the bullpen," he explained. He then heads for the stands, where he'll wipe down three sections of seats before returning to his bullpen post for batting practice. First, he makes a quick stop in the media workroom to pick up the visiting team's roster. Towels, water cooler, and cups are supplied by the Phillies clubhouse. "You have to be very alert during BP because the balls come flying out here," he said while his eyes were glued to the field. "I need to know the visiting team's bullpen coach, always introduce myself, and let them know I'm here to help anyway I can." Know thy enemy.

On this day the Boston Red Sox are the visiting team. The padded gate to the bullpen is open during BP and closed once the game begins. It can only be opened or locked by pushing a couple of green control buttons on the back of the door. In other words no one can get in or out of the bullpen by pushing or pulling the door. When one enters the bullpen area, there are seven steps, a level area of about six feet in length, and three more steps. Up the first flight of steps is a chain-link fence and a door on the right, which is the visiting bullpen. On the level area, an opening on the right leads to a long row of green colored, high-top, patio-like chairs. Three more steps takes you to the back of the pen and another chain-link area, where the Phillies' bullpen is.

The pitching mounds are made out of dirt and clay while catchers will do their work on an artificial surface that looks like Mother Nature's dirt. In between there is rich, green grass. Two pitchers can warm up in each pen. A tarp is rolled up behind the mounds in case of rain. The players sit on the green high chairs. The first 12 are for the Red Sox; the last 12 (toward center field) are for the Phillies. A large trash can, a small gate to the Phillies pen, and a pile of towels separates the two groups. Each seating area has three red umbrellas, and each displays a Budweiser logo to try and shield the sun. On this particular day, the temperature at game time is 82 degrees with plenty of sun and sparse clouds. Tommy Layne, a Boston pitcher, carefully hung a towel over the edge of the umbrella in an effort to steal more shade. Another teammate followed. The walls that contain the bullpen area are concrete, which adds to the warmth, sort of like an outside sauna. A big, blue Powerade cooler sits on top of a concrete ledge between the two bullpens and is very popular.

Although Rand has his own high chair, he seldom sits. He's in constant motion. If you stand on the flat area on top of the seven steps, you can barely see the batter. The big videoboard is behind, but the line score can't be seen. The auxiliary scoreboard mounted on the upper first-base level is his link to the score and inning. A better glimpse of the field can be found standing at the back of the Phillies bullpen. The only other sightline is peeking through a three-inch opening in the bullpen door. Rand will station himself there when there are two outs. After the third out, he opens the door and stands on the warning track.

After the Red Sox hit, someone from their bullpen crew entered the field with two baseballs, one for the center fielder, who'll play catch with the right fielder, and another for the bull-penner to do the same with the left fielder. The same takes place when the Phillies are taking the field. For this particular game, the Phillies brought eight minor leaguers from Carpenter Complex as they had another roster playing a split-squad game in Tampa the same afternoon. Extra bodies were needed. One was Scott Harris, a left-handed pitcher who was the 27th round pick by the Phillies the previous summer. He didn't get in the game, but he did play catch with Grady Sizemore between innings. If he doesn't make it to the majors, he can at least tell his grandchildren he was on the field.

Rod Nichols was the Phillies' bullpen coach; Dana LeVangie was Boston's. Rand explains, "We have a phone line to the dugout for each team." The visitor's is mounted on a concrete wall outside their bullpen, and it's the same for the Phillies. On top of each gray box is a blue light. It will flash when the phone rings. The dugout phone also has a flashing light when ringing. It's sort of like being in K-Mart for the blue-light specials. Sometimes the phones don't work. Rod and Dana are armed with walkie-talkies. When Boston's phone rang, Dana was at the far end of the bullpen, standing behind a pitcher warming up. He didn't hear it or see the flashing light and didn't move. Rand got the attention of Dana, who yanked a walkie-talkie out of his back pocket.

Starting pitchers this particular day were Miguel Gonzalez for the Phillies and Justin Masterson for the Red Sox. Gonzalez did some long-tossing in the outfield before moving to the bullpen. The digital clock on the scoreboard registered 12:41. Carlos Ruiz was Miguel's catcher. Pitching coach Bob McClure stood behind the chain-link fence behind Ruiz. With his arms folded, Nichols was behind Miguel. Ken Giles stood off to the side watching every pitch. Masterson was a few minutes behind with his warm-up as his team batted first. After the Red Sox hit in the top of the first, Masterson began heading for the stairs. Before he did each of his 19 teammates in the pen gave him a fist bump.

"Things are pretty quiet early in the game," Rand volunteered. "About the third to fourth inning, it begins to get busy. They'll be a lot of moving around." Starting pitchers early in spring training are usually limited to two to three innings, and Rand was right-on. The next pitcher began stretching, loosening his arm before starting to throw.  By the fourth inning, both bullpens began to stir. Rand made sure the chain-link gates behind the catchers were closed so he wouldn't get nailed by a wild pitch. "We had a college game earlier this spring. The gate was open, a pitch came through the gate, and smashed the visiting bullpen phone," he said with eyes glued to each bullpen pitch.

After the second inning, more Phillies relievers came into their clubhouse. Meanwhile fans of all sorts were lined up by the fence above the Phillies' bullpen and were peeking down at the players. More fans were looking over the fence from the tiki bar and at the other end from the outfield berm. Cell phone cameras were in full use. They were wearing all kinds of Phillies gear, making it obvious who they were rooting for. "Hey, buddy, give me a ball," pleaded a man to anyone who would listen." Another said, "I could have caught that ball" after the Red Sox left fielder didn't, and "Go get 'em, Pap" after Papelbon finished his warm-up pitches. "Once in a while, one of the coaches will point out a rowdy fan," Rand said. "I'll ask the fan to back off or call security." On the whole, the fans were in line this day.

Rand is a huge baseball fan. Throughout his career, he's met a lot of players. "Relievers are the greatest. They have more personality. Remember M&M? [Brett Myers and Ryan Madson]? What a pair of crazies. College kids are the best. They are just having fun, enjoying the game, being in the bullpen. These guys are all about work," he said before laughing about one difference between the two. "College kids pick up their cups, pros toss 'em on the ground."

Big league bullpens have bathrooms. But that's not the case at Bright House Field. The nearest toilet is tucked under the stands in the left-field corner, adjacent to the entrance to the Phillies clubhouse. So relievers make their dashes between innings. "I always tell them they can come back quickly between batters," Rand said. "I'll be there to open the door, or they can wait until the half-inning is over." Once the game has ended, Rand has a few clean-up chores and then he's outta there. Most gameday staff get a break during the game. Rand doesn't. What about lunch? Pointing to a cooler in the concrete corner behind the Red Sox bullpen, "Peanut butter and jelly," he said.

## EXTENDED SPRING TRAINING

Once the seasons started for the Phillies and their top four affiliates (Lehigh Valley, Reading, Clearwater, and Lakewood), there was still baseball going on at the Carpenter Complex in Clearwater. It is called extended spring training. Prospects not advanced enough for the four affiliates continued working on their skills. In addition 22 young and inexperienced players from the Dominican Republic and Venezuela were brought aboard. By the middle of April in 2015, the number totaled 53. The players were divided into two teams, No. 5 and No. 6. More players will report to the complex once the Phillies begin signing players selected in the annual summer draft in early June.

The Williamsport staff of Pat Borders (manager), Les Lancaster (pitching coach), and Eddie Dennis (hitting coach) was in charge of one team. The Gulf Coast League staff—Roly deArmas (manager), Brian Sweeney (pitching), and Rafael DeLima (hitting)—had the other team. They were joined from time to time by Doug Mansolino (field coordinator), Mike Compton (senior advisor, player development), Carlos Arroyo (roving pitching instructor), and other roving instructors.

A fluctuating number of players worked out six days a week. Sundays were off. Why a fluctuating number? One player returned home to Mexico to play. Some returned to the Dominican Republic; others went to Venezuela. On occasion, a player was sent to Lakewood or Clearwater to fill in for an injured player and then returned. A few were told they no longer are members of the Phillies organization and bluntly released. The extended spring training players were housed in a motel on Route 19 not far from the complex. They walked to and from the hotel. Some rode bikes they purchased. A few had cars. Breakfast and lunch were served at the complex and dinner at Lenny's, a famous restaurant that serves breakfast and lunch only to the public. Borders, Lancaster, and Dennis stayed at the hotel. Curfew was 11:00 PM. The staff did room checks. By feeding the players, the Phillies were sure that players were eating balanced, nutritious meals, rather than fast food. They were schooled on proper diet, getting their rest, and drinking plenty of water during the hot days. Players had to sign in at dinner, a way for the staff to check.

The camp roster included seven players from the states. The rest were from Venezuela, Dominican Republic, Puerto Rico, Panama, and Colombia. The youngest was a 16-year-old infielder from Panama named Jonathan Arauz. Two 23-year-olds, right-handed pitchers Manaure Martinez and Nathan Thornhill, were the senior citizens, so to speak. The smallest was middle infielder Jose Antequera, a 19-year-old from Venezuela. He was listed at 5'3", 148 pounds.

Players were expected to be on time for extra work at 8:00 AM. An hour later they underwent stretching, batting practice, infield fundamentals, and pitchers' fielding practice (PFP). With so many players in camp, doubleheaders were scheduled six days a week. Games were at 1:00 PM except for Saturdays at 10:00 AM. Games were played against three other organizations with similar programs, the Yankees (Tampa), Blue Jays (Dunedin), and Pirates (Bradenton). Home games and road games alternated daily. Two young, inexperienced minor league umpires worked the games.

For early workouts, players were required to wear a red T-shirt, blue shorts, red stirrups, and spikes. They switched to gray T-shirts (name on back) for other drills. Gray pants and red mesh jerseys with their name and number on the back were the game uniform. Caps were red with a blue bill.

The instructional staff usually arrived around 5:00 AM and departed 12 hours later. "We need to finalize plans for the day, review yesterday," deArmas explained. "Today, I had to chew out a player who was late for his early work." Ten of the Latin players had no previous pro experience. Many had never been away from home or flown before. "The staff serves as dads. We're here to help them adjust, help them if they have problems, like girlfriend problems or whatever," deArmas added. "With young players like these guys, all of us on the staff need patience...a lot of patience." The staff, including athletic trainers and conditioning coaches, are the unsung heroes of the organization. Long hours of working away from any limelight. Their results may not be known for years as extended is a long way from the major leagues.

On a day when the Blue Jays brought two squads to Carpenter Complex, one game was played on the Richie Ashburn Field on the south side of the clubhouse and the other on the Robin Roberts Field located on the other side. "We use these fields because they are wired with four cameras, center field, home, first, and third," he explained. "Video is part of their instruction. By next year all four fields will be equipped with video cameras, which is huge."

Players not playing this day were dressed in blue shorts and their red game jersey. One manned the radar gun. Another charted pitches. Another served as a bat boy while others were assigned to retrieve foul balls. "We don't keep stats of the games," deArmas said. "We do file a report to baseball administration about each game and how the players did. Mainly, we're here for instruction. We'll have base runners break on pitches in the dirt, no matter the game situation. If they are thrown out, that's okay. We'll bunt for base hits. It's a matter of repetition, repetition, repetition. We're also getting them acclimated to pro ball. We want to have fun playing games, but laughing on the bus after a loss is a no-no." Following his game, deArmas gathered all his players by third base. "[It's] just a review of things we did right, emphasizing the positives but also letting them know of the mistakes," he said. Borders did the same after his game.

With so many Latin players, the Phillies conducted twice-a-week English lessons, utilizing a bilingual Clearwater teacher. Mansolino went one step further during the minor league camp, and it spilled over to the extended program. Young Latino players roomed with English-speaking players or older Spanish players who had mastered the English language. "Being in the states is such a cultural change for the kids. We want to help them learn the English lessons for their personal lives and also as a player. Kids who learn English quicker will advance quicker with their baseball skills. Chooch [Carlos Ruiz] is a perfect example," Mansolino said. "Once he learned the language, he took off as a player. There's so much talk in a dugout during a game: 'That slider had bite', 'We can run on this guy', 'Look how deep the left fielder is playing', 'As a base runner you got to see that.' If you don't understand the language, your progress will be slower." "Without a doubt, Doug is right," deArmas added. "Players who aren't interested in learning the language will fall behind and not make it."

The program doesn't last all summer. During the summer draft, the Phillies selected 40 players from the high school and college levels and at every position from ages 18 to 24. The final extended game was June 12. Some youngsters remained there as members of the Gulf Coast League that began play on June 22. Others were assigned to the Williamsport Crosscutters in the New York-Penn League, a season that started June 19. The GCL season ended August 29. Williamsport and the Phillies' other four minor league clubs ended on September 7.

Signed players from this draft reported to Clearwater and the start of a minicamp on June 15, the same day the Crosscutters flew to Philadelphia for a bus ride to Williamsport. The signees from 2015, who were assigned to Williamsport, flew there on June 20. The others continued minicamp until the GCL opener. All new players underwent a complete physical either in Philadelphia or Clearwater before they could put on a uniform. Once the Williamsport club left Clearwater, deArmas spoke to his squad. "I told them, 'This is the toughest level in pro ball. Six days a week we're going to work your off asses, play games at 1:00 in the afternoon in Florida, you will be homesick, it will be hot, the stands will be empty. I don't want to hear any complaints about the heat.' It's the same for everybody. Get your rest, eat properly, and drink a lot of water. Otherwise you won't be able to perform, be evaluated, and make it to the next level."

The players are young and lack polish. They need to learn how to play the game, how to overcome failure, how to keep grinding it out. They are doing something they haven't done in their athletic lives, playing games six days a week. They will get tired physically and mentally but need to perform the next day. Only a few will reach the big leagues. It's a long grind, a steep ladder to climb. Among the graduates are Ruiz, Freddy Galvis, Cesar Hernandez, Odubel Herrera, Luis Garcia, Jenmar Gomez, and Placido Polanco, who spent two years in the Cardinals extended spring training. Come late March of 2016, the process will start over again. More new faces with dreams of finding a place in the major leagues.

## REHABBING INJURED PLAYERS

The life of an injured Phillies player on a rehabilitation assignment in Clearwater, Florida, is six days a week, 11 months a year at Carpenter Complex, which is next door to Bright House Field. Minor league athletic training and rehabilitation coordinator Joe Rauch oversees the program. Working very closely with Rauch is Jason Meredith (minor league strength and conditioning coordinator) and an intern. "Each player has a specific plan and timeline in place for their recovery and rehabilitation. Treatment is daily, and each is constantly monitored by the whole sports medicine team," Rauch explained. "We work hand-in-hand with each injured player. Sometimes it includes texting each other after hours with changes in the next day's program. The ultimate goal is to get our injured players back on the field. The responsibility of keeping them healthy rests with the athletic trainers and conditioning coaches at each level. It's a total team effort from top to bottom."

Rauch and the staff generally arrive as early as 5:30 AM and won't call it a day until late in the afternoon. They are stationed in the building that houses a huge weight room, six batting cages, and an athletic trainer's room large enough to accommodate three work stations. Rauch's office has views of the athletic trainer's room, weight room, and Mike Schmidt Field. There's also a three-laptop work station for players to view video coaching. Injured players begin arriving at 6:30 AM and can depart after five innings of a Gulf Coast League home game or about three in the afternoon.

Injured players are housed in two different hotels with the exception of players on the Triple A or major league roster. They are permitted to live elsewhere. Players from the area are allowed to live at home.

Dr. Michael Ciccotti (director, medical services) and Scott Sheridan (head athletic trainer) map out a rehab program for each injured major league player. Rauch designs programs for the minor league players. He files a report daily to numerous people in the organization, including all the athletic trainers and conditioning coaches. "Everybody needs to know the status of each individual player in rehab, including a new injury or illness," Rauch said. He provides each player with a printed workout schedule one week at a time, including conditioning, therapy, and baseball activities. The players share the responsibility of staying on point. After three to four weeks, adjustments in the schedule are made to break up the monotony.

At the start of the 2015 seasons of the major league Phillies and four minor league teams, 18 players were in the program. "The number constantly changes," Rauch said, smiling. "We're better off as an organization if we're not busy." Injured players on the seven-day or 15-day disabled list in the majors or seven-day DL in the minors remain with their respective clubs. Those needing long-term rehab are sent to Clearwater. Most common injuries that require rehab include shoulders and elbows, muscle pulls plus sprains, oblique injuries, and hamstrings. Three of the injured pitchers were rehabbing from Tommy John surgery. Following surgery the player will return to his home until the stitches are removed. Clearwater is next. Generally speaking, a shoulder-elbow program for a pitcher includes conditioning, therapy, and baseball activity that begins with playing catch. Over time, it progresses to long toss, longer tossing, throwing off the mound, throwing batting practice, simulated innings, simulated games, and pitching in a game. The game action often starts with the Gulf Coast League and progresses to other levels.

Position players generally start with conditioning and therapy. Their baseball activity is a progressive program. Routine fielding drills, which increase in difficulty, include dry swinging a bat, hitting off a tee, hitting against a coach, live batting practice, game activity as a designated hitter, and finally full-game action. Pitchers' programs are lengthier in that they cannot throw every day. Position players can progress more quickly, but caution is required. Rushing an injured player can create a more serious injury. Time off the playing field is detrimental to the player and organization. Players are required to wear blue shorts and a plain red or gray T-shirt (name on back in white letters) while at the Complex. Caps are red with a blue bill. Sneakers are a must in the weight room. Spikes are required for on-field activities. That's their uniform until they are back playing games, at which time they return to a full baseball uniform. Lunch is served in the Carpenter Complex clubhouse along with the players in the Gulf Coast League and staff. Players are on their own for dining. Baseball is like any sport. Injuries occur. Whether you are Chace Numata or Chase Utley, rehabbing in Clearwater is a vital phase of the organization. Rehabbing players have the finest physical facilities and staff in the game, and it's first class all the way.

# Acknowledgments

Outside of my family, so many people to acknowledge, especially my colleagues at the Phillies: Chris Wheeler, Dennis Lehman, Tina Urban, Susan Ingersoll-Papaneri, Adele MacDonald, Christine Negley, Debbie Nocito, Greg Casterioto, Debbie Rinaldi, Kurt Funk, Ed Wade, Scott Brandreth, Scott Palmer, John Brazer, and Bonnie Clark. All the vice presidents who shared their Phillies passion and sometimes, endless meetings.

Hal Bodley, MLB.com's senior correspondent and a friend since 1963. A former assistant and lifelong friend, Vince Nauss. A special friend, Paul Hagen, the 2013 J.G. Taylor Spink Award baseball writer, and John Timberlake, Lee McDaniel, Jason Adams, Doug Kemp, and Dan McDonough, my Clearwater Threshers friends.

Very grateful that Larry Andersen, one of the "misfits" from 1993, would donate his time and editorial skills to pen the foreword. Two baseball historians were extremely helpful, Rich Westcott and Bob Warrington. Bodley, Hagen, Westcott, and Warrington each contributed a story, which is greatly appreciated. Casterioto provided two stories. He gets two pats on the back.

Endless biographies from SABR BioProjects were of tremendous assistance. Thanks to all the authors. Dan Goroff and Skip Clayton lent hands in research and proofreading.

A huge thank you to Matt Rothenberg, manager of the Giamatti Research Center, at the Baseball Hall of Fame and Museum in Cooperstown, New York, for his willingness to provide information. I pestered him often and he batted 1.000.

Hundreds of interviews through the years with Phillies players, managers, coaches, alumni, and executives were so invaluable. So were opportunities to interview people behind the scenes of Phillies baseball, a small sampling of employees who have been involved during the Veterans Stadium era and current times at Citizens Bank Park as well as Clearwater.

Photos would haven't been possible without the gracious assistance of Urban, Miles Kennedy, Westcott, Warrington, and John Horne, coordinator of rights and reproductions of the Photo Archives at the Baseball Hall of Fame and Museum.

After the New York Mets ended the 1962 season with their 120th loss, manager Casey Stengel told the team, "This has been a real team effort. No one or two people could have done this." Well, I echo Casey. This was a total team effort. Unlike the Mets, my team roster is filled with All-Stars.

# Sources

## BOOKS

Bunning, Jim; Dolson, Frank—*Jim Bunning, Baseball and Beyond*; Temple University Press, Philadelphia, 1998.

De Quesada, Alejandro M—*Spring Training in Clearwater*; The History Press, Charleston, South Carolina, 2007.

Green, Dallas; Maimon, Alan—*The Mouth That Roared*; Triumph Books, Chicago, 2013.

Lewis, Allen and Westcott, Rich—*No-Hitters*; McFarland & Company, Inc., Jefferson, North Carolina, 2000.

Ritter, Lawrence S.—*Lost Ballparks*; Penguin Books, New York, 1992.

Roberts, Robin; C. Paul Roders III—*The Whiz Kids and the 1950 Pennant*; Temple University Press, Philadelphia, 1996.

Shenk, Larry; Gummer, Scott—*Phillies: An Extraordinary Tradition*; Insight Editions, San Rafael, California, 2010.

Shenk, Larry—*If These Walls Could Talk: Stories from the Philadelphia Phillies Dugout, Locker Room, and Press Box*; Triumph Books, Chicago, 2014.

Shenk, Larry; Clayton, Skip; Bostrom, Don—*This Date in Philadelphia Phillies History*; Camino Books, Philadelphia, 2014.

Siwoff, Seymour—*The Elias Book of Baseball Records*; New York, 2014.

Smith, Ron—*The Ballpark Book*; The Sporting News, a Times-Mirror Company, St. Louis, Missouri, 2000.

Tieman, Robert L.; Rucker, Mark—*Nineteenth Century Stars*; The Society for American Baseball Research, Kansas City, Missouri, 1989.

Westcott, Rich—*Philadelphia's Old Ballparks*; Temple University Press, Philadelphia, 1996.

Westcott, Rich—*Splendor on the Diamond*; University Press of Florida, Gainesville, Florida, 2000.

Westcott, Rich; Bilovsky, Frank—*Phillies Encyclopedia*; Temple University Press, Philadelphia, 2004.

Westcott, Rich—*Tales from the Phillies Dugout*; Sports Publishing, New York, 2003.

Westcott, Rich—*Great Stuff*; Sports Publishing, New York, 2014.

## ORGANIZATIONS

Broadcast Pioneers of Philadelphia
Clearwater Threshers
Philadelphia Phillies
SABR BioProjects

## PERIODICALS

*Phillies Magazines*
*Phillies Media Guides*
*Phillies Yearbooks*
*"After The Game," Phillies Alumni Newsletter*
*Philadelphia Daily News*

*Phillies Report*
*St. Petersburg Times*
*The New York Times*
*The Philadelphia Inquirer*

## WEBSITES

Baseballalmanac.com
Baseballencyclopedia.com
Baseball-reference.com
CSNPhilly.com
ESPN.com
MLB.com
National Baseball Hall of Fame and Museum.com
Phillies Insider Blog
Phillies.com/alumni
PhoulBallz.com
Phl17.com
SI.com
SpringTrainingOnline.com
Yahoo.com

# About the Author

Affectionately known as "The Baron," Larry Shenk is a longtime Phillies executive. His hobby is writing about his passion—Phillies baseball. His passion for the Phillies began as a youngster. A dream came true when he was hired by the Phillies as the publicity director following the 1963 season.

During 44 seasons with the Phillies, The Baron's had more titles than World Series rings, including director of public relations; vice president, public relations; vice president, alumni relations; alumni relations and team historian; and team historian.

*The Fightin' Phillies: 100 Years of Philadelphia Baseball from the Whiz Kids to the Misfits* is his fourth publication since leaving a full-time position. It follows *If These Walls Could Talk: Stories from the Philadelphia Phillies Dugout, Locker Room, and Press Box*, another Triumph Books publication (2014). He co-authored *This Date In Philadelphia Phillies History* (1979 and 2014) and *Phillies: An Extraordinary Tradition* (2010).

During his Phillies career, he authored the Phillies' first media guide in 1964 and served as editor/author of numerous annual

Left to right: Larry Shenk, Julie Shenk, Tyler Shenk, Mike Mosel, Debi Mosel, Audrey Shenk, Andy Shenk, and Renee Shenk.

publications such as *Yearbook*; *Phillies Magazine*; spring training programs; special occasion publications, including National League Championship Series and World Series programs; *A Century of Phillies Baseball, Final Innings*, celebrating 33 years of Phillies baseball at Veterans Stadium; and the Opening Day program for Citizens Bank Park.

He has received numerous awards, including the Robert O. Fishel Award (1983) for excellence in the field of public relations; Philadelphia Sports Writers Association Good Guy Award (1995); the Richie Ashburn Special Achievement Award (2003); the Dallas Green Special Achievement Award (2007) from the Philadelphia chapter of the Baseball Writers Association of America; and Lifetime Achievement Awards (2007) from both the Philadelphia chapter of the Public Relations Society of America and the Philadelphia Sports Writers Association. In addition he was inducted into the Central Pennsylvania Sports Hall of Fame (1992), the City All-Star chapter of the Pennsylvania Sports Hall of Fame (2004), and the Delaware Baseball Hall of Fame (2005).

A graduate of Myerstown (Pennsylvania) High School (1956) and Millersville State College (1961), The Baron was a general reporter with the *Lebanon Daily News* (1961–63) and a sports-writer at *The Wilmington News-Journal* (1963) before joining the Phillies.